HOW YOUR HOUSE WORKS

Charlie Wing

WILEY

. . . for Wid

HOW YOUR HOUSE WORKS

Visual Guide to Understanding and Maintaining Your Home

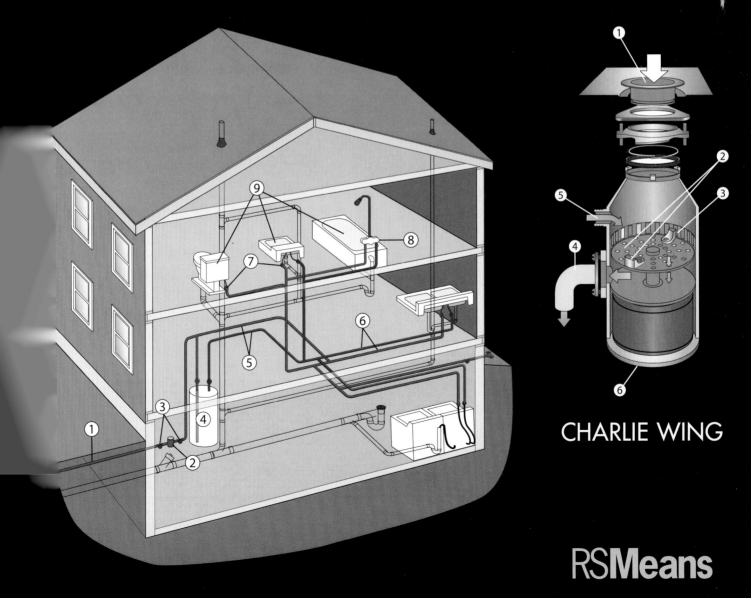

CHARLIE WING

RSMeans

Published by John Wiley & Sons, Inc., Hoboken, New Jersey

Published simultaneously in Canada

For general information about our other products and services, please contact our Customer Care Department within the United States at (800) 762-2974, outside the United States at (317) 572-3993 or fax (317) 572-4002.

Wiley publishes in a variety of print and electronic formats and by print-on-demand. Some material included with standard print versions of this book may not be included in e-books or in print-on-demand. If this book refers to media such as a CD or DVD that is not included in the version you purchased, you may download this material at http://booksupport.wiley.com. For more information about Wiley products, visit www.wiley.com.

Library of Congress Cataloging-in-Publication Data:

Wing, Charles, 1939-
  How your house works : a visual guide to understanding & maintaining your home / Charlie Wing. -- 2nd ed.
    p. cm. -- (RSMeans)
  Includes index.
    ISBN 978-1-118-09940-7 (pbk.); ISBN 978-1-118-28549-7 (ebk); ISBN 978-1-118-28580-0 (ebk); ISBN 978-1-118-28607-4 (ebk); ISBN 978-1-118-28616-6 (ebk); ISBN 978-1-11828736-1 (ebk); ISBN 978-1-11828737-8 (ebk)

  1. Dwellings--Maintenance and repair. I. Title.
  TH4817.W56 2012
  643'.7--dc23

                              2011046745

Printed in the United States of America

10 9 8 7 6 5 4 3 2

CONTENTS

1377

127419

INTRODUCTION

This book offers a unique approach to home improvement, maintenance, and repair. It describes how virtually everything in a house is put together, and how each item functions – from plumbing to electrical, heating and air conditioning, appliances, doors and windows, and even the home's foundation and wood framing.

The key to the book is the easy-to-understand, see-through drawings. Each one is backed up by clear, brief explanations from a nationally known home improvement expert. It's a formula for a quick understanding of what you're dealing with when troubleshooting a problem, talking to your repairman, or planning your new home, addition, or remodeling project, and selecting new fixtures, appliances, or materials.

The illustrations show how the components of a system fit together and how each item is intended to function – whether it's an air conditioner, a hot water heater, the foundation, or a faucet. The author breaks down the workings of all of the plumbing, electrical, and heating/air conditioning systems, and other house parts, and shows not only what the parts look like and how they interact, but the sequence in which things work. Even complex systems are explained in simple terms and diagrams.

Throughout the book, you'll also see "Before Calling for Help" boxes – guidance on simple things to check, in many cases solving the problem quickly and inexpensively without having to hire a repairman. If you do find that you need a contractor or serviceman, the book will help you understand your options and be better informed about having the correct elements installed or replaced.

Maintenance tips and other helpful guidance throughout the book will help you keep your home running smoothly.

Not only homeowners, but handymen and contractors will benefit from the easy-to-interpret information presented here, especially for getting up to speed on items that are not their specialty.

If you would like the confidence of knowing more about how your house works and what to do if something breaks down, read this book. It just may change your life.

Note: *This book is intended to provide useful information for understanding the systems, fixtures, and appliances in a house, but it is not a substitute for professional construction, engineering, or repair evaluations, recommendations, or services. Readers should obtain assistance from appropriate experts, as needed.*

ABOUT THE AUTHOR

Charlie Wing is a nationally recognized home improvement/repair expert. He has written or co-written more than 20 books on these topics, including Home Depot's *Decorative Painting, Tiling, and Plumbing 1-2-3* books, *Better Homes & Gardens' Complete Guide to Home Repair*, Taunton Press's *The Visual Handbook of Building and Remodeling*, Reader's Digest's *The Big Book of Small Household Repairs*, and many others, including *Ortho's Home Improvement Encyclopedia* and *How to Build Additions*.

An MIT PhD, Charlie has been a guest more than 400 times on home improvement radio and television shows, including on the Discovery Channel, PBS, and NBC's *Today Show*. He developed and hosted a national PBS series on home remodeling for energy efficiency. He was founding and technical editor for *Smart Homeowner* magazine from 2001 to 2004.

A Note from the Author

After observing neighbors, friends, and family through decades of home ownership, I'm convinced that most of today's homeowners live in a perpetual state of anxiety. The log cabin with a privy, a fireplace, and a bucket for hauling water has been replaced by homes with sophisticated wiring, plumbing, and appliances. What happens if something goes wrong?

No wonder we live in fear. While school has taught us math, foreign languages, and computer sciences, most of us have no idea how our furnace, refrigerator, or even kitchen faucet works. This is an expensive omission in our educations. In metropolitan areas, the minimum charge for a plumber or appliance repairperson to come to your home is about $150. In fact, repair services are now so expensive that the leading consumer magazine recommends replacing, rather than repairing, appliances over five years old.

Why don't more people attempt simple repairs themselves? Because they're convinced that only professional tradespeople have the required tools and special knowledge. The truth, however, is the opposite. Let me tell you my favorite home repair story.

A few years back, I was visiting a friend who happened to own a plumbing repair service. His considerable success was built on the promise that a repair would be accomplished the same day, or the repair would be free. He had built a fleet of 75 trucks and licensed plumbers on that simple promise. The promise also allowed him to charge a minimum of $150 just for showing up.

During my visit, my friend's dishwasher began making a strange whirring sound. Convinced that the sound indicated an impending complete breakdown, he called the repair center listed for the brand.

A day later the doorbell rang, and there appeared an appliance repairman with an intimidating tool belt and service manual the size of the New York City phone book. Before starting repairs, he informed my friend he would have to sign a work order agreeing to a minimum charge of $150, regardless of the problem or the success of the work.

That agreed to, my friend said, "The dishwasher makes a weird whizzing sound, like the motor bearings are gone."

Without a word, the repairman plucked a simple Phillips screwdriver from his tool belt and unscrewed the perforated cover of the dishwasher's drain. He reached in with two fingers and plucked out a pistachio shell. "Here is the culprit," he beamed.

He replaced the drain cover and turned on the machine. The noise had disappeared. "That will be $150," the serviceman said.

Now what enabled the serviceman to go so directly to the problem? First, he understood how a dishwasher worked—that, for example, it had a drain and a pump impeller to circulate water. Second, he knew from experience that well over half of all appliance "repairs" involve tightening a loose connection, adjusting a screw or knob, or removing a foreign object.

When you go to a doctor with a complaint, the result is most often the same. The doctor has studied anatomy. He or she knows what is inside you and how your different parts relate. Most often the prescription is, "Go to bed, stay warm, and drink lots of water," not, "I think we'd better replace your heart."

These two principles: that repair requires understanding how things work, and that many repairs are surprisingly simple, are what led me to create this book. I hope that it saves you many times $150 and relieves some of your homeowner anxiety.

1 PLUMBING

If you are like most homeowners, the maze of hot and cold supply pipes and waste pipes in your basement resembles nothing more meaningful than a plate of spaghetti. This chapter will show you that, in fact, your house contains three separate systems of pipes, all making perfect sense.

Understanding their purpose and how each one works will enable you to decide which projects are in the realm of a homeowner, and which ones require a plumber. If you're planning to build a new home or do major remodeling, this chapter will also help you to visualize the plumbing requirements, and how they'll fit into your space.

A visit to the plumbing aisle of your local home center will show you that do-it-yourself plumbing repair has never been easier. There you will find kits, including illustrated instructions, for just about every common repair project.

Plumbing is not dangerous, unless you're dealing with gas pipes. In fact, call a licensed professional if your repair or installation involves any change to existing gas piping. But plumbing mistakes can be damaging to the finishes and contents of your home, just by getting them wet. The force and weight of water are also something to be reckoned with, if many gallons flow where they should not. Before starting a project involving the supply system, locate the shut-off valve for the fixture you're working on. If you can't find one, shut off the main valve where the supply enters the house.

The Supply System

Cold water supply
Hot water supply

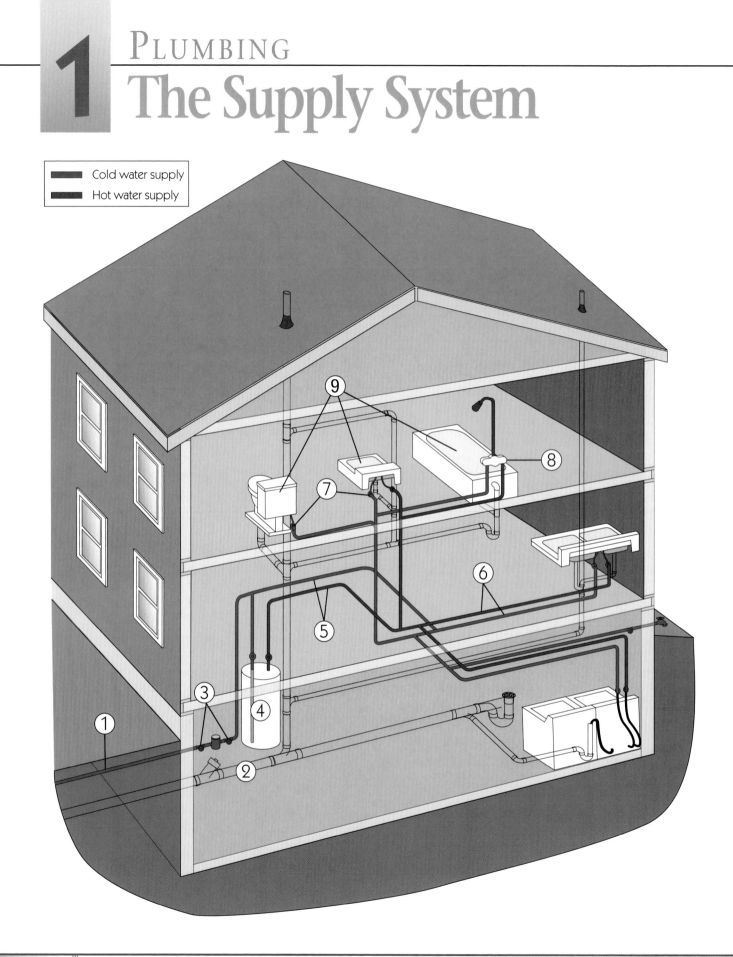

How It Works

The supply system is the network of pipes that delivers hot and cold potable water under pressure throughout the house.

1. Water enters underground from the street through a ³/₄" or 1" metal pipe. In houses built prior to 1950, the metal is usually galvanized steel; after 1950, copper. In the case of a private water supply, the pipe is usually polyethylene.

2. If you pay for water and sewage, your home's usage is measured and recorded as the water passes through a water meter. If you find no meter inside the house, one is probably located in a pit between the house and the street. You can monitor your consumption, measured in cubic feet, by lifting the cap and reading the meter.

3. Next to the water meter (before, after, or both), you will find a valve, which allows shutting off the water supply, both cold and hot, to the entire house. If you have never noted this valve, do so now. When a pipe or fixture springs a leak, you don't want to waste time searching for it.

4. Water heaters are most often large, insulated, vertical tanks containing from 40 to 120 gallons. Cold water enters the tank from a pipe extending nearly to the tank bottom. Electric elements, a gas burner, or an oil burner heat the water to a pre-set temperature. When hot water is drawn from the top, cold water flows in at the bottom to replace it.

If the home is heated hydronically (with circulating water), the water heater may consist of a heat-exchange coil inside the boiler, or it may be a separate tank (BoilerMate™) heated with water from the boiler through a heat exchange coil.

Wall-mounted tankless water heaters provide a limited, but continuous, supply of hot water through a coil heated directly by gas or electricity.

5. Supply pipes—both cold and hot—that serve many fixtures are called "trunk lines," and are usually ³/₄" in diameter. Pipes serving hose bibbs and other fixtures with high demands may be ³/₄" as well.

6. Pipes serving only one or two fixtures are called "branch lines." Because they carry less water, they are often reduced in size to ¹/₂" and, in the case of toilets, ³/₈". Exceptions are pipes serving both a shower and another fixture.

7. Every fixture should have shutoff valves on both hot and cold incoming supplies. This is so that repairing the single fixture doesn't require shutting off the entire house supply at the meter valve.

8. A pressure-balanced anti-scald valve or thermostatic temperature control valve prevents the hot and cold temperature shocks we have all experienced when someone suddenly draws water from a nearby fixture. They are not inexpensive, but they provide insurance against scalds and cold-water shocks, which may trigger a fall in the elderly.

9. "Fixture" is the generic plumbing term for any fixed device that uses water.

Drain pipes are sized according to the rate of flow they may have to carry. One fixture unit (FU) is defined as a discharge rate of one cubic foot of water per minute. Plumbing codes assign bathroom sinks (lavatories) 1 FU, kitchen sinks 2 FU, and toilets (water closets) 4 FU.

The Waste System

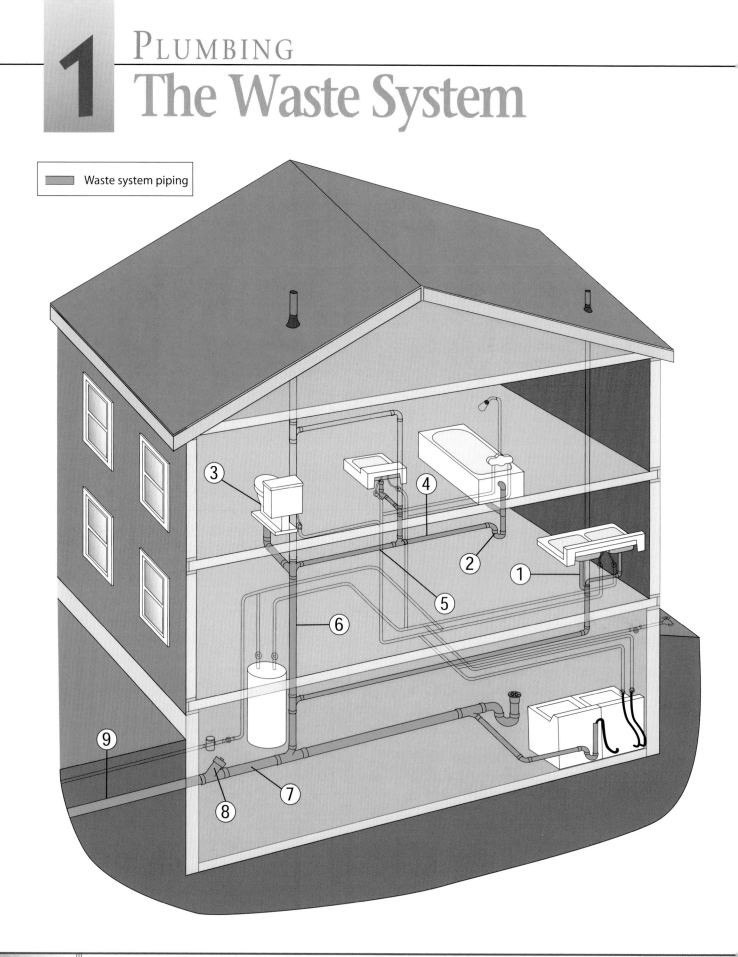

Waste system piping

How It Works

The waste system is the assemblage of pipes that collects and delivers waste (used) water to either the municipal or private sewage system.

1. The pipe that drains away a fixture's waste water is its drain. The minimum diameter of the drain is specified by code and is determined by the rate of discharge of the fixture.

2. Each and every fixture drain must be "trapped." A trap is a section of pipe that passes waste water, but retains enough water to block the passage of noxious sewer gases from the sewage system into the living spaces of the house.

3. Toilets (water closets) have no visible trap, but one is actually there, built into the base of the toilet.

4. The horizontal section of drain pipe between the outlet of a trap and the first point of the drain pipe that is supplied with outdoor air is called the "trap arm." The plumbing code limits the length of the trap arm in order to prevent siphon action from emptying the trap. The allowed length is a function of pipe diameter.

5. As with a river, the smaller tributary drain pipes that feed into the main "house drain" are called "branches."

6. The largest vertical drain pipe, extending from the lowest point through the roof, and to which the smaller horizontal branch drains connect, is called the "soil stack." The term "soil" implies that the drain serves human waste. If it does carry human waste, and/or if it serves enough fixture units, it must be at least 3 inches in diameter. In a very horizontally-extended house, there may be more than one soil stack.

7. The largest, bottom-most horizontal waste pipe is the "house drain." In a delicate balance between too-slow and too-rapid flow of waste, the house drain (and all other horizontal waste pipes) must be uniformly inclined at between $^1/_8$" and $^1/_4$" per foot. In a basement or crawl space, the house drain is usually exposed. With a slab-on-grade foundation, the house drain is beneath the slab.

8. To facilitate unclogging of drain pipes, Y-shaped "cleanouts" are provided. At a minimum, there will be a 4" diameter cleanout at the point where the house drain exits the building. This cleanout is utilized when tree roots invade the exterior drains and special drain-reaming equipment must be called in to cut the roots. Additional cleanouts are required throughout the waste system for every 100' of horizontal run and every cumulative change of direction of 135 degrees.

9. Waste pipe outside of the building line is termed the "house sewer." It is always at least 4" in diameter.

Vent system piping

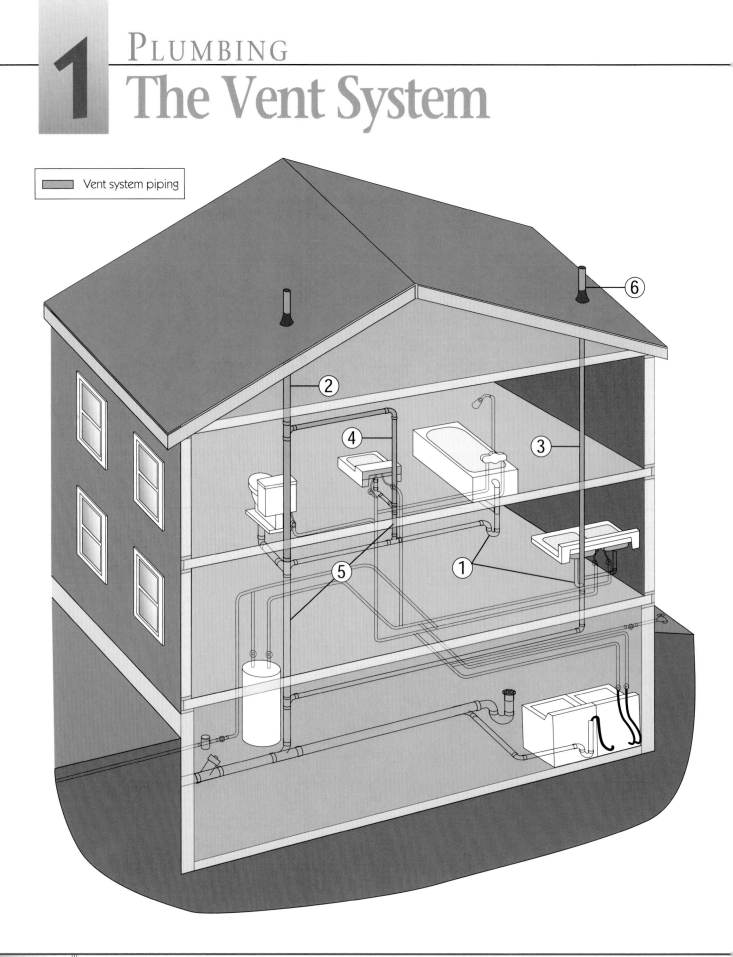

How It Works

As you can see on pages 14 and 15, fixture drains must be kept at atmospheric pressure so that the water seals in their drain traps are not siphoned away, thereby exposing the interior of the house to noxious sewer gases. The vent system consists of the pipes that relieve pressure differences within the drain system.

1. All plumbing fixtures (things that use and discharge waste water into the drain system) possess traps. To prevent waste water from forming a siphon during discharge, air must be introduced into the drain pipe near the outlet of the trap (maximum distance determined by the drain pipe diameter).

2. The primary vent is part of a large-diameter vertical pipe termed the "stack." Below the highest point of waste discharge into it it is the "waste stack." Above that point it is the "vent stack." If a waste stack also serves one or more toilets (and it usually does), it is sometimes called the "soil stack." Because it provides a direct air passage to the municipal sewer pipe or private septic tank, a vent stack must be terminated in the open air. And to keep the sewer gas as far as possible from people, it is usually terminated through the roof.

3. The permitted length of drain pipe from a trap to a vent (the trap arm) is specified by code as a function of the pipe diameter. (See page 15.) If the horizontal run of the drain is very long, a smaller-diameter vent stack is usually provided close after the trap.

4. Another solution to the too-long horizontal drain is to break it into legal lengths with "revents." To guarantee that they are never blocked with water, revents connect to the vent stack at least 6" above the flood level of the highest fixture on the drain. A horizontal drain may be revented as many times as required.

Where reventing is impractical—such as in the case of an island sink—a "loop vent" can be provided. The loop vent (also known as a "barometric vent") does not connect to the vent stack. Instead, it provides pressure relief simply by the volume of its contained air.

Another solution, allowed only for single fixtures in locations precluding regular venting, is the "automatic vent." This is an air check valve, which allows house air to flow into the drain, but prevents sewer gas from escaping.

5. A vertical vent pipe is allowed to serve as a combined waste and vent, provided its diameter is sufficiently large. Sections of pipe serving both purposes are called "wet vents."

6. The air in vent pipes is at 100% humidity. In northern states, where the average daily temperature is below freezing for extended periods, frost can build up on the inside of exposed vents. To avoid complete frost blockage, local codes may specify a larger diameter for the section of vent above the roof. In addition, so that snow does not cover the vent pipe, a local code may also call for a vertical extension of the pipe beyond the code minimum of 6".

Lavatory Pop-up Drain

How It Works

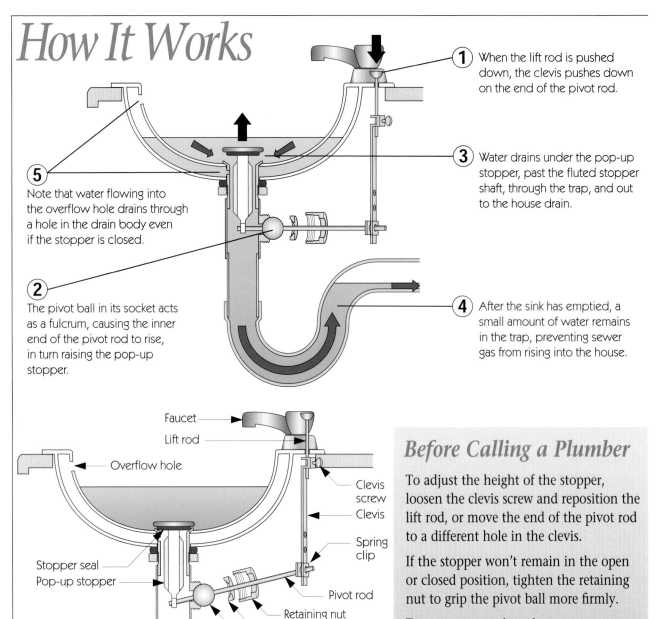

1 When the lift rod is pushed down, the clevis pushes down on the end of the pivot rod.

3 Water drains under the pop-up stopper, past the fluted stopper shaft, through the trap, and out to the house drain.

5 Note that water flowing into the overflow hole drains through a hole in the drain body even if the stopper is closed.

2 The pivot ball in its socket acts as a fulcrum, causing the inner end of the pivot rod to rise, in turn raising the pop-up stopper.

4 After the sink has emptied, a small amount of water remains in the trap, preventing sewer gas from rising into the house.

Faucet
Lift rod
Overflow hole
Clevis screw
Clevis
Spring clip
Stopper seal
Pop-up stopper
Pivot rod
Retaining nut
Gasket
Pivot ball
Tailpiece
Trap

Before Calling a Plumber

To adjust the height of the stopper, loosen the clevis screw and reposition the lift rod, or move the end of the pivot rod to a different hole in the clevis.

If the stopper won't remain in the open or closed position, tighten the retaining nut to grip the pivot ball more firmly.

To remove or replace the pop-up stopper, or to insert a drain auger, unscrew the retaining nut, remove the pivot rod, and lift the stopper out.

Replacement kits are available for entire pop-up assemblies at hardware stores and home centers.

Sink Drain

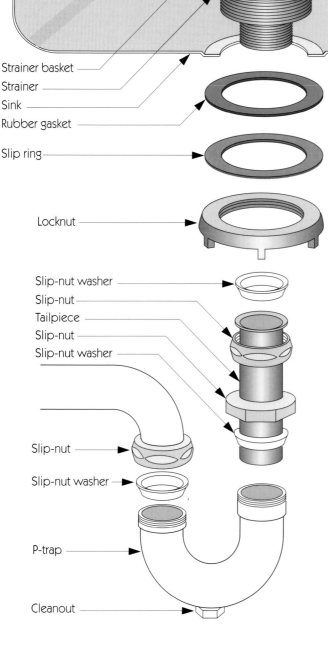

Strainer basket

Strainer

Sink

Rubber gasket

Slip ring

Locknut

Slip-nut washer

Slip-nut

Tailpiece

Slip-nut

Slip-nut washer

Slip-nut

Slip-nut washer

P-trap

Cleanout

Before Calling a Plumber

If you have cleaned the rubber disk at the bottom of the strainer basket, and the sink still will not retain water, replace the strainer. Replacement strainers can be found at any home center.

If your ring or other small item has accidentally gone down the drain, place a pot beneath the trap and remove the cleanout plug. If the ring is not in the pot, it is gone forever.

If you replace the sink, it is best to replace the entire drain assembly down to the trap. If you want to keep the old drain, however, at least replace the two slip washers.

To clear a clogged sink or lavatory drain, remove the strainer basket or the pop-up stopper, and insert a sink auger as far as it will go. Turn the auger clockwise while pulling it out.

Plunger-Type Tub Drain

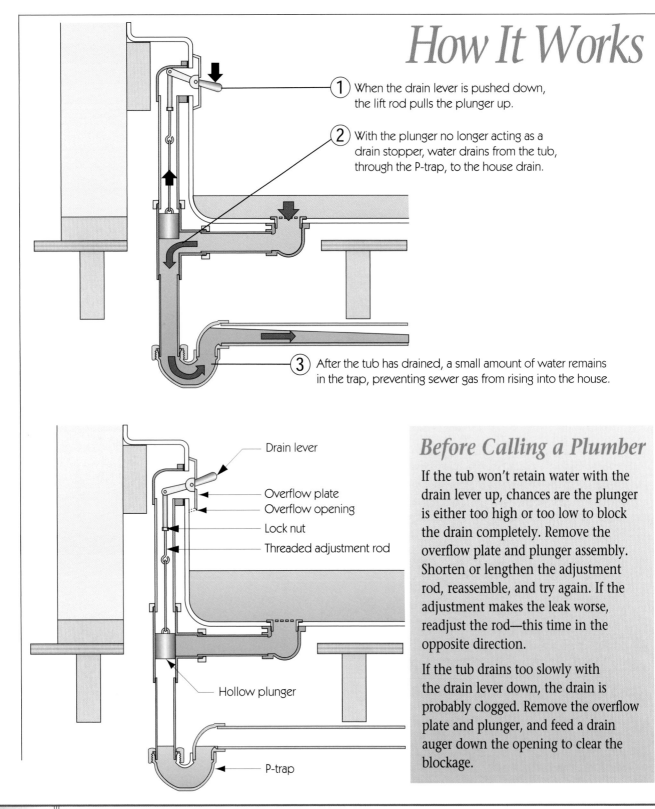

How It Works

① When the drain lever is pushed down, the lift rod pulls the plunger up.

② With the plunger no longer acting as a drain stopper, water drains from the tub, through the P-trap, to the house drain.

③ After the tub has drained, a small amount of water remains in the trap, preventing sewer gas from rising into the house.

Drain lever
Overflow plate
Overflow opening
Lock nut
Threaded adjustment rod
Hollow plunger
P-trap

Before Calling a Plumber

If the tub won't retain water with the drain lever up, chances are the plunger is either too high or too low to block the drain completely. Remove the overflow plate and plunger assembly. Shorten or lengthen the adjustment rod, reassemble, and try again. If the adjustment makes the leak worse, readjust the rod—this time in the opposite direction.

If the tub drains too slowly with the drain lever down, the drain is probably clogged. Remove the overflow plate and plunger, and feed a drain auger down the opening to clear the blockage.

Pop-up Tub Drain

How It Works

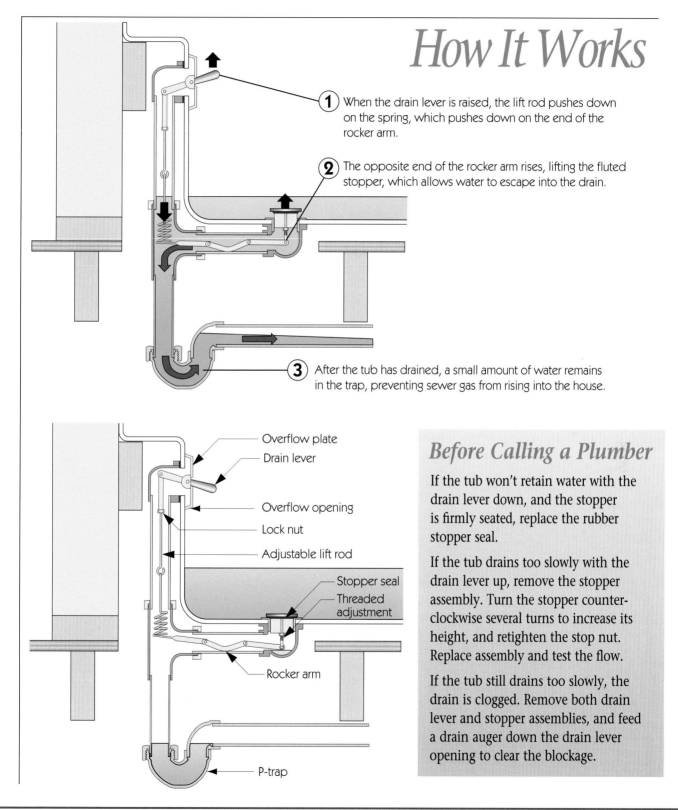

1 When the drain lever is raised, the lift rod pushes down on the spring, which pushes down on the end of the rocker arm.

2 The opposite end of the rocker arm rises, lifting the fluted stopper, which allows water to escape into the drain.

3 After the tub has drained, a small amount of water remains in the trap, preventing sewer gas from rising into the house.

Overflow plate
Drain lever
Overflow opening
Lock nut
Adjustable lift rod
Stopper seal
Threaded adjustment
Rocker arm
P-trap

Before Calling a Plumber

If the tub won't retain water with the drain lever down, and the stopper is firmly seated, replace the rubber stopper seal.

If the tub drains too slowly with the drain lever up, remove the stopper assembly. Turn the stopper counter-clockwise several turns to increase its height, and retighten the stop nut. Replace assembly and test the flow.

If the tub still drains too slowly, the drain is clogged. Remove both drain lever and stopper assemblies, and feed a drain auger down the drain lever opening to clear the blockage.

How It Works

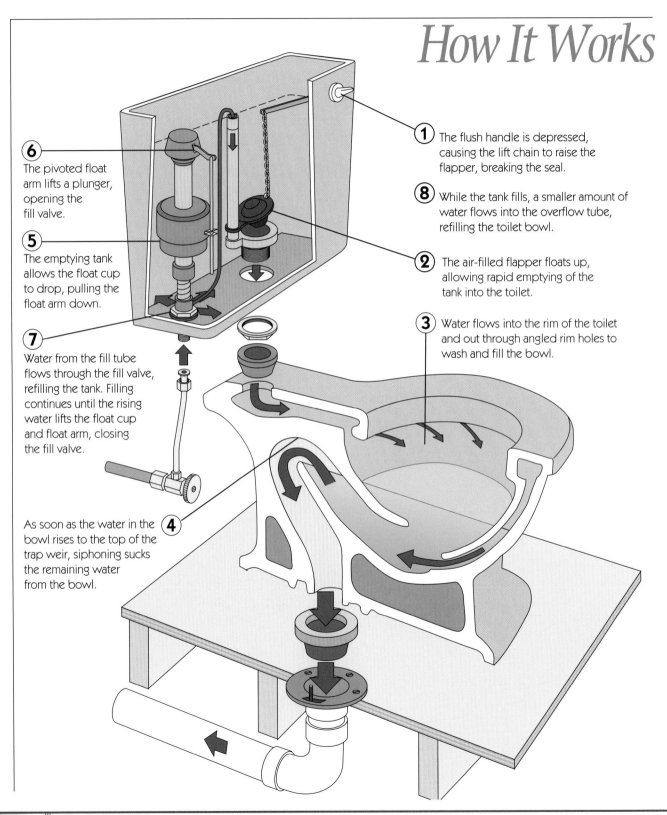

6 The pivoted float arm lifts a plunger, opening the fill valve.

5 The emptying tank allows the float cup to drop, pulling the float arm down.

7 Water from the fill tube flows through the fill valve, refilling the tank. Filling continues until the rising water lifts the float cup and float arm, closing the fill valve.

As soon as the water in the bowl rises to the top of the trap weir, siphoning sucks the remaining water from the bowl. **4**

1 The flush handle is depressed, causing the lift chain to raise the flapper, breaking the seal.

8 While the tank fills, a smaller amount of water flows into the overflow tube, refilling the toilet bowl.

2 The air-filled flapper floats up, allowing rapid emptying of the tank into the toilet.

3 Water flows into the rim of the toilet and out through angled rim holes to wash and fill the bowl.

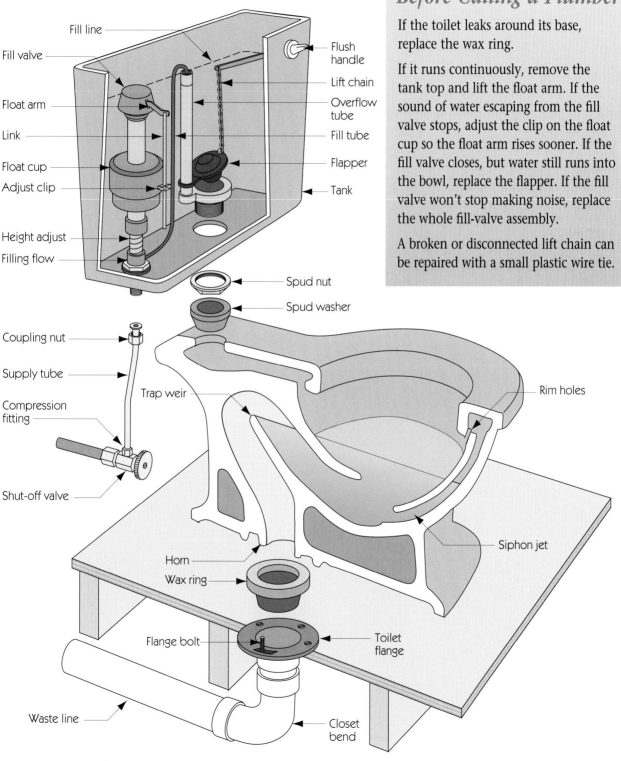

Fill line

Fill valve

Float arm

Link

Float cup

Adjust clip

Height adjust

Filling flow

Flush handle

Lift chain

Overflow tube

Fill tube

Flapper

Tank

Spud nut

Spud washer

Coupling nut

Supply tube

Compression fitting

Shut-off valve

Trap weir

Rim holes

Siphon jet

Horn

Wax ring

Flange bolt

Toilet flange

Waste line

Closet bend

Before Calling a Plumber

If the toilet leaks around its base, replace the wax ring.

If it runs continuously, remove the tank top and lift the float arm. If the sound of water escaping from the fill valve stops, adjust the clip on the float cup so the float arm rises sooner. If the fill valve closes, but water still runs into the bowl, replace the flapper. If the fill valve won't stop making noise, replace the whole fill-valve assembly.

A broken or disconnected lift chain can be repaired with a small plastic wire tie.

1

Traps & Vents

How They Work

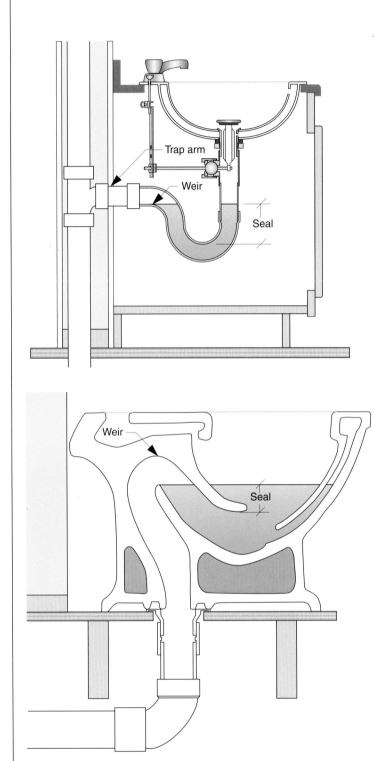

P-Trap

Older homes may contain many types of traps. (See "Prohibited Older Traps" on page 15.) Of all the traps, the "P" has proven most successful at resisting siphonage, so most codes now require it.

The reasons for its success are:

1) the depth of its water seal, and

2) its horizontal trap arm. Unless the arm is long enough to cause a friction backup to the top of the pipe, a siphon is never formed.

Water Closet Trap

Invisible to the eye, the water chambers inside a toilet base actually form an S-trap.

S-traps have been generally banned due to their propensity to siphon, leaving an imperfect water seal against sewer gases. The toilet gets around this problem by diverting a small flow of water to the bowl through the fill tube while the tank is refilling. (See page 12.)

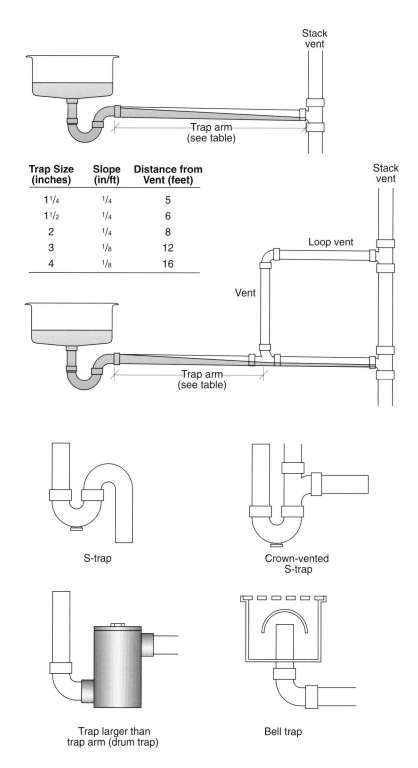

Trap Size (inches)	Slope (in/ft)	Distance from Vent (feet)
$1\frac{1}{4}$	$\frac{1}{4}$	5
$1\frac{1}{2}$	$\frac{1}{4}$	6
2	$\frac{1}{4}$	8
3	$\frac{1}{8}$	12
4	$\frac{1}{8}$	16

S-trap

Crown-vented S-trap

Trap larger than trap arm (drum trap)

Bell trap

Maximum Trap Arm

Just as with a river, friction causes flowing water to back up. If the water in a trap arm (the horizontal section of drain pipe between the outlet of the trap and the vertical drain) were to back up to the top of the pipe, a siphon would exist. In a siphon, the moving slug of water and absence of air create a suction, which can empty the water from the trap.

As a result, plumbing codes specify the maximum length of trap arm allowed for each pipe diameter. (See table at left.)

Prohibited Older Traps

If you live in a home built prior to 1950, look in the basement under your plumbing fixtures. If your plumbing hasn't been updated, you will probably find several examples of the now-banned traps shown at left. They are banned because, in rare instances, they may lose their water seals.

However, the grandfather provisions of the plumbing codes require their replacement with P-traps only in the case of new construction or extensive plumbing remodeling.

Ball-Type Faucet

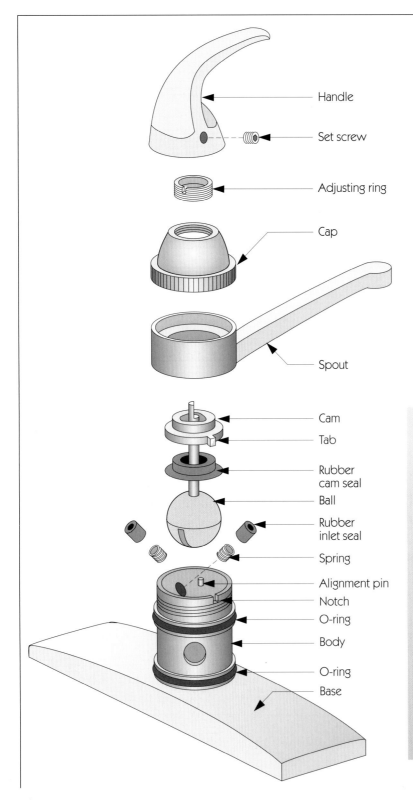

Handle

Set screw

Adjusting ring

Cap

Spout

Cam

Tab

Rubber cam seal

Ball

Rubber inlet seal

Spring

Alignment pin

Notch

O-ring

Body

O-ring

Base

How It Works

Inside the faucet body is a hemispherical recess with a fixed alignment pin and three holes: a cold-water inlet, a hot-water inlet, and a mixed water outlet. The hollow ball (plastic, brass, or stainless steel) is slotted. Moving the faucet handle rotates the ball up and down, and from side to side.

Up-and-down handle motion opens and closes the outlet, thus controlling the flow.

Side-to-side motion uncovers more or less of the two inlets, thus controlling the proportion of hot and cold and the resulting mixed temperature.

Before Calling a Plumber

If the faucet leaks from under the handle, remove the handle and tighten the adjusting ring inside the cap.

If water leaks from under the spout, remove handle, cap, and spout. Replace the two large body O-rings, lubricate with petroleum jelly, and reassemble.

If the spout drips, the rubber inlet seals are likely worn. To replace the seals, remove the handle and cap, and lift out the ball. Pluck out the seals (2) and springs (2) and replace them. If this doesn't work, replace the ball—preferably with a stainless steel one.

Cartridge-Type Faucet

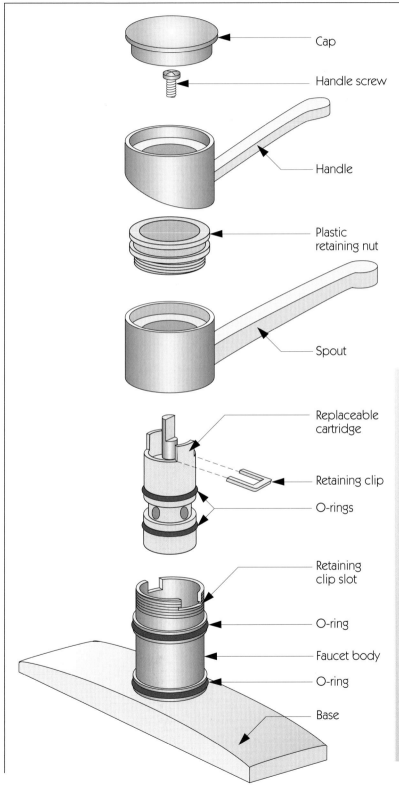

Cap

Handle screw

Handle

Plastic retaining nut

Spout

Replaceable cartridge

Retaining clip

O-rings

Retaining clip slot

O-ring

Faucet body

O-ring

Base

How It Works

Except for the compression-type, the cartridge-type faucet is the simplest because it has only one replaceable part—the cartridge.

There are dozens of differing cartridges, but all operate on the same principle: the cartridge is moved up and down and rotated to change the alignment of holes in the cartridge and faucet body, thus controlling the amounts of hot and cold water flowing to the spout.

If buying a replacement cartridge, take the old one with you to compare to the dozens you will find at the hardware store or home center.

Before Calling a Plumber

If the spout won't stop dripping, the cartridge is at fault. Remove the cap, handle, retaining nut, and retaining clip. Then extract the cartridge. This may require twisting and considerable force.

First, try replacing the O-rings on the cartridge. Make sure the new ones are identical to the old, and apply petroleum jelly before reassembly. If that doesn't work, replace the entire cartridge.

If, instead, the leak is from under the spout, remove the handle, cap, and spout. Replace the two large body O-rings, lubricate with petroleum jelly, and reassemble.

Disk-Type Faucet

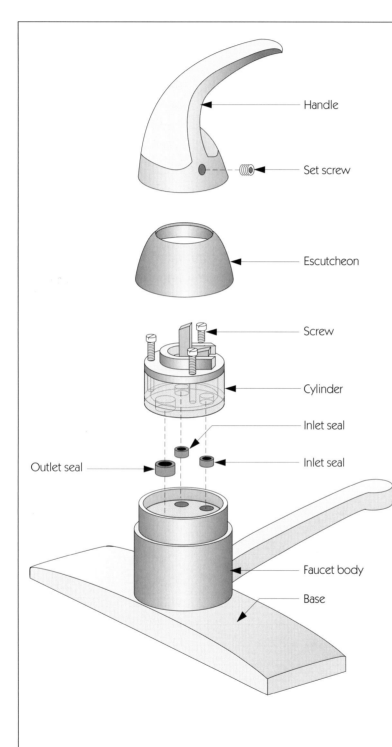

Handle

Set screw

Escutcheon

Screw

Cylinder

Inlet seal

Inlet seal

Outlet seal

Faucet body

Base

How It Works

The heart of the disk faucet is a cylinder containing two polished, fire-hardened ceramic disks, each containing two inlet and one outlet ports.

The bottom disk is fixed, while the handle rotates the upper disk, changing the proportion of incoming hot and cold water. Up-and-down handle motion opens and closes the outlet, thus controlling the flow.

Trouble rarely develops between the disks inside the cartridge. If a leak develops, it is likely due to the rubber seals under the cartridge or the spout O-rings.

Before Calling a Plumber

If the faucet won't stop dripping, remove the handle by loosening its set screw. Remove the escutcheon. Remove the screws in the cylinder, and lift the cylinder out. Take the cylinder to a home center for identification, and replace the three rubber seals on the bottom of the cylinder. After reassembling, lift the handle to its open position before turning on the water supply.

If water leaks from under the spout, remove the handle, escutcheon, cylinder, and spout. Replace the two large body O-rings, lubricate with petroleum jelly, and reassemble.

Compression-Type Faucet

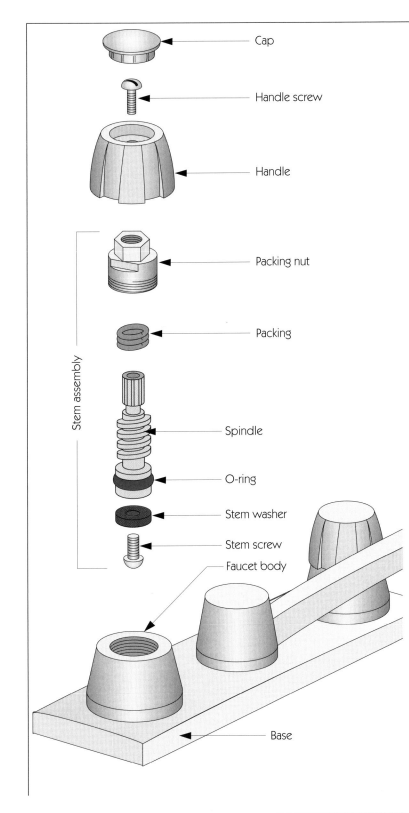

Cap

Handle screw

Handle

Packing nut

Packing

Stem assembly

Spindle

O-ring

Stem washer

Stem screw

Faucet body

Base

How It Works

Compression faucets have separate handles for hot and cold water. At the bottom of each stem assembly is a rubber washer. Turning the handle clockwise screws the stem in and down, reducing the space between the washer and the valve seat at the bottom. Turn the handle far enough, and the washer seats firmly against the valve seat, shutting off all flow.

The water that passes through the washers on both sides is mixed and emerges from the spout.

Before Calling a Plumber

If the spout won't stop dripping, or it requires excessive force to stop the dripping, the rubber washer(s) are worn out. Remove the caps and handles, remove the packing nuts, and turn the spindle assemblies out of the faucet bodies. Replace the stem washers and screws with identical parts, and reassemble.

If water leaks from under a handle, remove the handle and packing nut, and add a few turns of graphite or teflon packing inside the packing nut. Tighten the packing nut just until the leaking stops, and replace the handle.

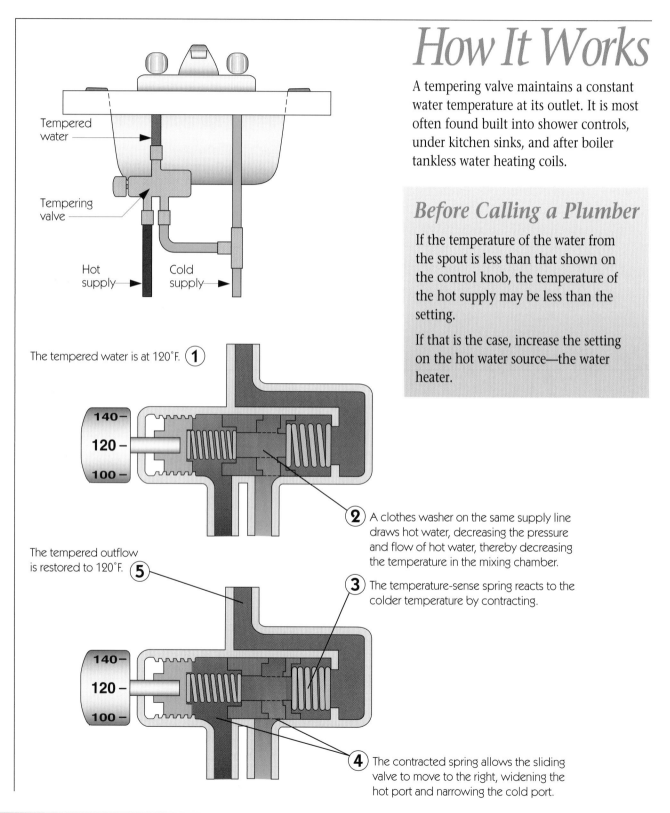

How It Works

A tempering valve maintains a constant water temperature at its outlet. It is most often found built into shower controls, under kitchen sinks, and after boiler tankless water heating coils.

Before Calling a Plumber

If the temperature of the water from the spout is less than that shown on the control knob, the temperature of the hot supply may be less than the setting.

If that is the case, increase the setting on the hot water source—the water heater.

Tempered water

Tempering valve

Hot supply

Cold supply

The tempered water is at 120°F. (**1**)

The tempered outflow is restored to 120°F. (**5**)

(**2**) A clothes washer on the same supply line draws hot water, decreasing the pressure and flow of hot water, thereby decreasing the temperature in the mixing chamber.

(**3**) The temperature-sense spring reacts to the colder temperature by contracting.

(**4**) The contracted spring allows the sliding valve to move to the right, widening the hot port and narrowing the cold port.

Tub/Shower Control

Compression Type

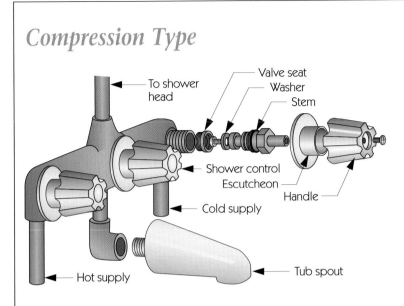

- To shower head
- Valve seat
- Washer
- Stem
- Shower control
- Escutcheon
- Handle
- Cold supply
- Hot supply
- Tub spout

Disk Type

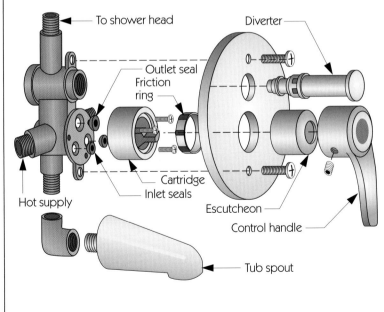

- To shower head
- Diverter
- Outlet seal
- Friction ring
- Cartridge
- Inlet seals
- Escutcheon
- Control handle
- Hot supply
- Tub spout

How It Works

Tub/shower controls are no different from sink faucets of the same type, with the exception of an additional diverter valve.

Compression-type controls (as on page 19) have separate valves for hot and cold supply, with the mixed temperature depending on both.

Disk-type controls (page 18) have a sliding and rotating disk, which alters the apertures of hot and cold inlets (temperature) and the aperture of the outlet (flow).

The diverter directs the outflow to either the tub spout or the shower head.

Before Calling a Plumber

If your tub/shower control has two or three handles, it utilizes compression valves. See page 19 for troubleshooting.

If the tub/shower control has a single handle, it likely contains a disk. In that case, see page 18 for further direction.

How They Work

Freeze-Proof Sillcock

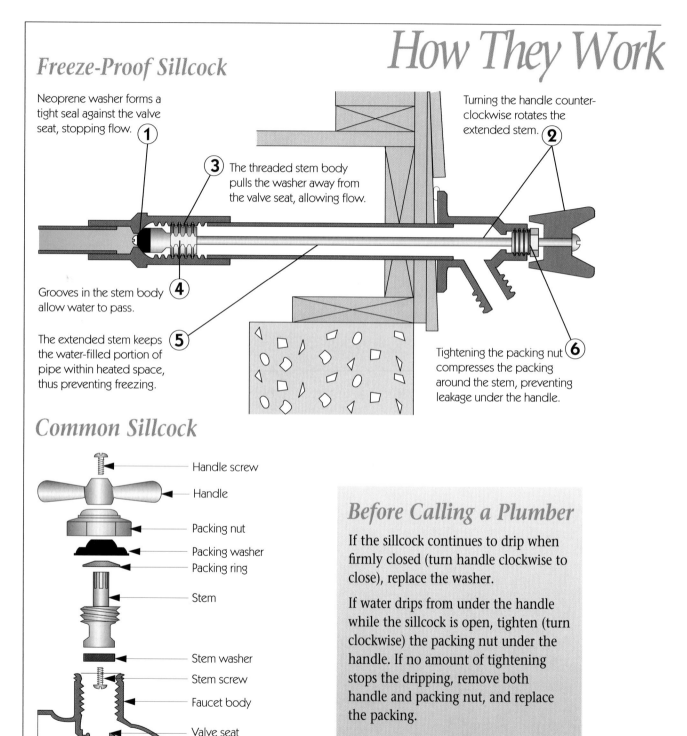

Neoprene washer forms a tight seal against the valve seat, stopping flow. ①

③ The threaded stem body pulls the washer away from the valve seat, allowing flow.

Turning the handle counter-clockwise rotates the extended stem. ②

Grooves in the stem body ④ allow water to pass.

The extended stem keeps ⑤ the water-filled portion of pipe within heated space, thus preventing freezing.

Tightening the packing nut ⑥ compresses the packing around the stem, preventing leakage under the handle.

Common Sillcock

- Handle screw
- Handle
- Packing nut
- Packing washer
- Packing ring
- Stem
- Stem washer
- Stem screw
- Faucet body
- Valve seat

Before Calling a Plumber

If the sillcock continues to drip when firmly closed (turn handle clockwise to close), replace the washer.

If water drips from under the handle while the sillcock is open, tighten (turn clockwise) the packing nut under the handle. If no amount of tightening stops the dripping, remove both handle and packing nut, and replace the packing.

Pitcher (Hand) Pump

How It Works

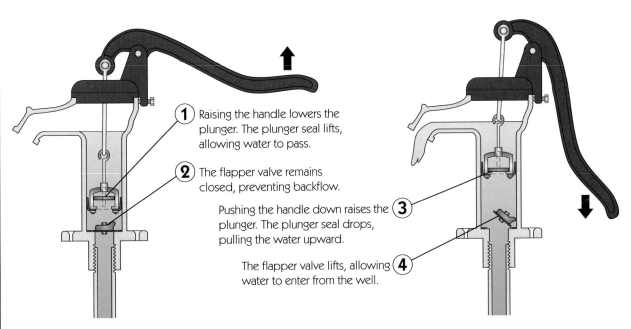

1 Raising the handle lowers the plunger. The plunger seal lifts, allowing water to pass.

2 The flapper valve remains closed, preventing backflow.

Pushing the handle down raises the **3** plunger. The plunger seal drops, pulling the water upward.

The flapper valve lifts, allowing **4** water to enter from the well.

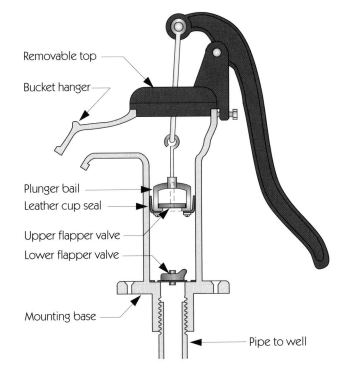

Removable top

Bucket hanger

Plunger bail

Leather cup seal

Upper flapper valve

Lower flapper valve

Mounting base

Pipe to well

Before Calling a Plumber

The leather plunger and flapper valves tend to dry out if left unused. If pumping produces no water, prime the pump by pouring water into the top of the pump. Wetting the leather softens it, allowing the plunger and flapper valves to form better seals.

If repeated priming produces no results, or if you have to prime after less than an hour of disuse, replace both leather seals.

Soaking the leather in mineral oil before installation will slow the drying process.

Jet Pump

Venturi Effect

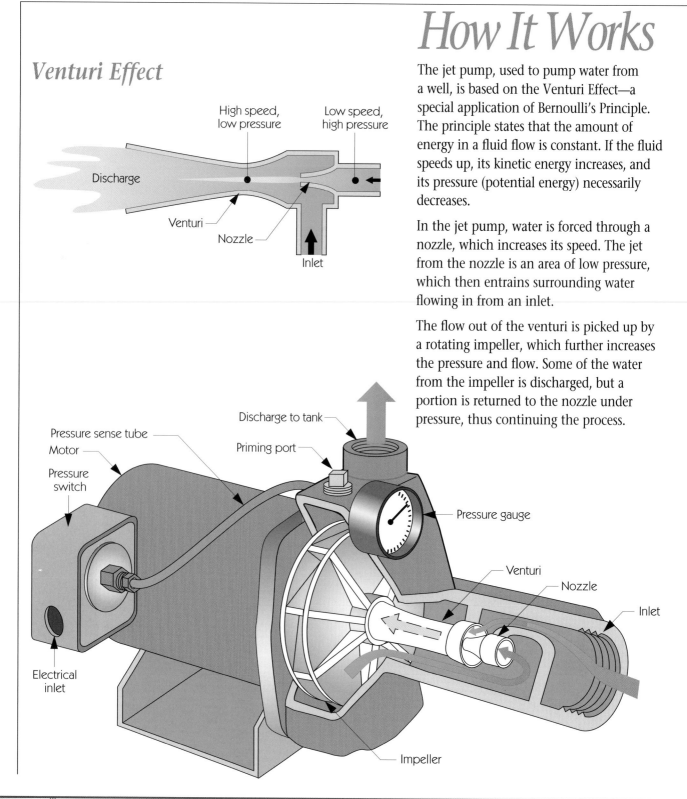

High speed, low pressure

Low speed, high pressure

Discharge

Venturi

Nozzle

Inlet

Pressure sense tube

Motor

Pressure switch

Discharge to tank

Priming port

Pressure gauge

Venturi

Nozzle

Inlet

Electrical inlet

Impeller

How It Works

The jet pump, used to pump water from a well, is based on the Venturi Effect—a special application of Bernoulli's Principle. The principle states that the amount of energy in a fluid flow is constant. If the fluid speeds up, its kinetic energy increases, and its pressure (potential energy) necessarily decreases.

In the jet pump, water is forced through a nozzle, which increases its speed. The jet from the nozzle is an area of low pressure, which then entrains surrounding water flowing in from an inlet.

The flow out of the venturi is picked up by a rotating impeller, which further increases the pressure and flow. Some of the water from the impeller is discharged, but a portion is returned to the nozzle under pressure, thus continuing the process.

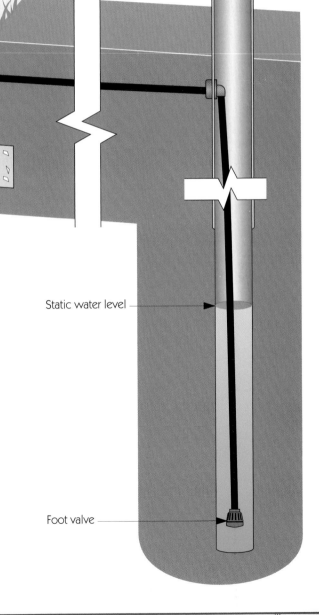

Priming port

Static water level

Foot valve

Before Calling a Plumber

If a jet pump fails to pump water, it is most likely air-bound, i.e. there is air in the pipe between the pump inlet and the well.

First, remove the plug from the priming port, and pour water into it until it stops bubbling. Be patient, as you may need to fill the entire length of pipe down to the level of water in the well. You may have to repeat the process several times.

If the pump still won't draw water, it is likely that the foot valve at the bottom of the well pipe is defective or clogged, allowing the water in the pipe to flow back into the well.

How It Works

The submersible pump is an elegant solution to the problem of lifting water from deep-drilled wells. The 4" diameter of residential-well models allow them to be lowered to the bottom of 6"-diameter wells. Since they push from below, rather than suck from above, these pumps can pump water from as deep as 1,000'. Since they are fully immersed in water, they never require priming and rarely overheat.

Water enters the pump through the intake screen, which filters out large particulates that could damage the pump.

The water is then picked up by the first stage. Each stage consists of a centrifugal impeller and a diffuser. The impeller creates about 15 psi of upward pressure, while the diffuser brakes the water's rotation. Each stage is driven by the same motor and shaft and adds 15 psi to the total pressure. Thus, a 5-stage pump can produce about 75 psi; a 20-stage pump, 300 psi.

In a shallow well, the pump may be suspended only by the 1" polyethylene pipe leading to the pitless adapter near the top of the well. Pumps in deep wells are supported by ropes to take the strain off the pipe's slip fittings.

The pitless adapter is a 2-piece coupling, which allows simple removal of the down-well assembly for repair or replacement.

The pressure switch at the storage tank supplies power to the sump in order to keep the tank pressure between 20 and 50 psi.

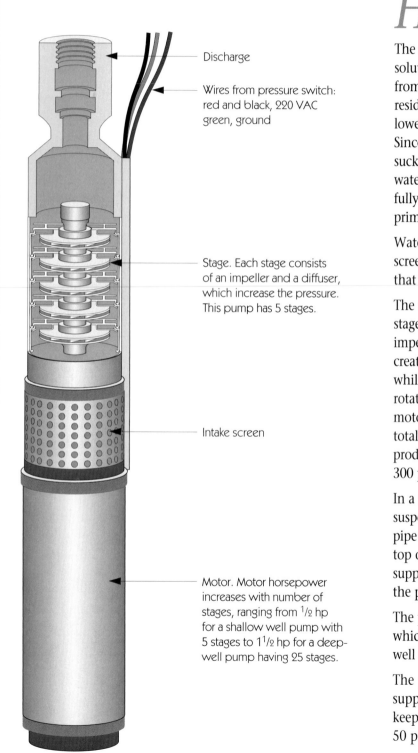

Discharge

Wires from pressure switch: red and black, 220 VAC green, ground

Stage. Each stage consists of an impeller and a diffuser, which increase the pressure. This pump has 5 stages.

Intake screen

Motor. Motor horsepower increases with number of stages, ranging from 1/2 hp for a shallow well pump with 5 stages to 1 1/2 hp for a deep-well pump having 25 stages.

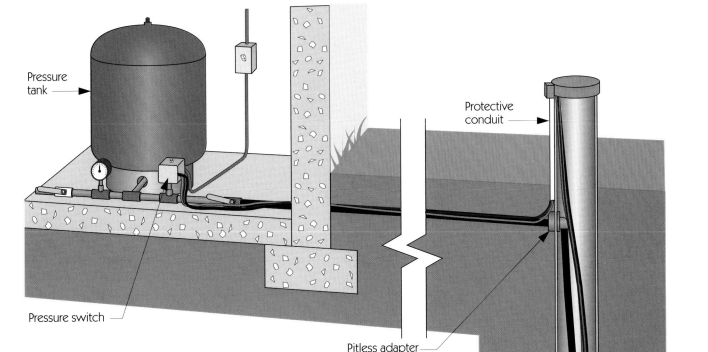

Pressure tank

Pressure switch

Protective conduit

Pitless adapter

6" well casing

Static water level

Snubber (centers pump)

Submersible pump

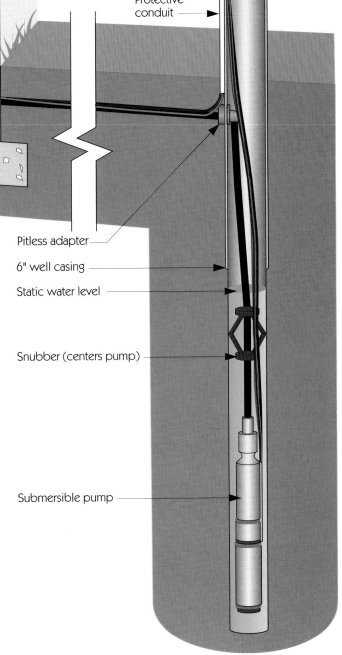

Before Calling a Plumber

Submersible pumps, being immersed in water, never require priming. They are, however, subject to abrasion from sand in the well water and burn-out from lightning strikes. (They make an excellent ground.)

A submersible pump may fail to pump water for several reasons: 1) the pressure switch is faulty and failing to trip; 2) the pressure switch contacts are dirty and not making electrical contact; 3) the circuit breaker supplying the pressure switch has tripped; 4) one of the wires supplying the pump is broken or has a corroded connection; 5) the well is dry; and 6) (most dreaded) the pump has burned out.

Sump Pump

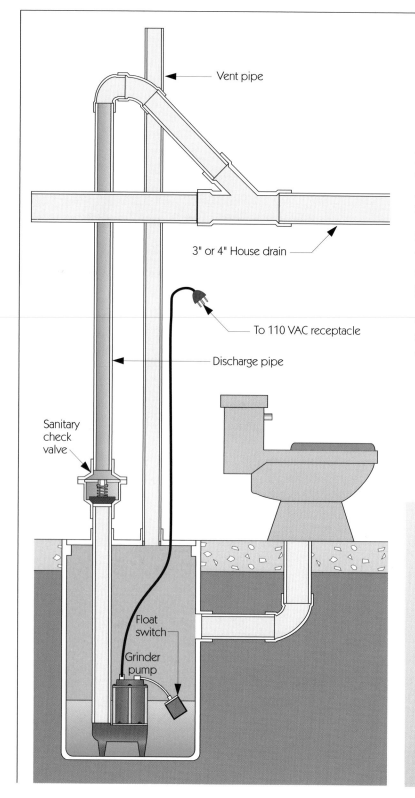

Vent pipe

3" or 4" House drain

To 110 VAC receptacle

Discharge pipe

Sanitary check valve

Float switch

Grinder pump

How It Works

House sewer drains usually exit the home above the basement floor level. This poses a dilemma when finishing a basement and adding a toilet. A sewage sump pump can provide the solution.

The toilet discharges into a plastic sump pit, containing the sewage sump pump. When the mixed solid and liquid waste rises, the float switch turns on the pump, which grinds the waste and ejects it upward through the discharge pipe and into the house drain.

A loop in the discharge pipe and a sanitary check valve prevent back-siphonage of waste from the house drain.

Before Calling a Plumber

Three things can cause a sump pump to stop working:

1) The pump may have stalled, drawing higher current and causing the circuit breaker to trip.

2) An object too tough for the pump to shred may have passed through the toilet and jammed the pump.

3) The pump motor or float switch may have burned out, requiring replacement.

Pressure Tank

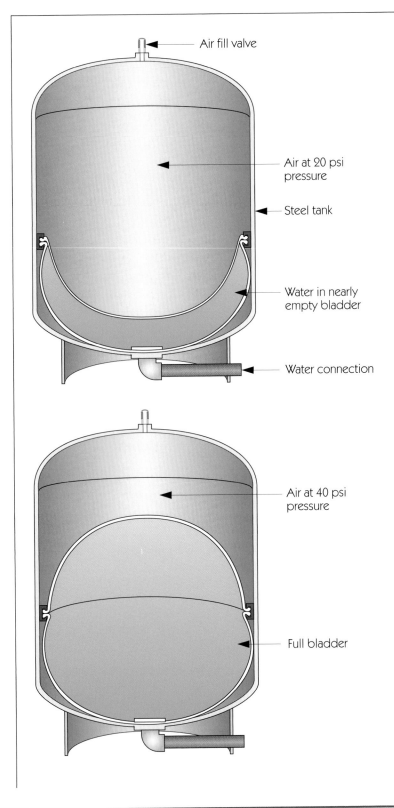

Air fill valve

Air at 20 psi pressure

Steel tank

Water in nearly empty bladder

Water connection

Air at 40 psi pressure

Full bladder

How It Works

In a private water supply, the pressure tank stores water under pressure so that the pump doesn't have to run every time a small amount of water is drawn.

Older tanks were simple vessels in which water entering from the bottom displaced and compressed the air in the tank to create pressure. A problem with this simple system was that, over time, the water absorbed the air, leaving little cushion. Eventually there was so little cushion that the pump cycled on and off every few seconds, leading to a premature failure.

Newer tanks contain the water in a vinyl or neoprene bladder. The air in the tank is separate from, and cannot be absorbed by, the water. In addition, the tank can be pressurized through an automotive-type fill valve at the top. By pre-pressurizing the tank to 20 psi and setting the pump's pressure switch to 20–40 psi, the volume per pump cycle can be maximized at roughly half the volume of the tank.

Before Calling a Plumber

If your pump turns on before the tank is nearly empty, turn off the pump, let the tank run dry, and pressurize the tank to 20 psi using a bicycle pump.

If the pump is cycling every few seconds, either the bladder has failed, allowing the air to be absorbed, or you have an older-style tank. In either case, replacement is recommended.

Electric Water Heater

How It Works

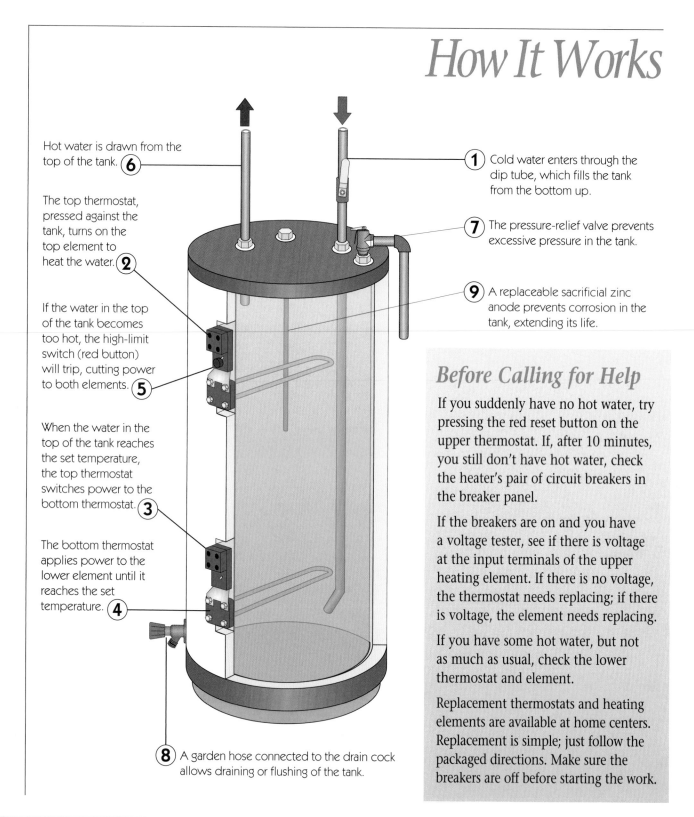

Hot water is drawn from the top of the tank. **6**

The top thermostat, pressed against the tank, turns on the top element to heat the water. **2**

If the water in the top of the tank becomes too hot, the high-limit switch (red button) will trip, cutting power to both elements. **5**

When the water in the top of the tank reaches the set temperature, the top thermostat switches power to the bottom thermostat. **3**

The bottom thermostat applies power to the lower element until it reaches the set temperature. **4**

1 Cold water enters through the dip tube, which fills the tank from the bottom up.

7 The pressure-relief valve prevents excessive pressure in the tank.

9 A replaceable sacrificial zinc anode prevents corrosion in the tank, extending its life.

8 A garden hose connected to the drain cock allows draining or flushing of the tank.

Before Calling for Help

If you suddenly have no hot water, try pressing the red reset button on the upper thermostat. If, after 10 minutes, you still don't have hot water, check the heater's pair of circuit breakers in the breaker panel.

If the breakers are on and you have a voltage tester, see if there is voltage at the input terminals of the upper heating element. If there is no voltage, the thermostat needs replacing; if there is voltage, the element needs replacing.

If you have some hot water, but not as much as usual, check the lower thermostat and element.

Replacement thermostats and heating elements are available at home centers. Replacement is simple; just follow the packaged directions. Make sure the breakers are off before starting the work.

Gas Water Heater

How It Works

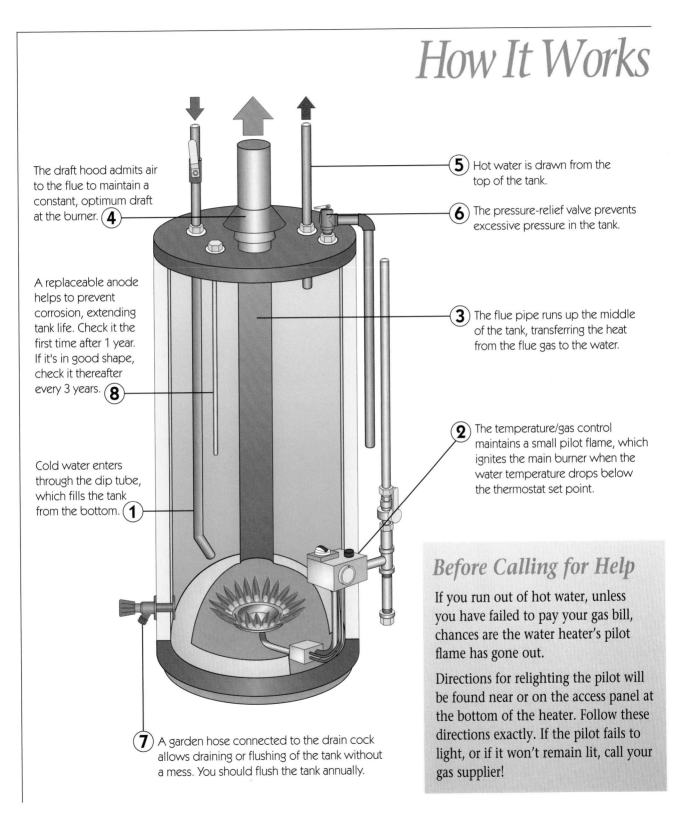

The draft hood admits air to the flue to maintain a constant, optimum draft at the burner. **(4)**

A replaceable anode helps to prevent corrosion, extending tank life. Check it the first time after 1 year. If it's in good shape, check it thereafter every 3 years. **(8)**

Cold water enters through the dip tube, which fills the tank from the bottom. **(1)**

(5) Hot water is drawn from the top of the tank.

(6) The pressure-relief valve prevents excessive pressure in the tank.

(3) The flue pipe runs up the middle of the tank, transferring the heat from the flue gas to the water.

(2) The temperature/gas control maintains a small pilot flame, which ignites the main burner when the water temperature drops below the thermostat set point.

(7) A garden hose connected to the drain cock allows draining or flushing of the tank without a mess. You should flush the tank annually.

Before Calling for Help

If you run out of hot water, unless you have failed to pay your gas bill, chances are the water heater's pilot flame has gone out.

Directions for relighting the pilot will be found near or on the access panel at the bottom of the heater. Follow these directions exactly. If the pilot fails to light, or if it won't remain lit, call your gas supplier!

How It Works

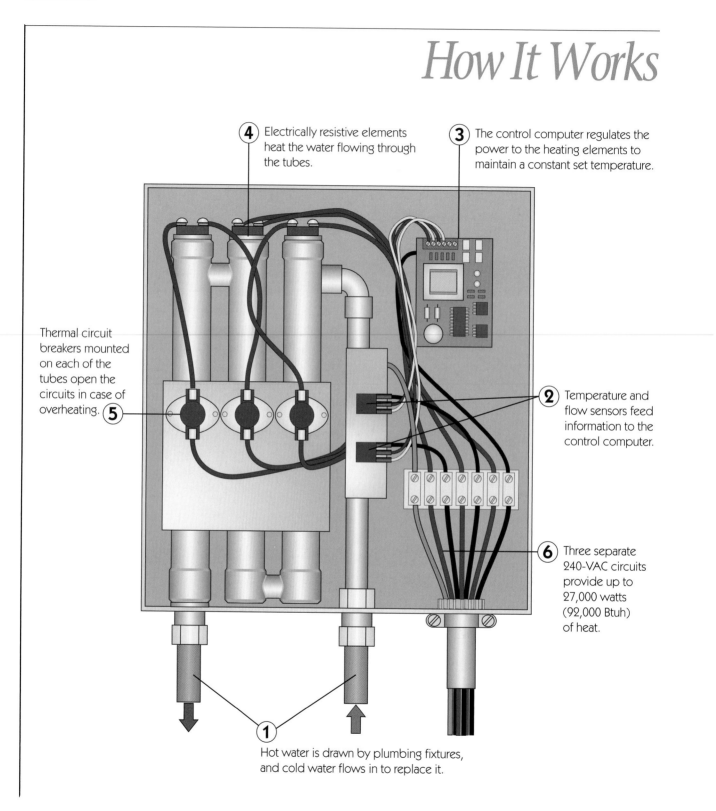

4 Electrically resistive elements heat the water flowing through the tubes.

3 The control computer regulates the power to the heating elements to maintain a constant set temperature.

Thermal circuit breakers mounted on each of the tubes open the circuits in case of overheating. **5**

2 Temperature and flow sensors feed information to the control computer.

6 Three separate 240-VAC circuits provide up to 27,000 watts (92,000 Btuh) of heat.

1 Hot water is drawn by plumbing fixtures, and cold water flows in to replace it.

Gas Tankless Heater

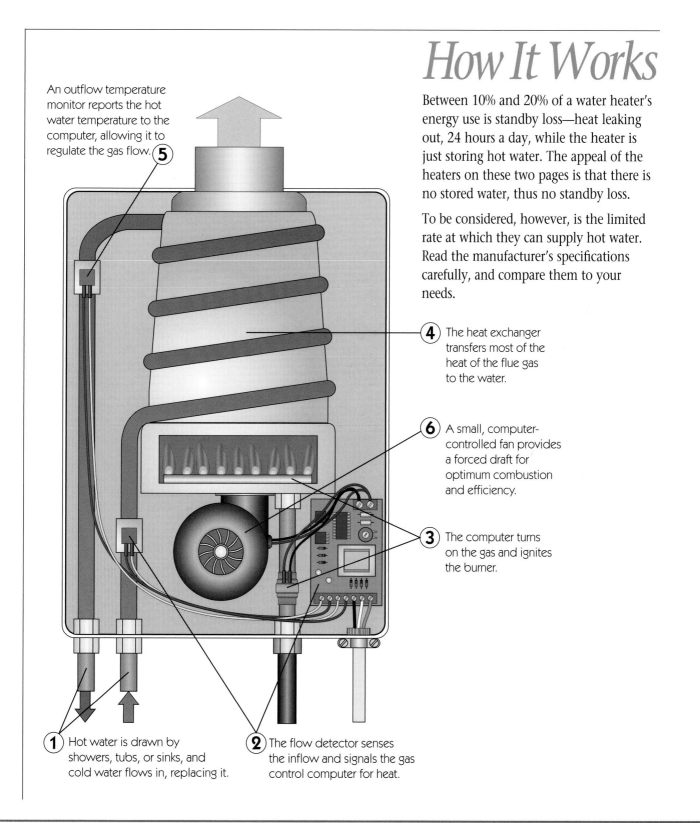

How It Works

Between 10% and 20% of a water heater's energy use is standby loss—heat leaking out, 24 hours a day, while the heater is just storing hot water. The appeal of the heaters on these two pages is that there is no stored water, thus no standby loss.

To be considered, however, is the limited rate at which they can supply hot water. Read the manufacturer's specifications carefully, and compare them to your needs.

An outflow temperature monitor reports the hot water temperature to the computer, allowing it to regulate the gas flow. **(5)**

(4) The heat exchanger transfers most of the heat of the flue gas to the water.

(6) A small, computer-controlled fan provides a forced draft for optimum combustion and efficiency.

(3) The computer turns on the gas and ignites the burner.

(1) Hot water is drawn by showers, tubs, or sinks, and cold water flows in, replacing it.

(2) The flow detector senses the inflow and signals the gas control computer for heat.

How It Works

Heating domestic hot water in a boiler with a tankless coil is inefficient during the off-heating season. Much of the heat is wasted through the boiler's limited insulation and up the vent flue.

The BoilerMate™ hot water storage tank reduces heat losses by half by requiring the boiler to fire only a couple of times a day and by being completely encased in thick insulation.

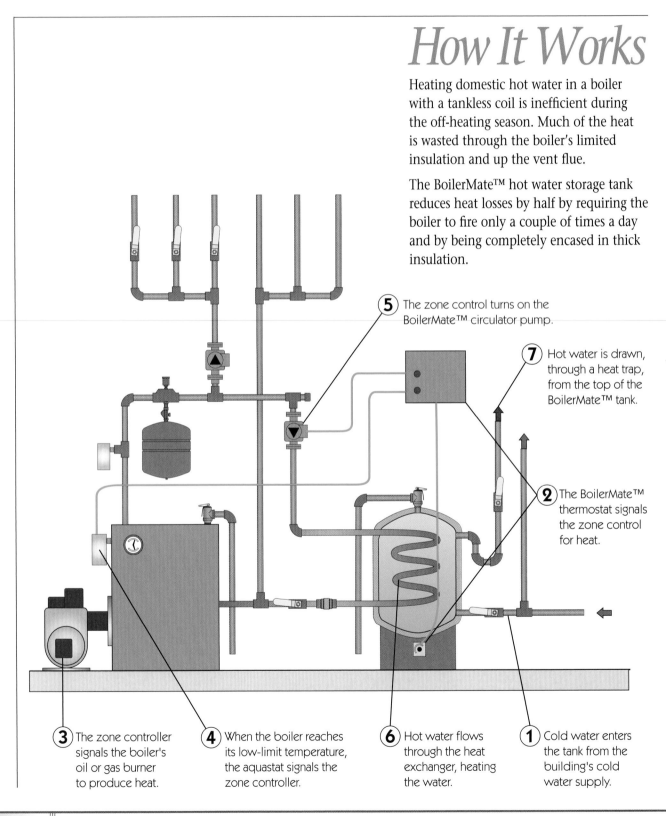

5 The zone control turns on the BoilerMate™ circulator pump.

7 Hot water is drawn, through a heat trap, from the top of the BoilerMate™ tank.

2 The BoilerMate™ thermostat signals the zone control for heat.

3 The zone controller signals the boiler's oil or gas burner to produce heat.

4 When the boiler reaches its low-limit temperature, the aquastat signals the zone controller.

6 Hot water flows through the heat exchanger, heating the water.

1 Cold water enters the tank from the building's cold water supply.

Solar Water Heater

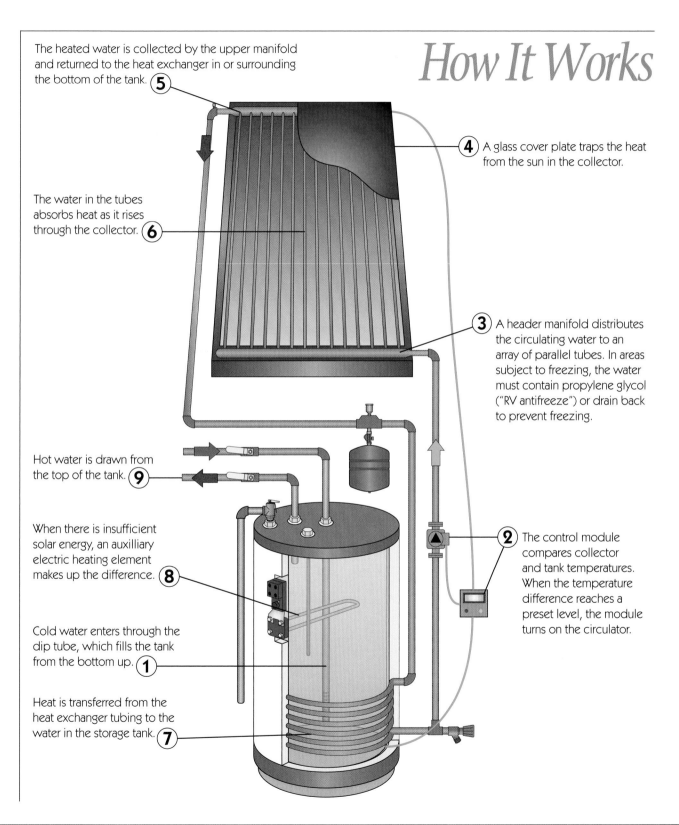

The heated water is collected by the upper manifold and returned to the heat exchanger in or surrounding the bottom of the tank. **(5)**

(4) A glass cover plate traps the heat from the sun in the collector.

The water in the tubes absorbs heat as it rises through the collector. **(6)**

(3) A header manifold distributes the circulating water to an array of parallel tubes. In areas subject to freezing, the water must contain propylene glycol ("RV antifreeze") or drain back to prevent freezing.

Hot water is drawn from the top of the tank. **(9)**

When there is insufficient solar energy, an auxilliary electric heating element makes up the difference. **(8)**

(2) The control module compares collector and tank temperatures. When the temperature difference reaches a preset level, the module turns on the circulator.

Cold water enters through the dip tube, which fills the tank from the bottom up. **(1)**

Heat is transferred from the heat exchanger tubing to the water in the storage tank. **(7)**

How It Works

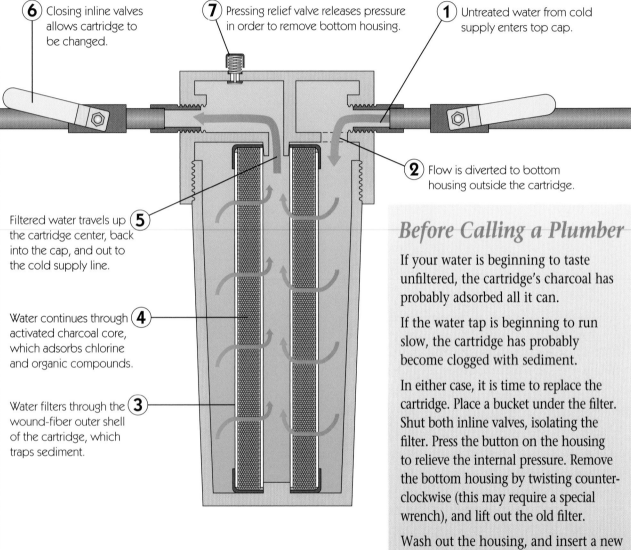

6 Closing inline valves allows cartridge to be changed.

7 Pressing relief valve releases pressure in order to remove bottom housing.

1 Untreated water from cold supply enters top cap.

2 Flow is diverted to bottom housing outside the cartridge.

5 Filtered water travels up the cartridge center, back into the cap, and out to the cold supply line.

4 Water continues through activated charcoal core, which adsorbs chlorine and organic compounds.

3 Water filters through the wound-fiber outer shell of the cartridge, which traps sediment.

Before Calling a Plumber

If your water is beginning to taste unfiltered, the cartridge's charcoal has probably adsorbed all it can.

If the water tap is beginning to run slow, the cartridge has probably become clogged with sediment.

In either case, it is time to replace the cartridge. Place a bucket under the filter. Shut both inline valves, isolating the filter. Press the button on the housing to relieve the internal pressure. Remove the bottom housing by twisting counter-clockwise (this may require a special wrench), and lift out the old filter.

Wash out the housing, and insert a new cartridge and O-ring (first wiping O-ring with petroleum jelly). Replace the bottom housing by twisting clockwise until hand-tight.

Open the two inline valves, and run water at the tap until it runs clear with no bubbles.

Tank Filter

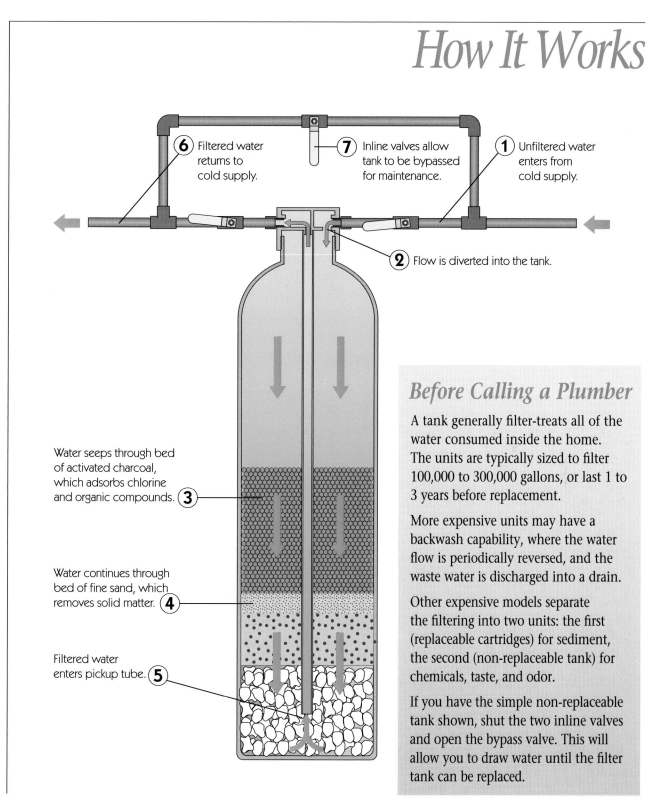

How It Works

6 Filtered water returns to cold supply.

7 Inline valves allow tank to be bypassed for maintenance.

1 Unfiltered water enters from cold supply.

2 Flow is diverted into the tank.

Water seeps through bed of activated charcoal, which adsorbs chlorine and organic compounds. **3**

Water continues through bed of fine sand, which removes solid matter. **4**

Filtered water enters pickup tube. **5**

Before Calling a Plumber

A tank generally filter-treats all of the water consumed inside the home. The units are typically sized to filter 100,000 to 300,000 gallons, or last 1 to 3 years before replacement.

More expensive units may have a backwash capability, where the water flow is periodically reversed, and the waste water is discharged into a drain.

Other expensive models separate the filtering into two units: the first (replaceable cartridges) for sediment, the second (non-replaceable tank) for chemicals, taste, and odor.

If you have the simple non-replaceable tank shown, shut the two inline valves and open the bypass valve. This will allow you to draw water until the filter tank can be replaced.

How It Works

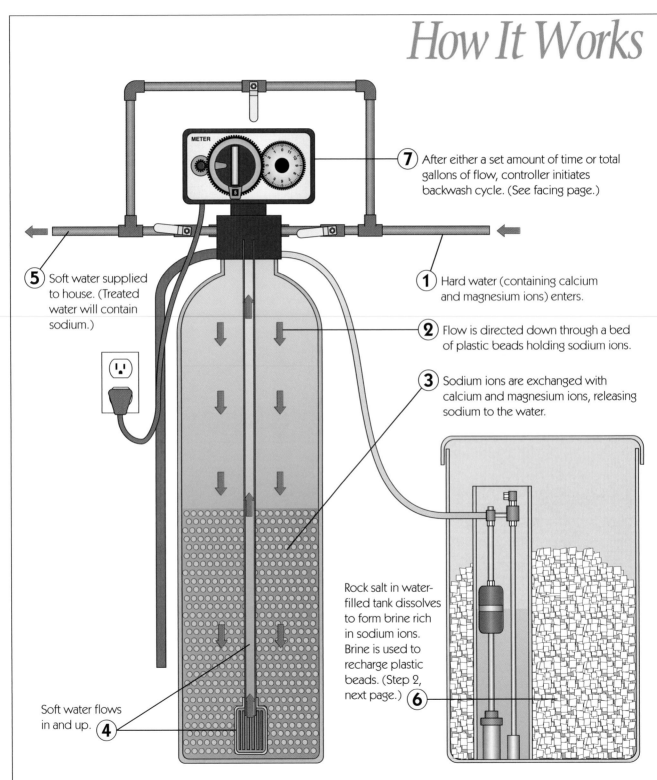

7 After either a set amount of time or total gallons of flow, controller initiates backwash cycle. (See facing page.)

5 Soft water supplied to house. (Treated water will contain sodium.)

1 Hard water (containing calcium and magnesium ions) enters.

2 Flow is directed down through a bed of plastic beads holding sodium ions.

3 Sodium ions are exchanged with calcium and magnesium ions, releasing sodium to the water.

Rock salt in water-filled tank dissolves to form brine rich in sodium ions. Brine is used to recharge plastic beads. (Step 2, next page.) **6**

Soft water flows in and up. **4**

METER

Recharging the Resin

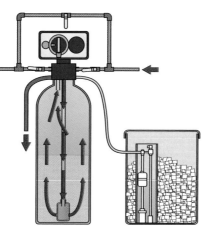

1

Controller initiates backwash cycle. Untreated water flows in reverse direction through resin bed and is discharged into drain.

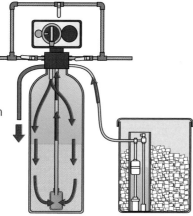

2

Controller switches to recharge cycle. Concentrated sodium solution (brine) pumped through resin bed forces replacement of calcium and magnesium ions by sodium ions. Altered solution is discharged into drain.

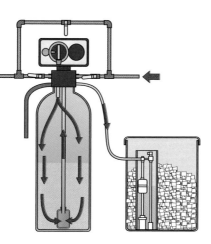

3

Resin bed is again rinsed with untreated water, but overflow this time refills brine tank with fresh water.

4

Rock salt in brine tank is slowly dissolved and must be manually replenished.

Before Calling a Plumber

If your water gradually turns hard again and never regains softness, check the brine tank. It may have run out of rock salt. (You can buy more at the hardware store.)

If there is plenty of salt left, check the water level in the brine tank. It should be about halfway up the tank. If not, add water directly to the tank.

If your water hardness cycles on a regular schedule, resin is becoming saturated, and the controller must be reset to recharge more often. See the operator's manual for instructions on resetting.

Reverse Osmosis Filter

How It Works

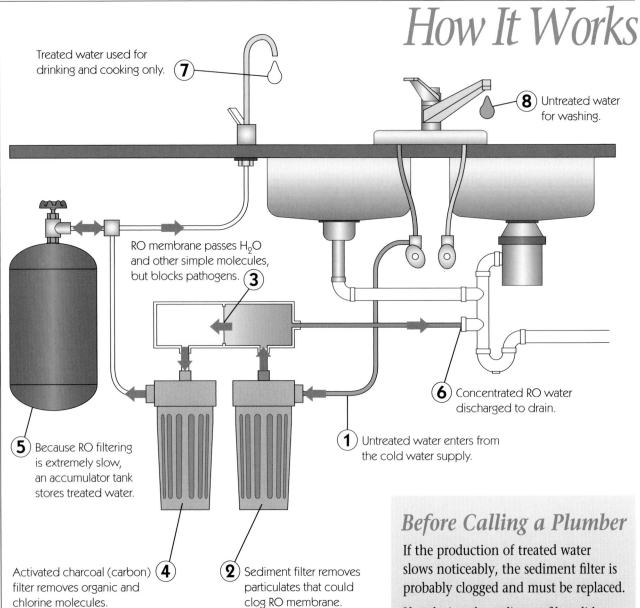

Treated water used for drinking and cooking only. **7**

8 Untreated water for washing.

RO membrane passes H₂O and other simple molecules, but blocks pathogens. **3**

5 Because RO filtering is extremely slow, an accumulator tank stores treated water.

Activated charcoal (carbon) **4** filter removes organic and chlorine molecules.

2 Sediment filter removes particulates that could clog RO membrane.

6 Concentrated RO water discharged to drain.

1 Untreated water enters from the cold water supply.

Reverse osmosis (RO) filters combine three filtering components: a sediment filter to remove large particles, a plastic reverse-osmosis membrane to remove dissolved salts and metals, and an activated charcoal canister to remove tastes and odors. No home system provides a greater degree of filtering.

Before Calling a Plumber

If the production of treated water slows noticeably, the sediment filter is probably clogged and must be replaced.

If replacing the sediment filter did not correct the loss of production, the RO filter may be fouled and require cleaning or replacement. Refer to your owner's manual.

If the water begins to taste or smell of chemicals, the charcoal filter may be used up and require replacement.

UV Purifier

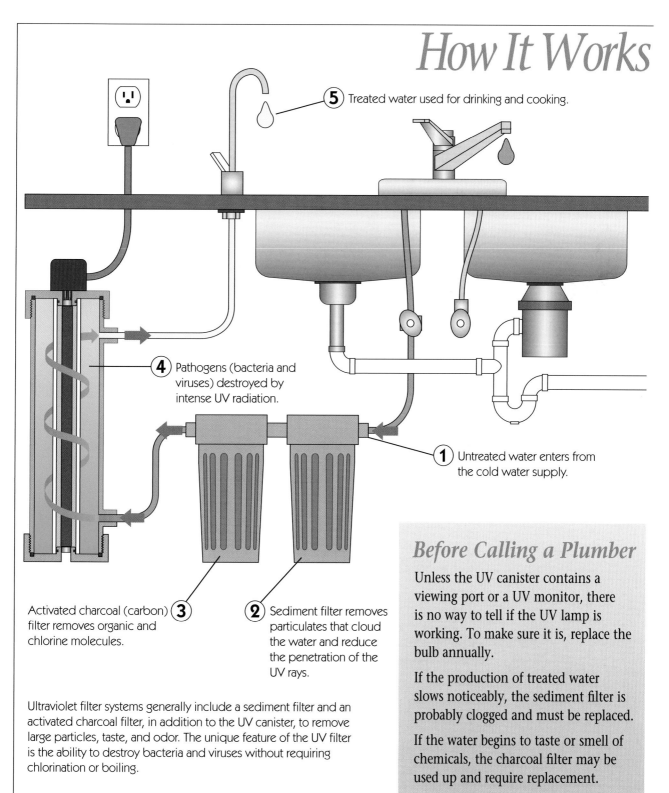

How It Works

5 Treated water used for drinking and cooking.

4 Pathogens (bacteria and viruses) destroyed by intense UV radiation.

1 Untreated water enters from the cold water supply.

Activated charcoal (carbon) **3** filter removes organic and chlorine molecules.

2 Sediment filter removes particulates that cloud the water and reduce the penetration of the UV rays.

Ultraviolet filter systems generally include a sediment filter and an activated charcoal filter, in addition to the UV canister, to remove large particles, taste, and odor. The unique feature of the UV filter is the ability to destroy bacteria and viruses without requiring chlorination or boiling.

Before Calling a Plumber

Unless the UV canister contains a viewing port or a UV monitor, there is no way to tell if the UV lamp is working. To make sure it is, replace the bulb annually.

If the production of treated water slows noticeably, the sediment filter is probably clogged and must be replaced.

If the water begins to taste or smell of chemicals, the charcoal filter may be used up and require replacement.

Fire Sprinklers

A plug, held in place by a glycerine-filled ampule, seals the sprinkler outlet. **(1)**

As the ampule heats up, the glycerine expands. Within a minute or two of reaching 155F, the pressure shatters the glass ampule, releasing the plug. **(2)**

Water under pressure strikes the deflector plate and sprays radially over a large area. The cooling effect usually prevents other sprinkler heads from activating. **(3)**

How They Work

An unvented fire in an enclosed space produces heated air, which, because warm air is buoyant, rises to the ceiling. The air temperature at ceiling level steadily increases until it reaches the design temperature of the sprinkler head. This temperature, about 150°F, is well below the danger point for human respiration and the ignition points of furnishings and construction materials.

As soon as the closest sprinkler triggers, water striking the fire evaporates, absorbing its latent heat of evaporation and cooling the air and burning material. (Recall the cooling effect of a rain shower on a hot day.) Deprived of heat, the fire is usually extinguished.

Unfortunately, the sprinkler continues to spray until someone turns it off!

Typical Distribution of Sprinkler Heads

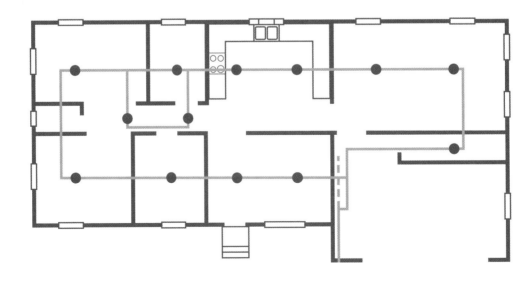

2 WIRING

Homeowners who have little understanding of electricity justifiably fear electrical wiring. However, a basic understanding of how electricity flows (which this chapter will help to give you) plus adherence to a single, simple safety rule, will help prepare you to troubleshoot and repair simple electrical problems without trepidation.

The basic safety rule when working on electrical circuits, fixtures, or devices is to **disconnect the power** before attempting any work. Unplug the device, turn off the circuit's breaker at the service panel, or flip the main breaker pair at the top of the service panel. And just to be doubly sure, use a circuit tester to make sure the power is definitely turned off before proceeding with a repair.

How It Works

Water Power Circuit

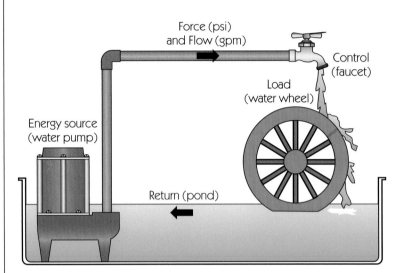

Force (psi)
and Flow (gpm)

Control
(faucet)

Load
(water wheel)

Energy source
(water pump)

Return (pond)

One of the basic laws of physics states that, except in nuclear reactions, matter can be neither created nor destroyed. Thus, in the waterworks at left, water lifted by the pump to turn the water wheel always returns to the pump.

A pump imparts energy in the form of pressure to the water in the pipe. The rate of flow of the pressurized water is measured in gallons per minute (gpm), and a faucet can be used to turn the flow on and off. The water, in falling, transfers its energy to the water wheel. Finally, the energy-depleted water flows back to its source.

The water circuit just described provides an excellent analogy to the flow of electricity. In an electrical circuit, electromotive force (voltage) is created by a power station. The rate of flow of the energized electrons is measured in amperes (1 ampere = $6.24 \cdot 10^{18}$ electrons per second). The switch, by closing and opening the circuit, can be used to turn the flow on and off. Instead of turning a water wheel, the energy in the electrons can be transferred to an electric motor or to a light bulb, as shown. And just as with the molecules of water, the now energy-depleted electrons return to their source through the conductive ground.

Electrical Power Circuit

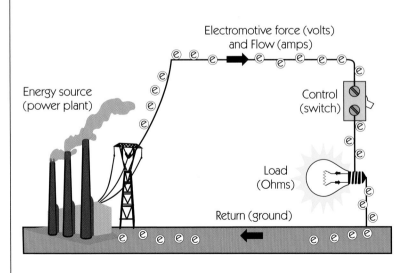

Electromotive force (volts)
and Flow (amps)

Energy source
(power plant)

Control
(switch)

Load
(Ohms)

Return (ground)

Without a complete return path (a closed circuit), electricity cannot flow. The zero-voltage return path in a circuit is always called the "ground," and may be earth or some conducting body that takes its place. The return path may also be a neutral wire.

Ohm's Law

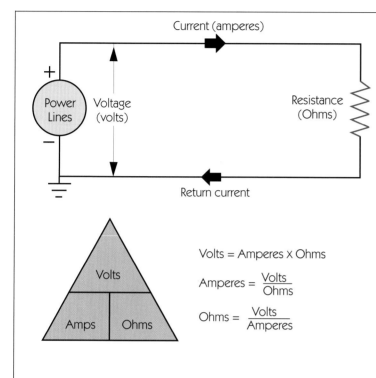

Current (amperes)

+
Power Lines

Voltage (volts)

Resistance (Ohms)

Return current

Volts = Amperes x Ohms

$$Amperes = \frac{Volts}{Ohms}$$

$$Ohms = \frac{Volts}{Amperes}$$

Volts / Amps / Ohms

How It Works

Georg Simon Ohm, in 1827, discovered and defined the relationship between the quantities in an electrical circuit. Ohm's Law is:

$$I = \frac{V}{R}$$

where:
- I = amperes of current flow
- V = volts of electromotive force
- R = ohms (Ω) of resistance

Ohm's Law can be rearranged to yield any one of the three quantities, given the other two. Place your thumb over the desired quantity in the green triangle at left, and the result shows the mathematical relationship between the remaining two.

Applying Ohm's Law to a Circuit

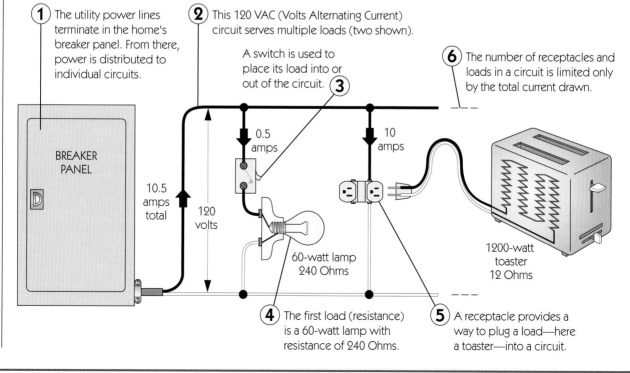

(1) The utility power lines terminate in the home's breaker panel. From there, power is distributed to individual circuits.

(2) This 120 VAC (Volts Alternating Current) circuit serves multiple loads (two shown).

A switch is used to place its load into or out of the circuit. **(3)**

(6) The number of receptacles and loads in a circuit is limited only by the total current drawn.

0.5 amps

10 amps

BREAKER PANEL

10.5 amps total

120 volts

60-watt lamp 240 Ohms

1200-watt toaster 12 Ohms

(4) The first load (resistance) is a 60-watt lamp with resistance of 240 Ohms.

(5) A receptacle provides a way to plug a load—here a toaster—into a circuit.

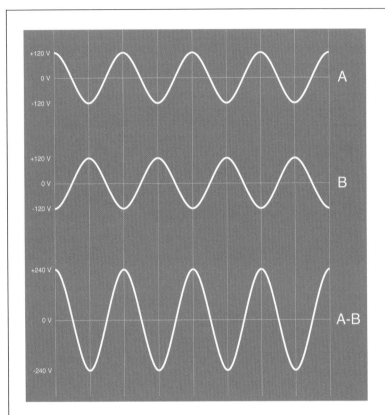

How It Works

We speak of the power in our homes as if it were all 120 VAC (Volts Alternating Current). Rather, it is three voltages. How else could we have both 120 VAC and 240 VAC appliances? In fact, some appliances, such as electric ranges and clothes dryers, run on both 120 VAC and 240 VAC.

Here is how it works. From a transformer on a pole, wires A, B, and C run to the house. As the voltage graphs at left show, wires A and B carry 120 VAC, but they are of opposite sign. Wire C is at neutral, or ground. Thus, we can have two different 120-VAC circuits by tapping into wire pairs A & C and B & C.

Now the tricky part. By connecting to wires A & B, due to their opposing signs, we get a third source—240 VAC.

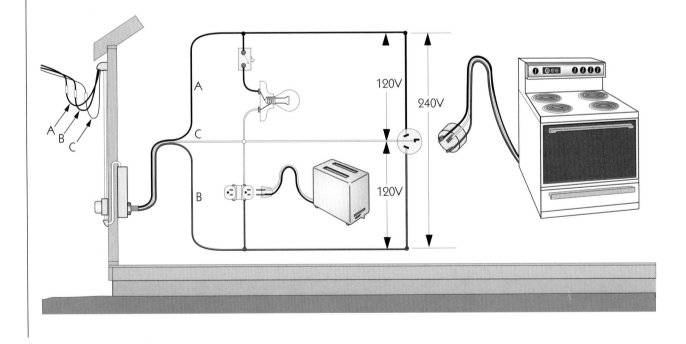

Circuit Breakers & Fuses

Magnetic Circuit Breaker

How They Work

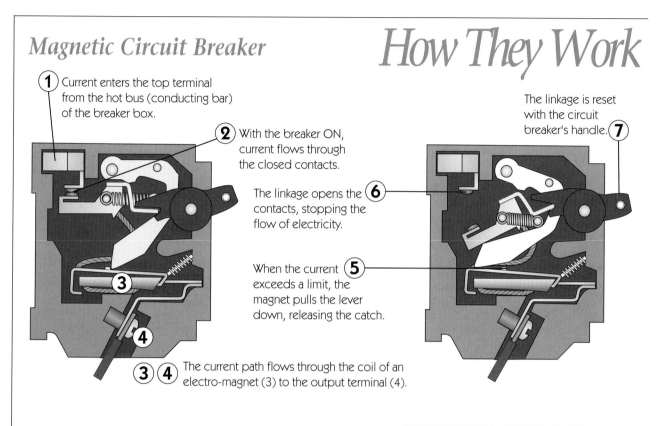

1 Current enters the top terminal from the hot bus (conducting bar) of the breaker box.

2 With the breaker ON, current flows through the closed contacts.

The linkage opens the **6** contacts, stopping the flow of electricity.

When the current **5** exceeds a limit, the magnet pulls the lever down, releasing the catch.

3 4 The current path flows through the coil of an electro-magnet (3) to the output terminal (4).

The linkage is reset with the circuit breaker's handle. **7**

Fuse

The current is conducted through the center post, through a bead of solder, then through the wire to the shell. **2**

The current heats the solder. When the current exceeds the limit, the solder melts, and the spring pulls the wire away, breaking the circuit. **3**

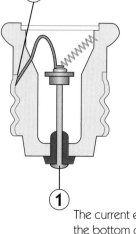

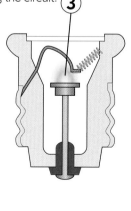

1 The current enters the fuse through the bottom center terminal.

Before Calling for Help

If the lights go out, the first place to look is in the main panel. (See page 52.) Blown see-through fuses are obvious. Either the glass will be cloudy, or the metal ribbon will be melted through.

Circuit breakers are not always so obvious. The handle usually flips all the way, but sometimes the movement is almost imperceptible. In any case, flip each breaker off and then on again. If there is an overload or short circuit, the breaker will immediately open again. If the breakers stay closed, and the lights are still out, the problem is not the breaker.

2 Service Drop

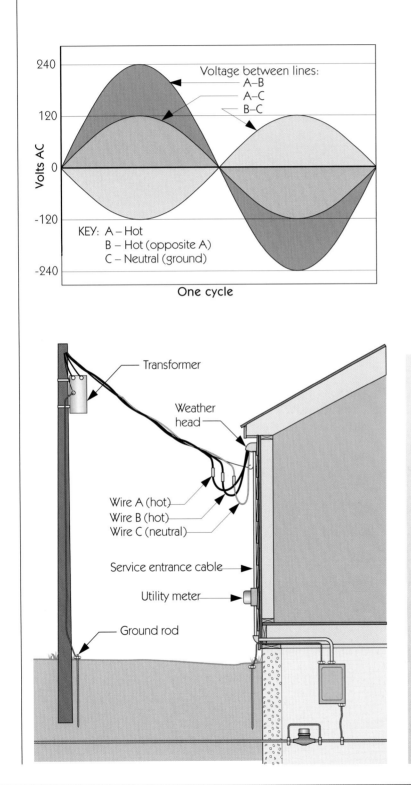

240

Voltage between lines:
A–B
A–C
B–C

120

Volts AC

0

-120

KEY: A – Hot
B – Hot (opposite A)
C – Neutral (ground)

-240

One cycle

Transformer

Weather head

Wire A (hot)
Wire B (hot)
Wire C (neutral)

Service entrance cable

Utility meter

Ground rod

How It Works

The service drop is the set of three wires from the utility's transformer to the home. As shown at left, and on page 46, wires A and B both carry 120 VAC, but when A is at its peak positive voltage, wire B is at its peak negative. Wire C (neutral or ground) is always at 0 VAC.

Circuits may be powered by the voltage difference between any two of the three wires, so the home can have three different power sources:

A–C = 120 VAC
B–C = 120 VAC
A–B = 240 VAC

Before Calling the Utility

If the power in a room suddenly goes out, before calling your utility to report a power outage:

- Call your next-door neighbor to see if they have also lost power.

- Check your circuit breaker panel(s) to see if any breakers have tripped off. If they have, try resetting. If they trip again, the circuit is overloaded.

- Check the house to see if there is power in any other circuit. If there is, the problem lies within the house.

- If there is no power in the house, reset the main disconnect breaker at the top of the circuit breaker panel.

- If there is still no power, call the utility to report a power outage.

Electromechanical Meter

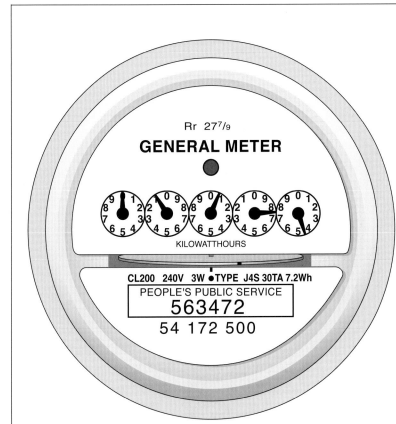

Rr 27⁷/₉

GENERAL METER

KILOWATTHOURS

CL200 240V 3W ●TYPE J4S 30TA 7.2Wh

PEOPLE'S PUBLIC SERVICE

563472

54 172 500

How It Works

Power is the rate at which energy is used or produced. Electrical power is measured in watts, where:

$$watts = amps \cdot volts$$

The total amount of energy consumed is the rate at which it is being used (watts times the length of time it has been used in hours). Because a watt-hour is so small, the utility company bills for kilowatt-hours, or thousand watt-hours.

The meter outside your home is actually a tiny motor whose rpm is proportional to the power running through it. Thus, the number of revolutions of its disk indicates the number of kilowatt-hours consumed.

On the face of the meter you will see a set of numbers indicating meter amp capacity, system voltage, meter type, and meter constant. In the illustration, the meter constant is *7.2 Wh*, meaning its disk spins once for every 7.2 watt-hours consumed.

Inside the meter case is a set of gears linking the disk to the set of indicator dials. Once per month a meter reader (some meters can be read remotely) records the dials, and you are billed on the difference between the present and previous month's readings.

The meter is read from left to right, always using the lower number when the pointer falls between two. For example, the meter in the illustration reads: 0 1 0 7 4.

Note that the directions of rotation of the dials alternate as in any gear-driven mechanism.

Before Calling the Utility

Some consumers concerned about high electric bills may suspect a malfunction in the meter. The chances of your meter being faulty are small, but checking its accuracy is a simple matter. Simply turn off all of the breakers in the main panel except one. Plug into that circuit an appliance of known wattage (a 5,000-watt heater, for example), and let it run for an hour. If the meter dial on the right changes by more than 5, call the utility.

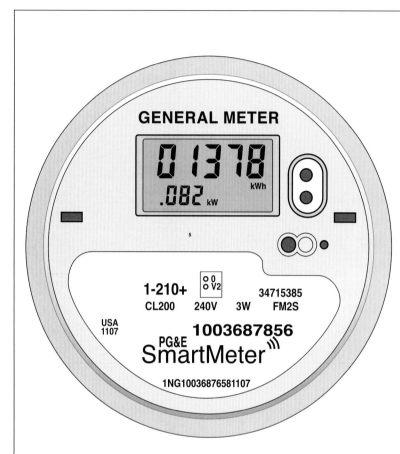

GENERAL METER

01378 kWh

.082 kW

5

1-210+   ○ 0   34715385
        ○ V2

CL200   240V   3W   FM2S

USA 1107

PG&E **1003687856**
SmartMeter

1NG10036876581107

How It Works

The Smart Meter is a combination digital watt-hour meter, computer, and two-way radio. Usage data, including contributions from solar and wind systems, are sampled several times per hour and transmitted by radio over networks to the electric utility company.

Having realtime access to data from individual homes allows the utility to spot power outages, as well as monitor time-of-day usage at different rates. The main selling point, however, is elimination of the human meter reader, resulting in savings to the customer.

In spite of the several advantages and savings, the smart meter faces strong resistance from consumer groups fearing possible health hazards from the radio-frequency radiation. The jury remains out.

Data Collection from Smart Meters

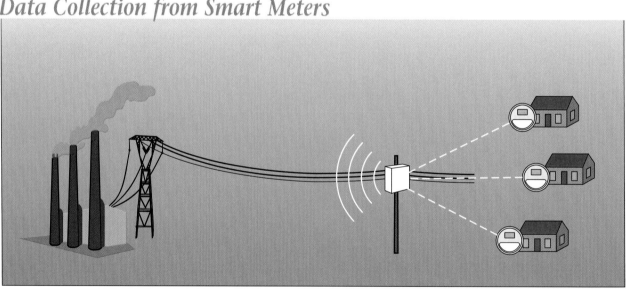

Circuit Grounding

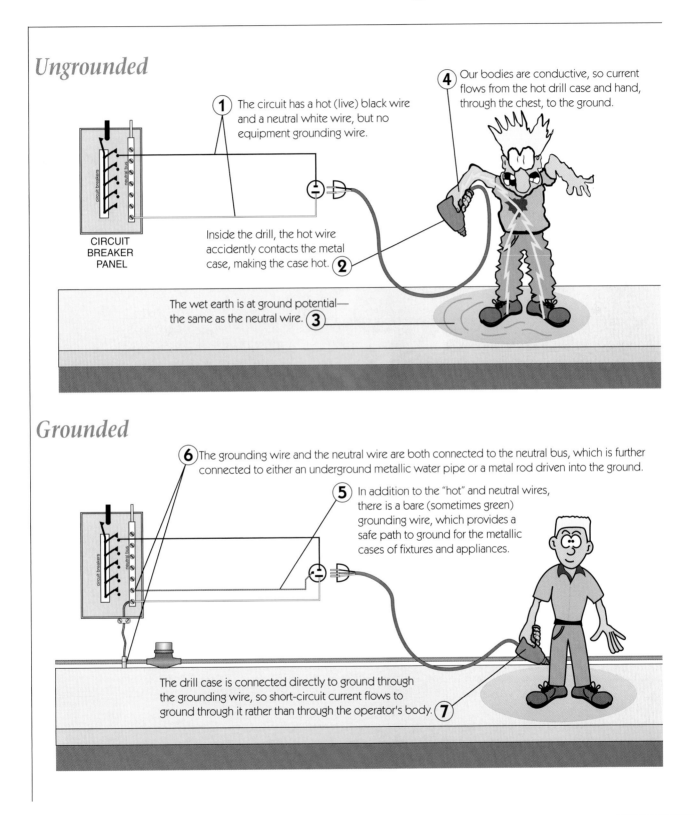

Ungrounded

(1) The circuit has a hot (live) black wire and a neutral white wire, but no equipment grounding wire.

(4) Our bodies are conductive, so current flows from the hot drill case and hand, through the chest, to the ground.

Inside the drill, the hot wire accidently contacts the metal case, making the case hot. **(2)**

CIRCUIT BREAKER PANEL

The wet earth is at ground potential—the same as the neutral wire. **(3)**

Grounded

(6) The grounding wire and the neutral wire are both connected to the neutral bus, which is further connected to either an underground metallic water pipe or a metal rod driven into the ground.

(5) In addition to the "hot" and neutral wires, there is a bare (sometimes green) grounding wire, which provides a safe path to ground for the metallic cases of fixtures and appliances.

The drill case is connected directly to ground through the grounding wire, so short-circuit current flows to ground through it rather than through the operator's body. **(7)**

How It Works

Main Panel

The main panel provides a single, convenient location for the distribution of power throughout the house. Sub-panels, fed from the main panel, are sometimes employed when a large amount of power is used far from the main panel.

The double-pole main breaker allows all power to the house to be switched off. **2**

One hot wire feeds Bus A, the other feeds Bus B. **3**

Smaller circuit breakers serving individual circuits are plugged into either Bus A or Bus B. **4**

Alternating the prongs of the bus bars guarantees that adjacent breakers are on different buses. **5**

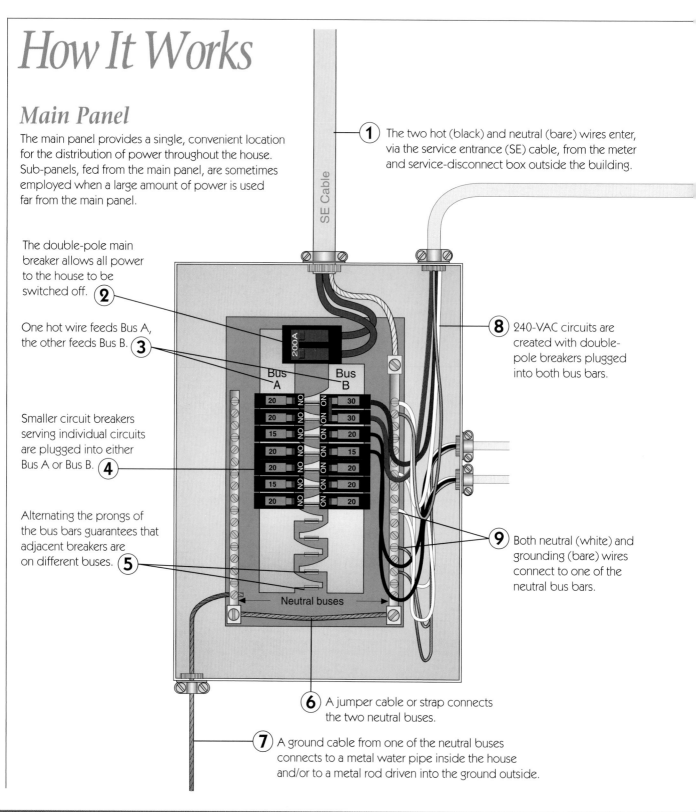

1 The two hot (black) and neutral (bare) wires enter, via the service entrance (SE) cable, from the meter and service-disconnect box outside the building.

8 240-VAC circuits are created with double-pole breakers plugged into both bus bars.

9 Both neutral (white) and grounding (bare) wires connect to one of the neutral bus bars.

6 A jumper cable or strap connects the two neutral buses.

7 A ground cable from one of the neutral buses connects to a metal water pipe inside the house and/or to a metal rod driven into the ground outside.

Sub-Panel

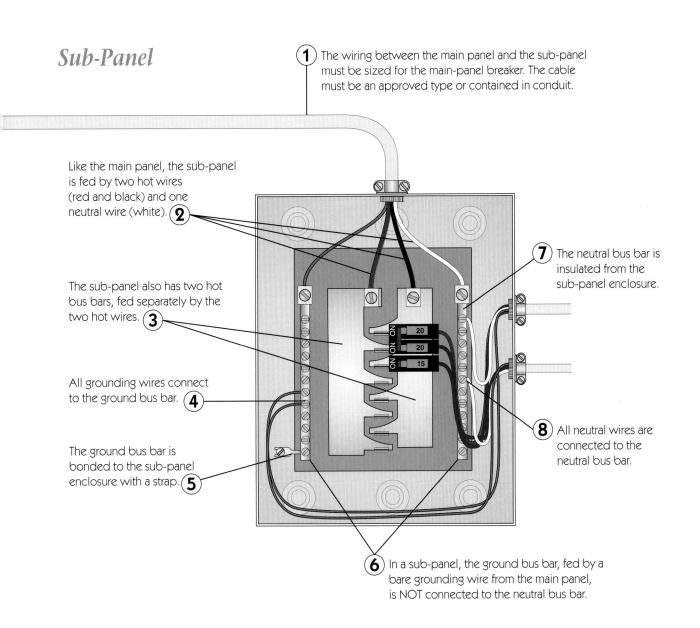

1 The wiring between the main panel and the sub-panel must be sized for the main-panel breaker. The cable must be an approved type or contained in conduit.

Like the main panel, the sub-panel is fed by two hot wires (red and black) and one neutral wire (white). **2**

The sub-panel also has two hot bus bars, fed separately by the two hot wires. **3**

All grounding wires connect to the ground bus bar. **4**

The ground bus bar is bonded to the sub-panel enclosure with a strap. **5**

7 The neutral bus bar is insulated from the sub-panel enclosure.

8 All neutral wires are connected to the neutral bus bar.

6 In a sub-panel, the ground bus bar, fed by a bare grounding wire from the main panel, is NOT connected to the neutral bus bar.

Receptacle

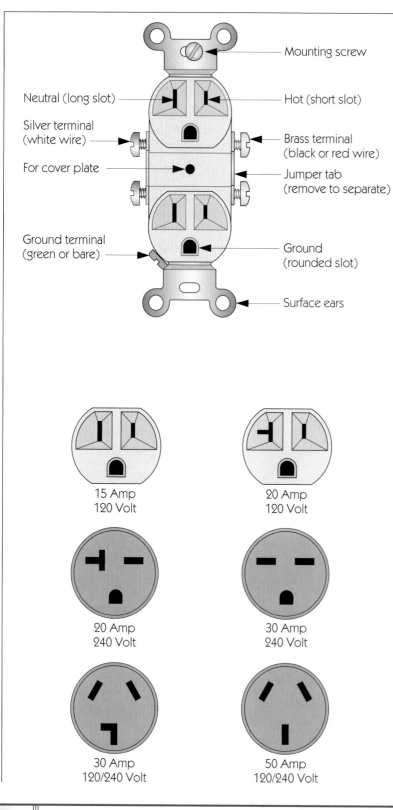

Mounting screw

Neutral (long slot)

Hot (short slot)

Silver terminal (white wire)

Brass terminal (black or red wire)

For cover plate

Jumper tab (remove to separate)

Ground terminal (green or bare)

Ground (rounded slot)

Surface ears

15 Amp 120 Volt

20 Amp 120 Volt

20 Amp 240 Volt

30 Amp 240 Volt

30 Amp 120/240 Volt

50 Amp 120/240 Volt

How It Works

A receptacle provides a way to connect lamps, appliances, or other electrical devices into a circuit. When plugged in, a device becomes an extension of that circuit.

To prevent wires in a circuit from being scrambled (hot wires plugged into neutral or grounding wires, etc.), a receptacle's sockets and its matching plug's prongs conform to standard patterns. In the common 15-Amp/120-VAC receptacle to the left, we see that the neutral slot is longer than the hot slot. The same is true of the prongs in the 15-Amp/120-VAC plug, so it is impossible to plug a cord in backward.

Similarly, the grounding socket is placed at the apex of a socket triangle. Older-style receptacles have no ground socket, so it is impossible to insert a 3-prong grounding plug into an ungrounded receptacle.

At left are the standard receptacles found in a home. Each has a standard geometry specified by the National Electrical Code (NEC). As with the 15-Amp/120-VAC receptacle described above, each has its matching plug.

Of special note is the difference between 15-Amp and 20-Amp/120-VAC receptacles. Unfortunately, 15-Amp receptacles are far less expensive than their 20-Amp cousins, so it is common (though illegal) practice to wire 20-Amp circuits with the cheaper 15-Amp receptacles. Fortunately, the plug of a 20-Amp appliance will not fit in the 15-Amp receptacle.

Typical Receptacle Circuits

SERIES OF RECEPTACLES

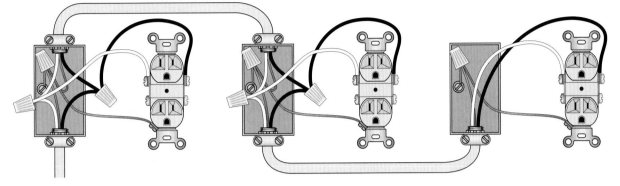

SPLIT-SWITCHED RECEPTACLE
(top receptacle switched)

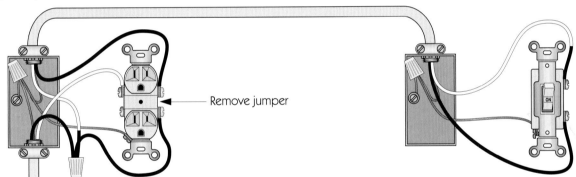

Remove jumper

SPLIT-CIRCUIT RECEPTACLE
(two separate circuits)

Remove
these
jumpers
on all 3

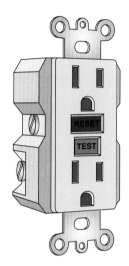

How It Works

The ground-fault circuit interrupter (GFCI) is required by code in potentially wet locations where the danger of shock is high.

AC current passing through a magnetic ring (toroid) generates a voltage in the GFCI's pickup coil. Normally, all current flows through the hot and neutral wires. Since the currents are equal and opposite, the voltages they generate cancel each other out. If any return current leaks to ground, however, the currents are unequal, and the coil generates a net voltage. This voltage is amplified by the fault sensor, which trips a solenoid to open the circuit and stop the current.

The maximum ground fault current before tripping, 0.005 amps, is not lethal, but could induce fibrillation.

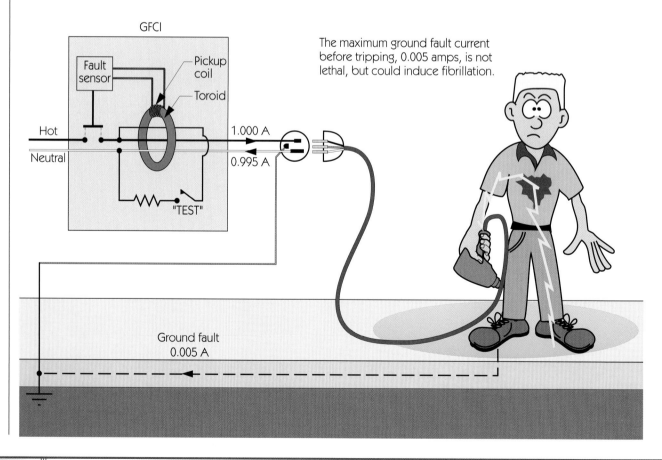

AFCI

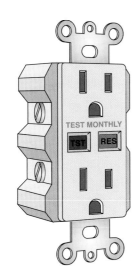

How It Works

Loose wires, broken wires, and wires contacting one another due to frayed insulation can all produce electric arcs—current jumping across small air gaps. Electric arcs are used to melt and weld metals; they can also start fires inside walls.

The arc-fault circuit interrupter (AFCI) is a circuit breaker containing a microprocessor (tiny computer) that constantly compares the current and voltage patterns in its protected circuit to those of a normal circuit. When it detects patterns typical of arcs, it trips a solenoid, opening the circuit, and stopping the flow of electricity.

AFCIs also contain standard magnetic or thermal circuit breaker mechanisms.

Arc Current and Voltage Patterns

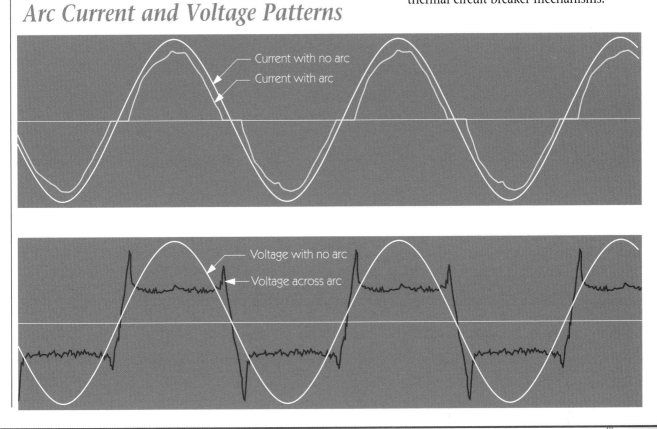

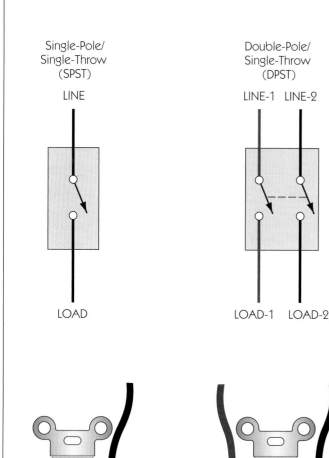

Single-Pole/
Single-Throw
(SPST)

LINE

LOAD

Double-Pole/
Single-Throw
(DPST)

LINE-1   LINE-2

LOAD-1   LOAD-2

LINE

ON

LOAD

GND

LINE-1   LINE-2

ON

LOAD-1   LOAD-2

How It Works

The single-pole, single-throw switch is the simplest and most common of switches. The toggle lever simply connects (ON) or disconnects (OFF) the hot (black *or* red) wires attached to its two terminals.

The double-pole, single-throw switch is essentially a pair of single-pole switches connecting or disconnecting both of the hot (black *and* red) wires in a 240-VAC circuit.

Note that the *National Electric Code* allows *only* the hot wires of a circuit to be switched. The danger in disconnecting the ground side of a circuit should be obvious.

Before Calling for Help

If a light or other switched electrical device fails to respond to its switch:

- Plug a lamp that you know is working into the circuit. If it works, the problem is not in the switch.

- If the substitute device doesn't work either, check the circuit breaker or fuse serving that circuit.

If you decide to replace the switch, first turn off the power to that circuit at the service panel. Label the wires as they are removed from the old switch, and reconnect them in exactly the same way.

Typical Single-Pole Switch Circuits

SPLIT-CIRCUIT RECEPTACLE

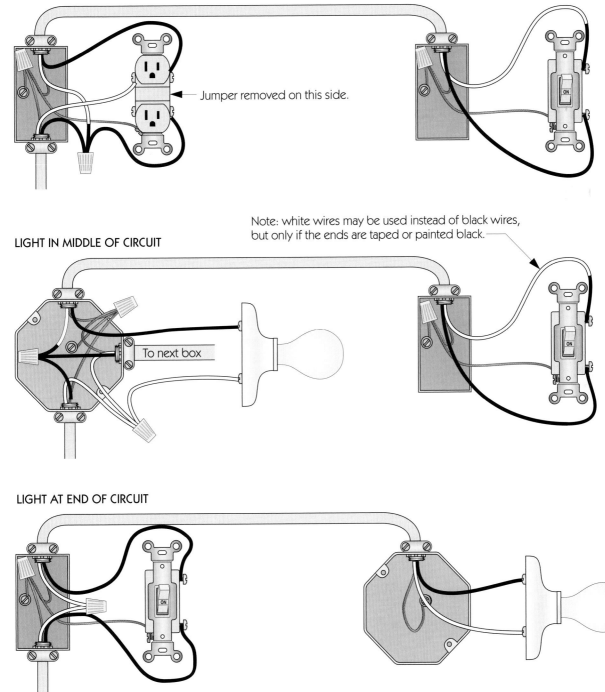

Jumper removed on this side.

LIGHT IN MIDDLE OF CIRCUIT

Note: white wires may be used instead of black wires, but only if the ends are taped or painted black.

To next box

LIGHT AT END OF CIRCUIT

3- & 4-Way Switches

How They Work

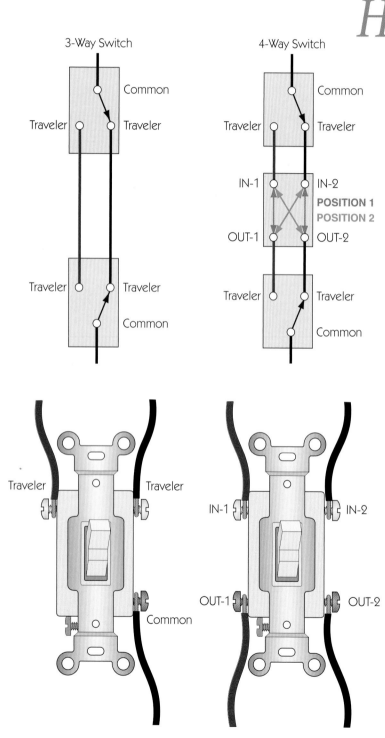

3-Way Switch

Common
Traveler — Traveler

Traveler — Traveler
Common

4-Way Switch

Common
Traveler — Traveler

IN-1 — IN-2
POSITION 1
POSITION 2
OUT-1 — OUT-2

Traveler — Traveler
Common

Traveler — Traveler

Common

IN-1 — IN-2

OUT-1 — OUT-2

The purpose of the 3-way switch is to control a light from two locations, such as at the head and the foot of a stairway. To see how a pair of 3-way switches operates, toggle either switch (as shown on left) off and on. You will see that, no matter what the position of the alternate switch, a connection can be established (ON) or broken (OFF) between the common terminals and, thus, to the light.

The 4-way switch goes one step further, allowing the control of a light from an unlimited number of locations. A 4-way switch is always sandwiched between 3-way switches. Inside a 4-way switch, the contacts toggle between position 1 (blue) and position 2 (green).

To understand the operation, imagine toggling any of the three switches back and forth. You will find, again, that a connection can always be made or broken at any one of the switches.

The 3-way switch has a *common* terminal, marked by a dark oxide screw, which can serve as either the power input or power output. The remaining pair of terminals, denoted by lighter colored screws, are for the *traveler* wires. The common wires must be black. The traveler wires may be red or black, and either may connect to either traveler terminal.

The 4-way switch also uses pairs of red and black wires. Both wires of a red/black pair must connect to terminals having the same color screws.

3-Way Switch Circuits

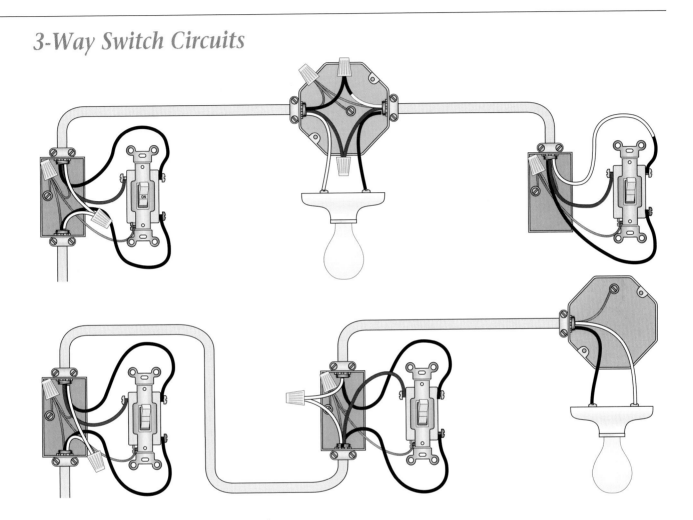

4-Way Switch Circuit

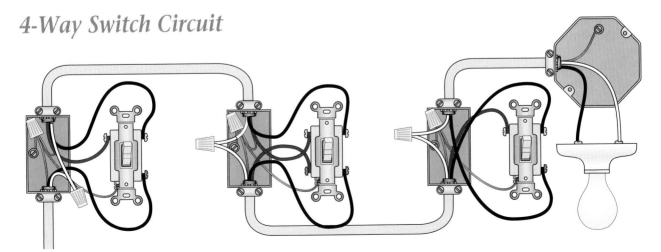

Ceiling Fan/Light Switch

Two Wall Switches

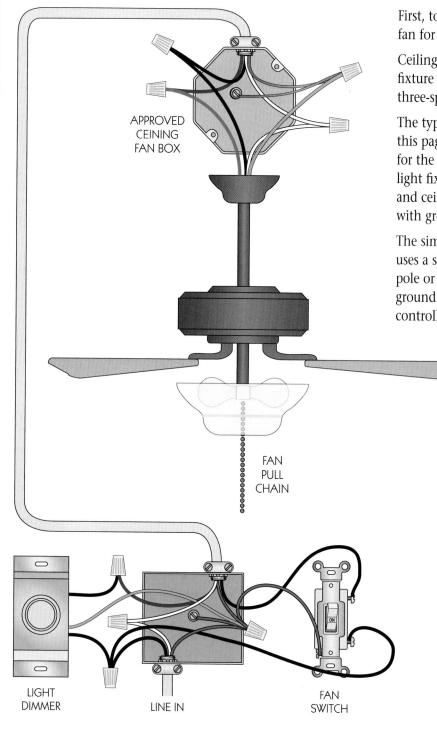

APPROVED
CEINING
FAN BOX

FAN
PULL
CHAIN

LIGHT
DIMMER

LINE IN

FAN
SWITCH

How It Works

First, to see how and why to use a ceiling fan for cooling, go to page 93.

Ceiling fans most often have both a light fixture (sometimes as an add-on kit) and a three-speed-pull-chain switch.

The typical wiring arrangement shown on this page has a single-pole on-off switch for the fan and a dimmer switch for the light fixture. The cable between the wall and ceiling must be either 14/3 or 12/3 with ground.

The simpler circuit on the following page uses a single wall switch (either single-pole or dimmer) and 14/2 or 12/2 with ground cable. In this case the fan is totally controlled by the pull chain.

Single Wall Switch

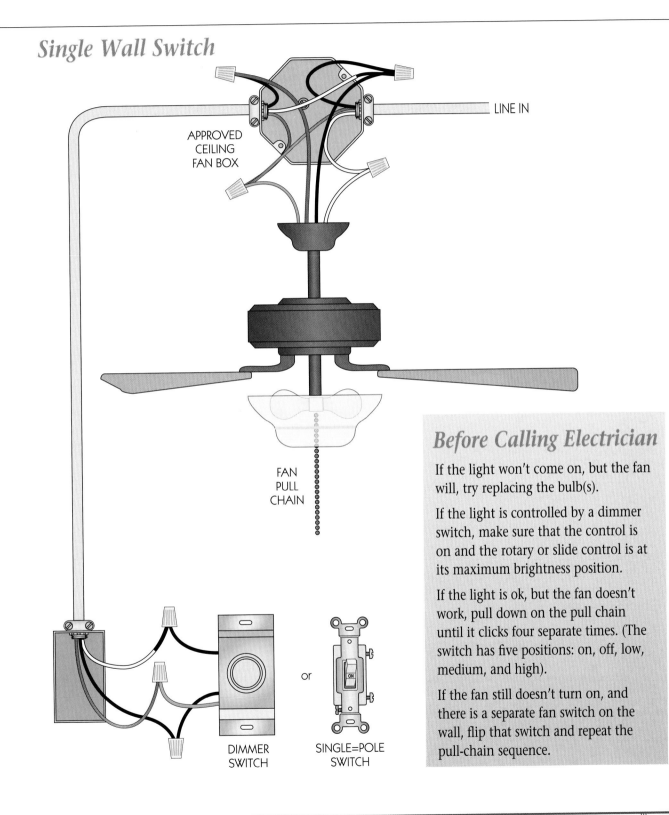

APPROVED
CEILING
FAN BOX

LINE IN

FAN
PULL
CHAIN

DIMMER
SWITCH

or

SINGLE=POLE
SWITCH

ON

Before Calling Electrician

If the light won't come on, but the fan will, try replacing the bulb(s).

If the light is controlled by a dimmer switch, make sure that the control is on and the rotary or slide control is at its maximum brightness position.

If the light is ok, but the fan doesn't work, pull down on the pull chain until it clicks four separate times. (The switch has five positions: on, off, low, medium, and high).

If the fan still doesn't turn on, and there is a separate fan switch on the wall, flip that switch and repeat the pull-chain sequence.

Dimmer Switch

Typical Dimmer

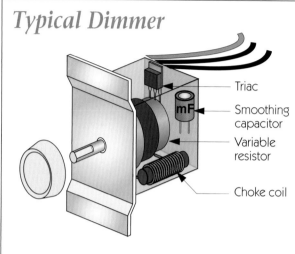

- Triac
- Smoothing capacitor
- Variable resistor
- Choke coil

How It Works

A dimmer switch does not decrease the voltage applied to a light bulb. As the graph shows, it decreases the fraction of time the bulb is on. The switching is not apparent, however, since it occurs more rapidly (120 times per second) than the eye can respond.

Both light output and energy consumed are nearly linear with the fraction of "on" time, so the savings resulting from dimming are significant. Dimming by 25% saves 20% on your electric bill; dimming by half saves 40%. Another saving is in bulb life. Dimming by 10% doubles the bulb's life span.

The common dimmer described here does not work with fluorescent bulbs. There are dimmers for fluorescent fixtures, but they must be matched to the type of ballast.

Switch On/Off Cycle

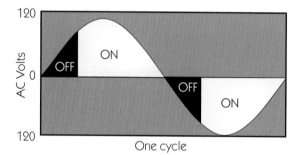

Dimmer Circuit

TO BULB

Smoothing capacitor

Variable resistor

Triac

Choke coil

Firing capacitor

LINE IN

On/Off

2 The variable resistor controls how quickly the voltage rises across the firing capacitor.

4 A triac is symmetrical, so the blocking/conducting action repeats on the negative half of the cycle.

3 When the capacitor voltage reaches the threshold voltage of the triac, the triac conducts current to the bulb. It continues to conduct until the line voltage passes through zero.

1 Voltage increases from zero on the hot wire to the dimmer switch.

5 To prevent vibration of the bulb's filament, the dimmer includes a smoothing capacitor and a choke coil to smooth the on/off spikes.

Typical Dimmer Switch Circuits

SINGLE-POLE DIMMER SWITCH

3-WAY SWITCH AND 3-WAY DIMMER SWITCH

TWO 3-WAY DIMMER SWITCHES

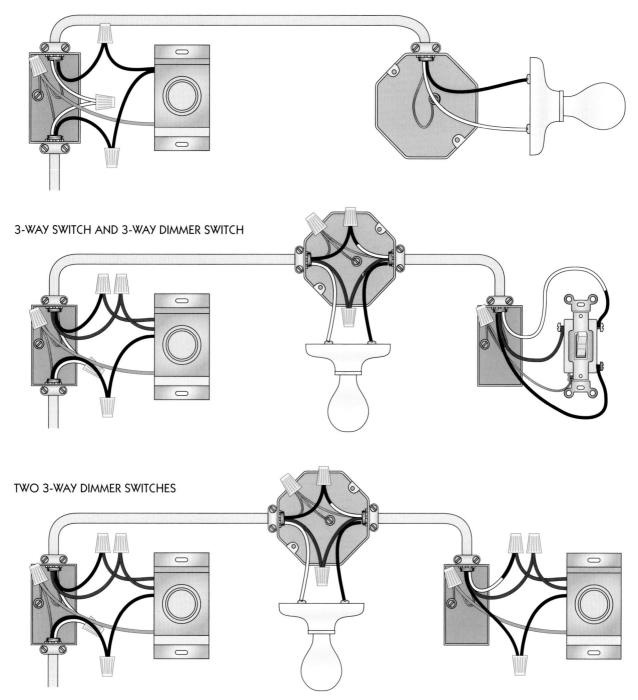

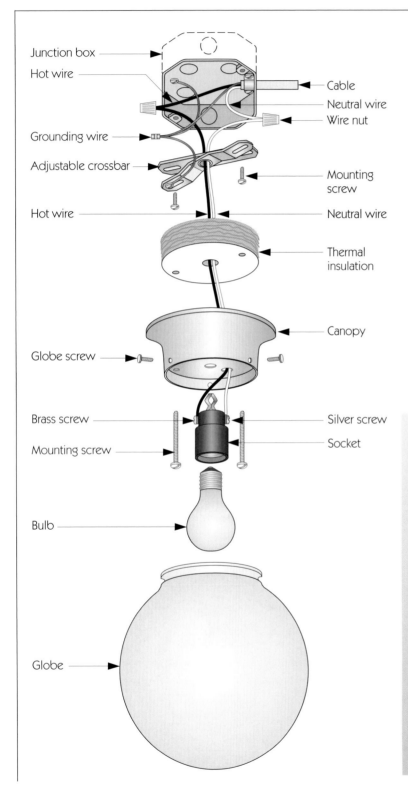

Junction box

Hot wire

Grounding wire

Adjustable crossbar

Hot wire

Globe screw

Brass screw

Mounting screw

Bulb

Globe

Cable

Neutral wire

Wire nut

Mounting screw

Neutral wire

Thermal insulation

Canopy

Silver screw

Socket

How It Works

Ceiling fixtures typically involve many parts, but most are standard and may be found in home centers.

All fixtures start with a junction box firmly mounted on or between the ceiling joists. Provided the canopy is large enough, a $1/2$"-thick "pancake" box allows mounting in a cut-out in the ceiling drywall.

Very heavy fixtures, such as chandeliers and some ceiling fans, may require support in addition to the junction box.

Although the fixture is out of reach, the wiring color code should be followed, with the hot (black) wire connecting to the darker terminal of the socket. This ensures that the socket shell is at ground potential.

Before Calling for Help

If a ceiling fixture won't light, the bulb is probably burned out. (Consider a compact fluorescent bulb for a longer-lasting replacement.) To replace the bulb, you usually unscrew the globe screws, and remove the globe.

Sometimes it is impossible to unscrew the bulb from the socket without the socket turning as well. If that happens, it may be necessary to turn off the power at the breaker box, remove the long mounting screws, and take the fixture apart. After separating the bulb and socket, the fixture is reassembled, the new bulb inserted, and the breaker turned back on.

Hanging Ceiling Fixture

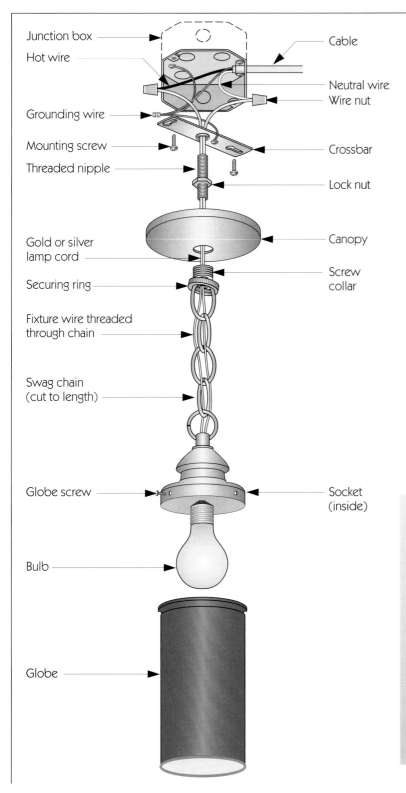

Junction box

Hot wire

Grounding wire

Mounting screw

Threaded nipple

Gold or silver
lamp cord

Securing ring

Fixture wire threaded
through chain

Swag chain
(cut to length)

Globe screw

Bulb

Globe

Cable

Neutral wire
Wire nut

Crossbar

Lock nut

Canopy

Screw
collar

Socket
(inside)

How It Works

Hanging fixtures have more parts than flush-mounts. In addition, you can change the fixture height by adding or removing links from the swag chain. The chain links are not welded, so they can be twisted open and closed using two sets of pliers.

Altering the length of the chain usually involves a similar change to the lamp cord. Both chain and lamp cord come in five colors: white, black, brown, clear gold, and clear silver. The cord conductors are not color-coded, so you must trace the conductors to make sure the socket shell (darker terminal screw) is connected to the circuit's hot (black) wire.

Replacing an incandescent bulb with an equivalent compact fluorescent bulb will save energy and, possibly, ever having to replace the bulb again.

Before Calling for Help

A broken bulb can often be safely removed from its socket by carefully pressing a raw potato into the remaining glass shards and twisting. First turn off the power, however, because potatoes conduct electricity.

Another trick frees both hands to work on the wiring in the junction box. Bend hooks into both ends of a section of wire coat hanger, and use it to suspend the chain and fixture from the box.

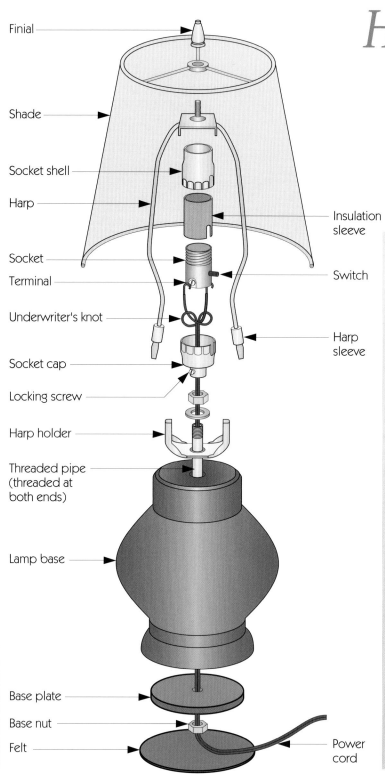

Finial
Shade
Socket shell
Harp
Socket
Terminal
Underwriter's knot
Socket cap
Locking screw
Harp holder
Threaded pipe
(threaded at
both ends)
Lamp base
Base plate
Base nut
Felt

Insulation
sleeve
Switch
Harp
sleeve
Power
cord

How They Work

Few projects are more satisfying than salvaging a dysfunctional heirloom lamp. Repairing the type of lamp shown is simple because replacements for all parts shown are readily available at home centers.

The cord is shown running through a pipe in the base. Sometimes the cord runs directly from the socket.

Before Calling for Help

The most common table and floor lamp repair is cord replacement. Cords can become worn and brittle, chewed by dogs, and damaged by vacuum cleaners. To make the repair simple, just buy an extension cord of the same color and length, and cut off the female end. Run the cut end up through the pipe at the base and through the socket cap. Using a utility knife, split the cord back about 6", and remove $5/8$" of insulation from the two conductors. Tie the two conductors into an underwriter's knot, as shown, then fasten the bare conductors under the terminal screws.

The conductor from the shorter blade of the plug should connect to the terminal with the darker screw, so it would be helpful to trace that conductor and mark it with a felt-tip pen before running it up the pipe.

The other common repair is socket replacement. There are several versions, so take the old one to the home center to get an exact replacement.

Fluorescent Lamps

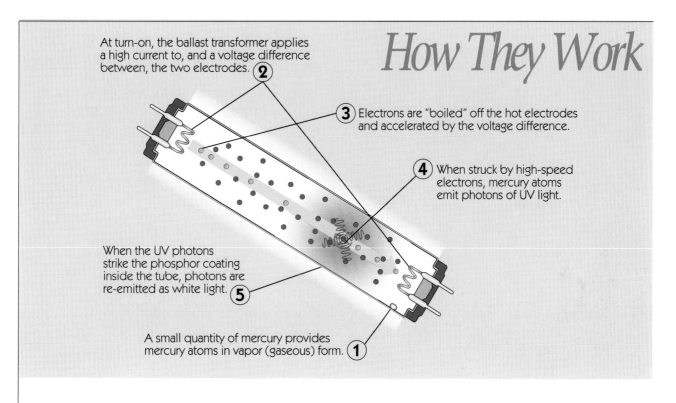

How They Work

At turn-on, the ballast transformer applies a high current to, and a voltage difference between, the two electrodes. **2**

3 Electrons are "boiled" off the hot electrodes and accelerated by the voltage difference.

4 When struck by high-speed electrons, mercury atoms emit photons of UV light.

When the UV photons strike the phosphor coating inside the tube, photons are re-emitted as white light. **5**

A small quantity of mercury provides mercury atoms in vapor (gaseous) form. **1**

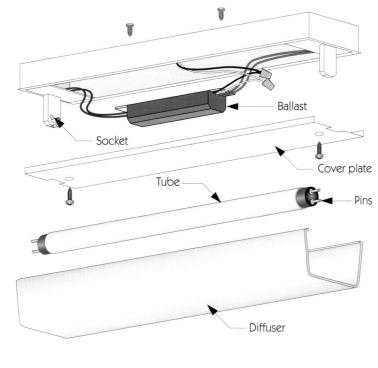

Ballast

Socket

Cover plate

Tube

Pins

Diffuser

Before Calling for Help

If the bulb flickers, but never fully lights, remove the bulb, lightly sand the pins, and reinsert the bulb. If the bulb still doesn't light, replace it.

If the bulb doesn't even flicker, and the fixture has a starter (small plug-in cylinder), turn off the power and replace the starter. If that doesn't work, replace the bulb, too.

If the bulb is blackened at one end, turn it end-for-end; if at both ends, replace both bulb and starter.

If there is a starter, and the bulb glows only at the ends, replace the starter.

How It Works

The heart of the most common carbon monoxide (CO) detector is a chemical reaction:

$$CO + H_2O \Rightarrow CO_2 + 2H^+ + 2e^-$$

The reaction takes place entirely within a cell containing electrodes and an electrolyte (conductive liquid or gel). Although the cell is closed, its walls contain a film that is permeable to gases, so it freely exchanges carbon monoxide (CO), carbon dioxide (CO_2), and oxygen (O_2) with the atmosphere.

Only atmospheric gases are used up, so the detector has a long life expectancy.

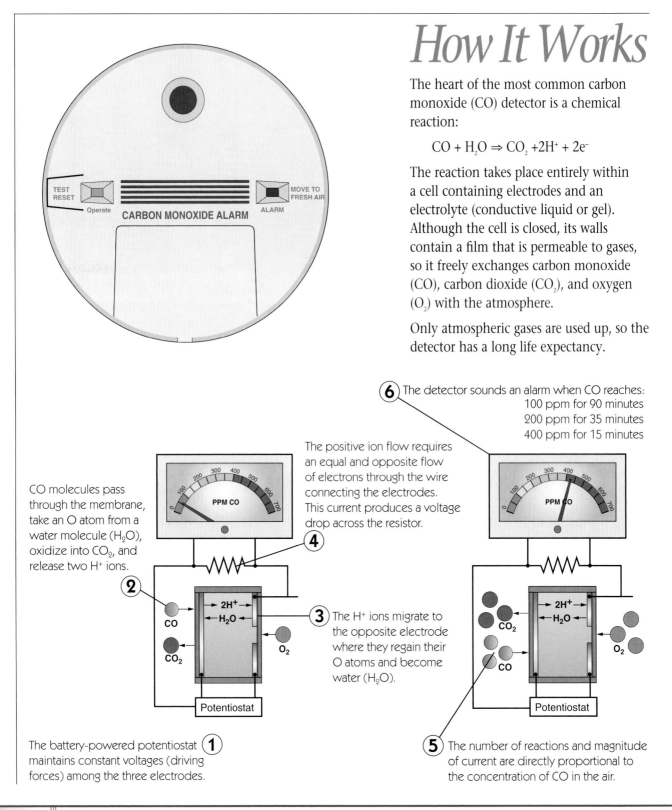

CARBON MONOXIDE ALARM

TEST RESET — Operate — ALARM — MOVE TO FRESH AIR

6 The detector sounds an alarm when CO reaches:
100 ppm for 90 minutes
200 ppm for 35 minutes
400 ppm for 15 minutes

The positive ion flow requires an equal and opposite flow of electrons through the wire connecting the electrodes. This current produces a voltage drop across the resistor. **4**

CO molecules pass through the membrane, take an O atom from a water molecule (H_2O), oxidize into CO_2, and release two H^+ ions. **2**

PPM CO

$2H^+$ → ← H_2O → CO → O_2 → CO_2

3 The H^+ ions migrate to the opposite electrode where they regain their O atoms and become water (H_2O).

Potentiostat

The battery-powered potentiostat **1** maintains constant voltages (driving forces) among the three electrodes.

5 The number of reactions and magnitude of current are directly proportional to the concentration of CO in the air.

Battery Smoke Detector

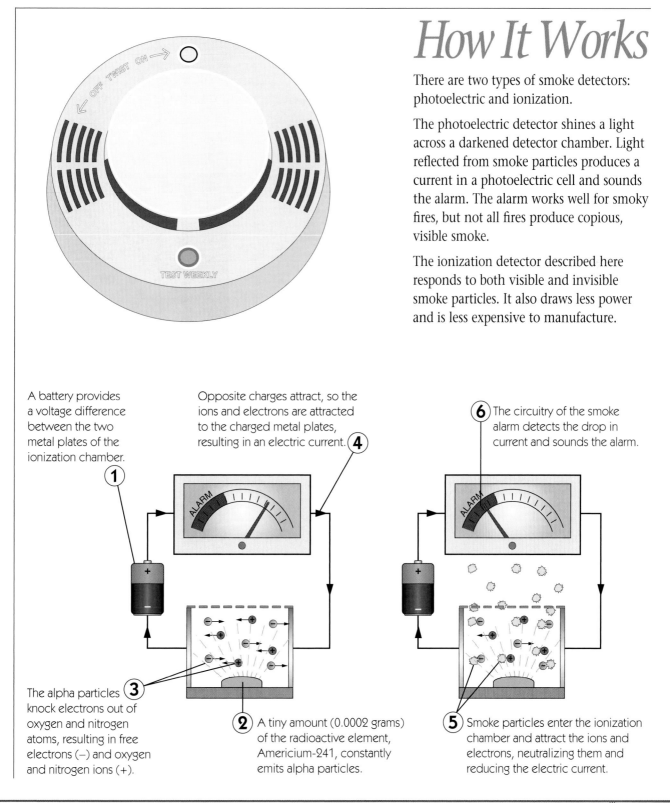

How It Works

There are two types of smoke detectors: photoelectric and ionization.

The photoelectric detector shines a light across a darkened detector chamber. Light reflected from smoke particles produces a current in a photoelectric cell and sounds the alarm. The alarm works well for smoky fires, but not all fires produce copious, visible smoke.

The ionization detector described here responds to both visible and invisible smoke particles. It also draws less power and is less expensive to manufacture.

A battery provides a voltage difference between the two metal plates of the ionization chamber. **(1)**

Opposite charges attract, so the ions and electrons are attracted to the charged metal plates, resulting in an electric current. **(4)**

(6) The circuitry of the smoke alarm detects the drop in current and sounds the alarm.

The alpha particles **(3)** knock electrons out of oxygen and nitrogen atoms, resulting in free electrons (−) and oxygen and nitrogen ions (+).

(2) A tiny amount (0.0002 grams) of the radioactive element, Americium-241, constantly emits alpha particles.

(5) Smoke particles enter the ionization chamber and attract the ions and electrons, neutralizing them and reducing the electric current.

How They Work

The most common method for detecting smoke is described in *Battery Smoke Detector* on page 71.

Because people often neglect to replace dead batteries, the Fire Code requires hard-wired (110 VAC) detectors in all new construction.

In addition, all of the detectors must be interconnected so that activation of one causes all to sound off.

The first detector is powered by an NM 14/2 with ground cable. From the first detector an NM 14/3 with ground cable is run to the rest. The black and white wires provide the power, while the red wires serves to interconnect the alarms.

The power may be tapped from an existing receptacle circuit, but not a lighting circuit, and it must not contain an on/off switch.

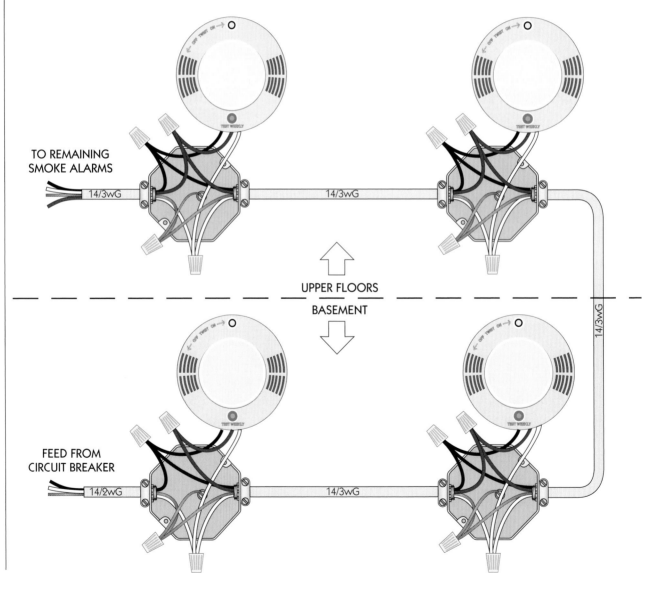

TO REMAINING SMOKE ALARMS

14/3wG

14/3wG

UPPER FLOORS

BASEMENT

14/3wG

FEED FROM CIRCUIT BREAKER

14/2wG

14/3wG

Typical Code Requirements

General

Smoke detectors are required:

- on every habitable level
- on the ceiling at base of each stairway
- on the ceiling outside every sleeping area

Smoke detectors may be either battery powered or hardwired.

Each location must have an ionization detector and a photoelectric detector or a single unit combining both.

Detectors within 20 feet of a kitchen or a bathroom containing a tub or shower must be photoelectric only.

New Construction

In addition to the general requirements above, smoke detectors in new residential construction must:

- be hardwired with battery backup

- be interconnected so activation of any detector results in all detectors sounding an alarm.

There must also be a detector inside each sleeping room.

At least one smoke detector must be installed for every 1,200 square feet of habitable space on each level.

Required Locations

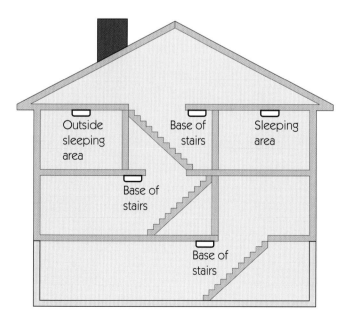

Outside sleeping area

Base of stairs

Sleeping area

Base of stairs

Base of stairs

Before Calling Electrician

Once a week test each smoke detector by pressing its "Test" button until it sounds. Station a helper at the detector furthest away to make sure all other detectors are interconnected.

Once a month switch off the circuit breaker that serves the detectors. Again, test each detector. If one doesn't sound, open its case and replace the battery. Don't forget to reset the circuit breaker!

If a detector still doesn't work after replacing its battery, replace it with one of the same type (battery only or line plus battery, dual or single detector type).

3 HEATING

Quality heating systems, properly installed, should provide 40 or more years of trouble-free service. Like teeth, however, they will do so only with proper maintenance. Cleaning and tuning up a furnace or boiler require specialized training and tools. Simpler tasks, such as changing furnace filters, adjusting temperature limits, and adjusting or replacing blower belts, do not. Regular maintenance will reduce energy costs and prevent unhealthy conditions, such as mold growth.

You will feel a lot more secure about your heating system if you do just two things. First, read the sections of this chapter that relate to your type of equipment. After that, ask your heating and air conditioning service person for a tour of your particular system: emergency switch, burner reset button, filter access panel, zone controls, thermostats, etc. Chances are, he or she will be glad to do this. Nothing is more annoying to a service person than to be called out at 2:00 AM on a winter night to do nothing more than push a burner reset button.

How It Works

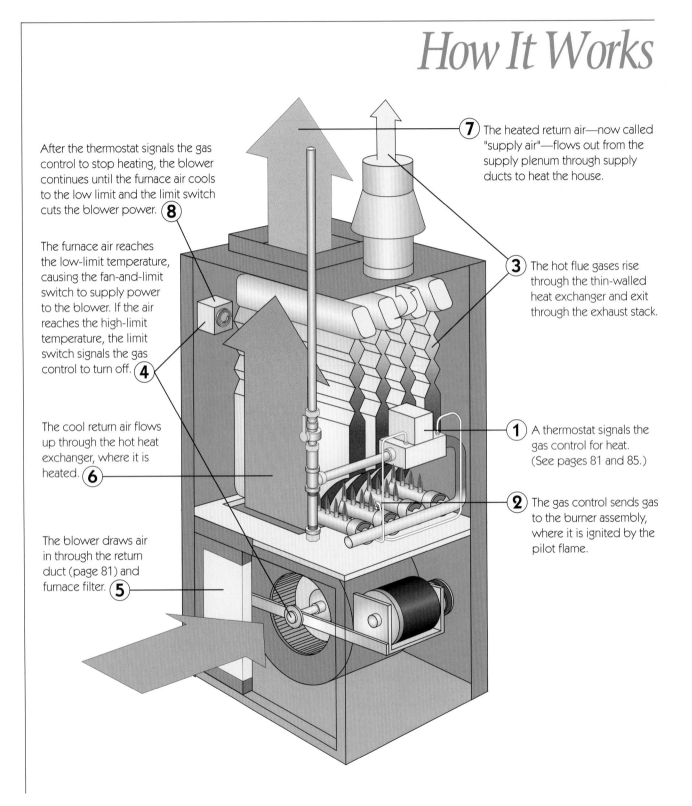

After the thermostat signals the gas control to stop heating, the blower continues until the furnace air cools to the low limit and the limit switch cuts the blower power. **8**

The furnace air reaches the low-limit temperature, causing the fan-and-limit switch to supply power to the blower. If the air reaches the high-limit temperature, the limit switch signals the gas control to turn off. **4**

The cool return air flows up through the hot heat exchanger, where it is heated. **6**

The blower draws air in through the return duct (page 81) and furnace filter. **5**

7 The heated return air—now called "supply air"—flows out from the supply plenum through supply ducts to heat the house.

3 The hot flue gases rise through the thin-walled heat exchanger and exit through the exhaust stack.

1 A thermostat signals the gas control for heat. (See pages 81 and 85.)

2 The gas control sends gas to the burner assembly, where it is ignited by the pilot flame.

Gas Hot Water Boiler

How It Works

When the water in the boiler reaches a low-limit temperature, the aquastat signals the circulator control (page 82) that the water is hot enough to circulate. If the boiler water reaches a high-limit temperature, the aquastat signals the gas control to turn off. **5**

4 The cooled flue gases are collected and discharged through the exhaust stack.

3 Hot flue gases rise through the honeycombed heat exchanger, where they are cooled as they heat the boiler water.

1 A thermostat signals the gas control for heat. (See pages 82 and 85.)

2 The gas control sends gas to the burner assembly, where it is ignited by the pilot flame.

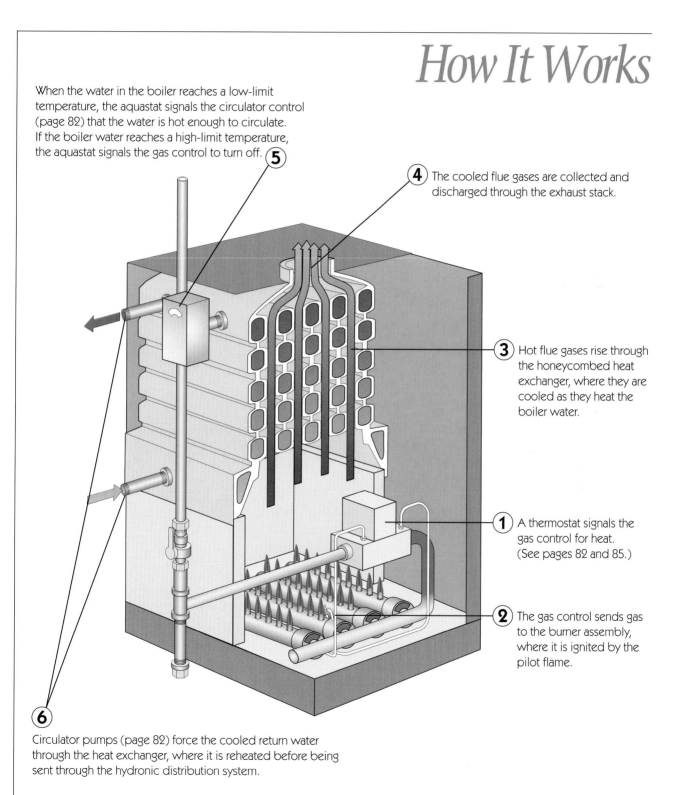

6 Circulator pumps (page 82) force the cooled return water through the heat exchanger, where it is reheated before being sent through the hydronic distribution system.

How It Works

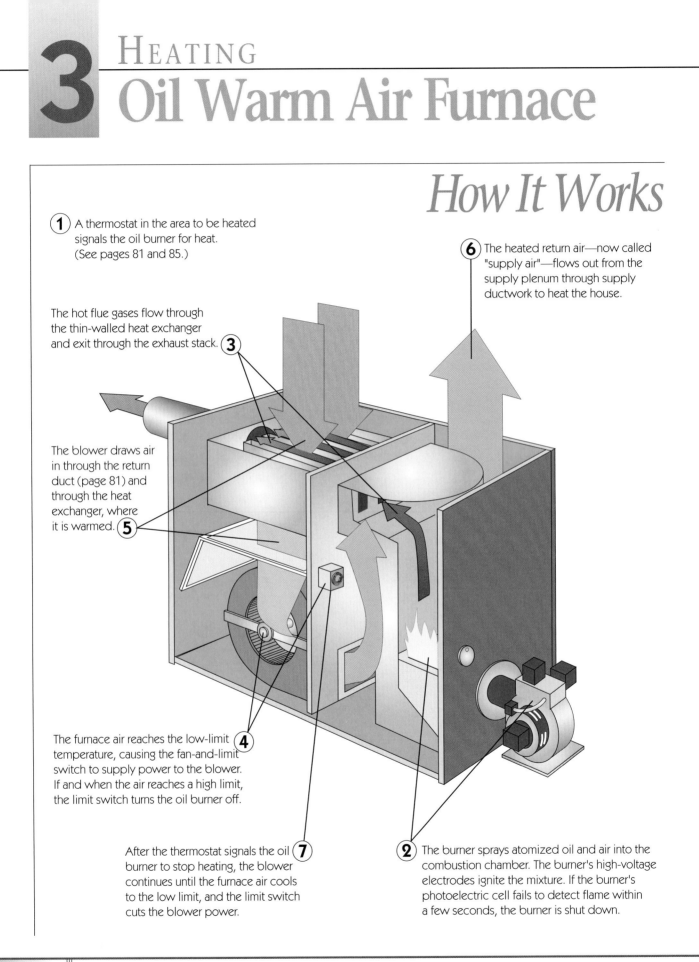

1 A thermostat in the area to be heated signals the oil burner for heat. (See pages 81 and 85.)

The hot flue gases flow through the thin-walled heat exchanger and exit through the exhaust stack. **3**

The blower draws air in through the return duct (page 81) and through the heat exchanger, where it is warmed. **5**

6 The heated return air—now called "supply air"—flows out from the supply plenum through supply ductwork to heat the house.

The furnace air reaches the low-limit temperature, causing the fan-and-limit switch to supply power to the blower. If and when the air reaches a high limit, the limit switch turns the oil burner off. **4**

After the thermostat signals the oil burner to stop heating, the blower continues until the furnace air cools to the low limit, and the limit switch cuts the blower power. **7**

2 The burner sprays atomized oil and air into the combustion chamber. The burner's high-voltage electrodes ignite the mixture. If the burner's photoelectric cell fails to detect flame within a few seconds, the burner is shut down.

Oil Hot Water Boiler

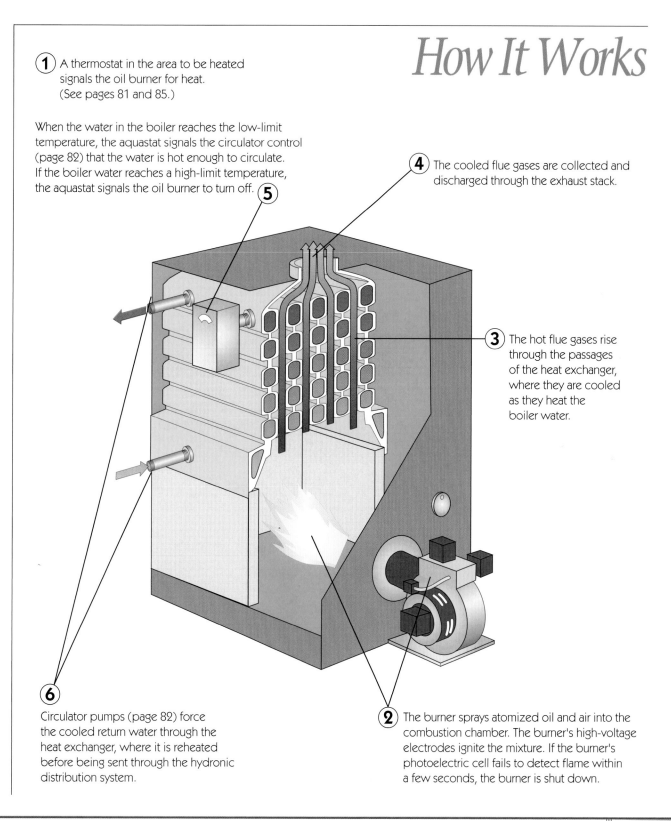

1 A thermostat in the area to be heated signals the oil burner for heat. (See pages 81 and 85.)

When the water in the boiler reaches the low-limit temperature, the aquastat signals the circulator control (page 82) that the water is hot enough to circulate. If the boiler water reaches a high-limit temperature, the aquastat signals the oil burner to turn off. **5**

4 The cooled flue gases are collected and discharged through the exhaust stack.

3 The hot flue gases rise through the passages of the heat exchanger, where they are cooled as they heat the boiler water.

6 Circulator pumps (page 82) force the cooled return water through the heat exchanger, where it is reheated before being sent through the hydronic distribution system.

2 The burner sprays atomized oil and air into the combustion chamber. The burner's high-voltage electrodes ignite the mixture. If the burner's photoelectric cell fails to detect flame within a few seconds, the burner is shut down.

Air-Source Heat Pump

R-410A Refrigerant

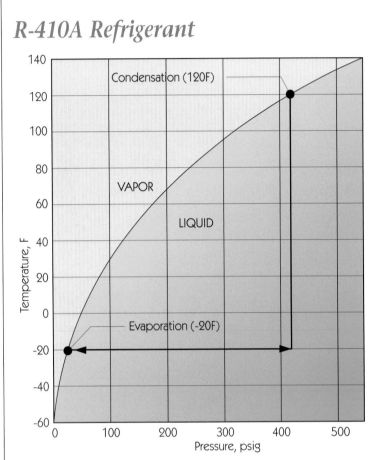

NOTE: psig is pounds per square inch gauge. Normal atmospheric pressure is 15 psi. A pressure gauge measures pressure above or below atmospheric. Thus, normal atmospheric pressure is 0 psig.

Before Calling for Help

If the heat pump doesn't run at all, check its circuit breaker or fuse.

If the unit runs, but it doesn't heat or cool as well as it used to, clean the inside filter and both inside and outside heat exchanger coils. At the same time, make sure shrubs or an accumulation of leaves is not blocking the air flow.

How It Works

If you know that water boils (turns from a liquid to a gas) at 212°F at atmospheric pressure, but that its boiling temperature rises at higher pressures (such as in a pressure cooker), and that evaporating water absorbs a lot of heat (think of exiting the water on a windy day), then you can understand how refrigerators, air conditioners, and heat pumps work.

As shown in the graph, R-410A refrigerant evaporates at -20°F at a pressure of 42 psi, or 27 psig. If we compress it to a pressure of 420 psig, however, its boiling temperature rises to about 120°F.

In the heat pump on the next page, top, the refrigerant is sucked into a compressor, where it is compressed to at least 420 psig, which raises its temperature to about 120°F.

The hot, compressed vapor then flows through a heat exchanger inside the house. The fan blows air through the coils, which cools it to below its condensation point and changes it back to a liquid.

The hot liquid flows from the heat exchanger to an expansion valve, then to a second heat exchanger and fan located outside the house. The expansion valve drops the pressure to 30 psig, causing the liquid to boil (evaporate) at temperatures above -20°F. Heat is absorbed from the outdoor air through the heat exchanger and is pumped from outside.

From the outside heat exchanger, the now cool vapor is again sucked into the compressor, and the cycle is repeated.

Heating Mode

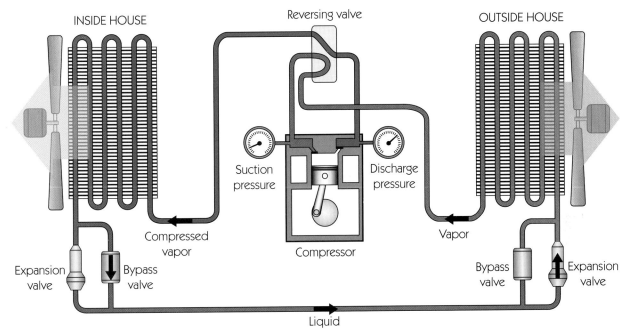

INSIDE HOUSE

Reversing valve

OUTSIDE HOUSE

Suction pressure

Discharge pressure

Compressed vapor

Compressor

Vapor

Expansion valve

Bypass valve

Bypass valve

Expansion valve

Liquid

Cooling Mode

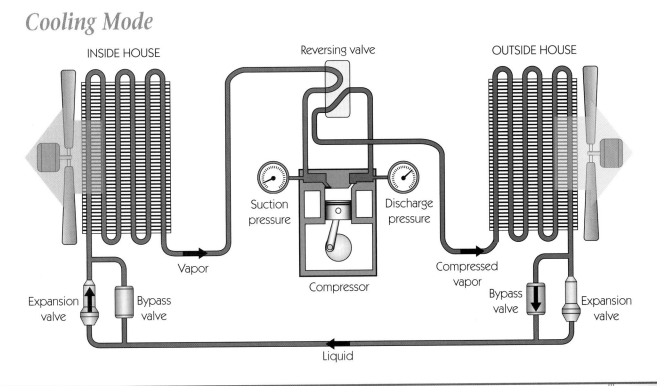

INSIDE HOUSE

Reversing valve

OUTSIDE HOUSE

Suction pressure

Discharge pressure

Vapor

Compressor

Compressed vapor

Expansion valve

Bypass valve

Bypass valve

Expansion valve

Liquid

Ventless Gas Heater

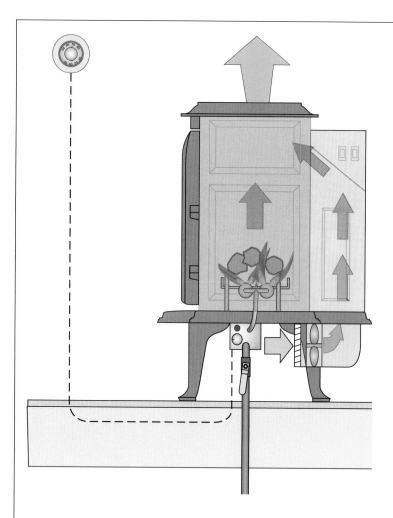

How It Works

The difference between ventless gas heaters and direct-vent gas heaters (page 84) is that the latter exchange air and combustion gases with the outside, while the former exhaust directly into the building.

The ventless heater raises two concerns:

- excess moisture (water vapor is one of two primary products of combustion) leading to the growth of mold
- dangerous levels of carbon monoxide, the product of incomplete combustion

In fact, ventless heaters raise relative humidities by 10 to 15%. Most homes are too dry in winter, so this poses a problem only in very tight new homes.

Modern ventless gas heaters prevent excess carbon monoxide by monitoring the percentage of oxygen in the air and shutting off the gas supply before it becomes dangerously low. How they do it is shown on the following page.

Sizing a Ventless Gas Heater

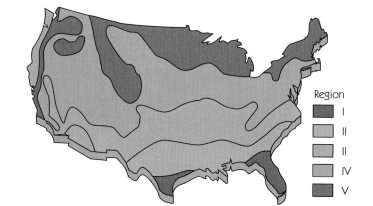

Region
- I
- II
- III
- IV
- V

Btuh/cu.ft. of Heated Volume*

| Region | House Construction | | |
	Loose	Average	Tight
I	2.3	1.9	1.5
II	3.4	2.2	1.8
III	4.3	2.6	2.2
IV	5.4	3.2	2.4
V	5.4	3.2	2.7

* Assumes heater is controlled by automatic thermostat

The Oxygen Depletion Sensor

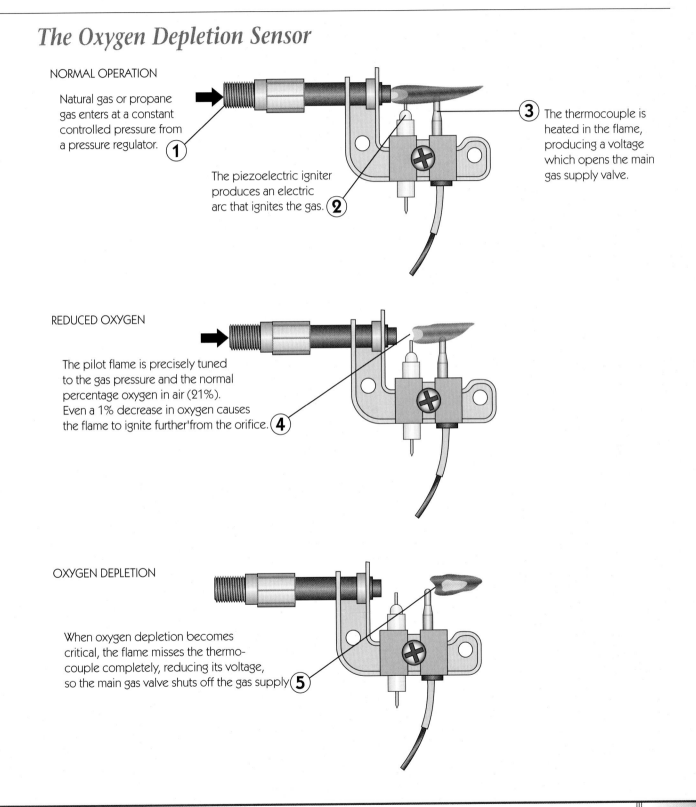

NORMAL OPERATION

Natural gas or propane gas enters at a constant controlled pressure from a pressure regulator. (1)

The piezoelectric igniter produces an electric arc that ignites the gas. (2)

(3) The thermocouple is heated in the flame, producing a voltage which opens the main gas supply valve.

REDUCED OXYGEN

The pilot flame is precisely tuned to the gas pressure and the normal percentage oxygen in air (21%). Even a 1% decrease in oxygen causes the flame to ignite further'from the orifice. (4)

OXYGEN DEPLETION

When oxygen depletion becomes critical, the flame misses the thermo-couple completely, reducing its voltage, so the main gas valve shuts off the gas supply (5)

3 HEATING
Direct-Vent Gas Heater

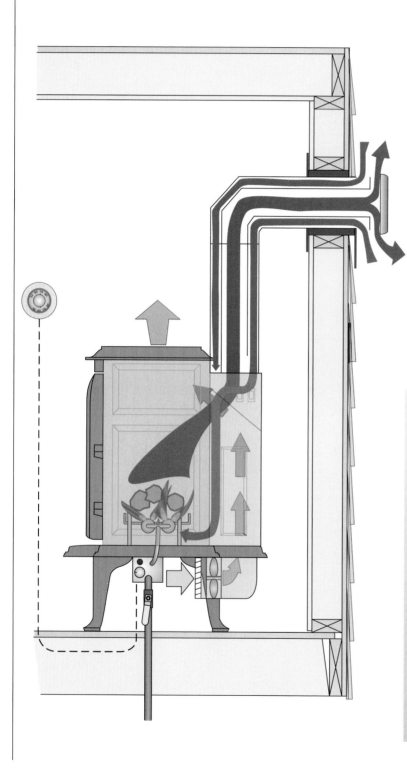

How It Works

Direct-vent heaters require no chimney flue. Instead, the hot combustion gas exhausts through an inner pipe cooled by outside supply air entering through a concentric outer shell. The supply air is warmed, and the combustion gas is cooled.

During the heating season, a small pilot flame stands by, waiting for the thermostat to call for heat. An oxygen depletion sensor (see page 83) monitors the shape of the pilot flame and cuts off the main gas supply if a short of oxygen is detected.

Room air is warmed either through natural convection or by a small fan, as shown in the illustration.

Before Calling for Help

If the pilot flame extinguishes, check first that there is a supply of gas. Make sure valves are in the open position.

If the gas is Propane (LP) or Compressed Natural Gas (CNG), check to see if the tank is empty.

Try reigniting the pilot light, following the step-by-step directions listed in the heater's owner's manual. If repeated attempts fail, call either the stove dealer or the gas supplier. Do not attempt any adjustments not listed in the manual.

If you ever smell gas, call the gas company. Do not try to light the pilot!

Direct-Vent Gas Fireplace

How It Works

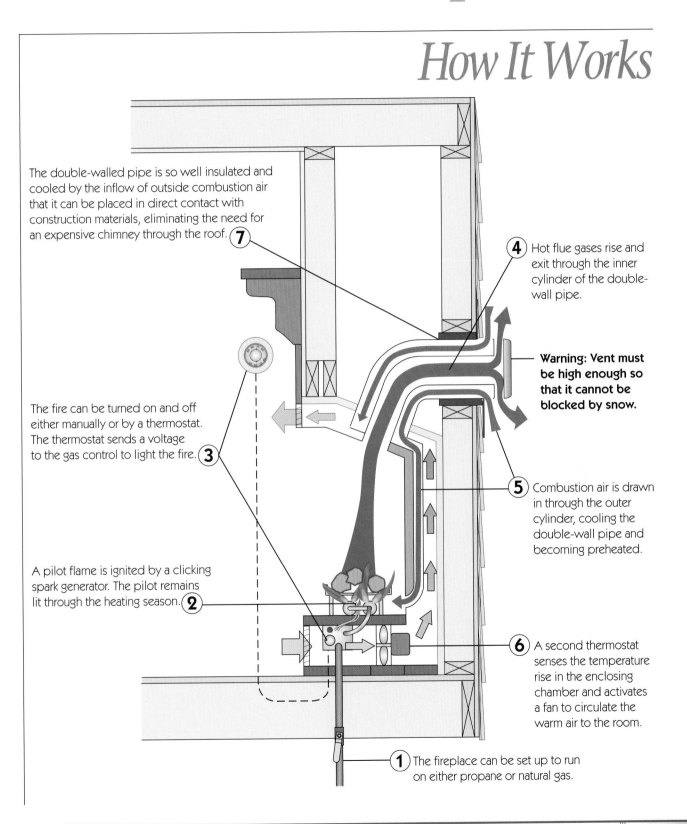

The double-walled pipe is so well insulated and cooled by the inflow of outside combustion air that it can be placed in direct contact with construction materials, eliminating the need for an expensive chimney through the roof. **7**

The fire can be turned on and off either manually or by a thermostat. The thermostat sends a voltage to the gas control to light the fire. **3**

A pilot flame is ignited by a clicking spark generator. The pilot remains lit through the heating season. **2**

4 Hot flue gases rise and exit through the inner cylinder of the double-wall pipe.

Warning: Vent must be high enough so that it cannot be blocked by snow.

5 Combustion air is drawn in through the outer cylinder, cooling the double-wall pipe and becoming preheated.

6 A second thermostat senses the temperature rise in the enclosing chamber and activates a fan to circulate the warm air to the room.

1 The fireplace can be set up to run on either propane or natural gas.

How It Works

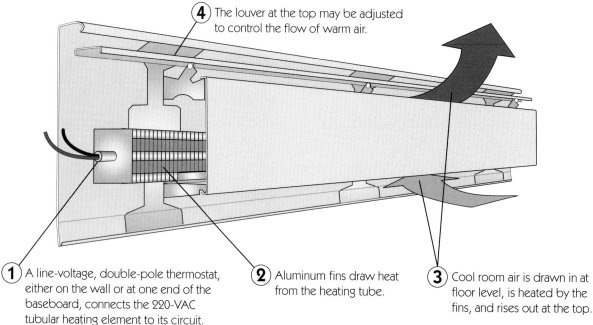

4 The louver at the top may be adjusted to control the flow of warm air.

1 A line-voltage, double-pole thermostat, either on the wall or at one end of the baseboard, connects the 220-VAC tubular heating element to its circuit.

2 Aluminum fins draw heat from the heating tube.

3 Cool room air is drawn in at floor level, is heated by the fins, and rises out at the top.

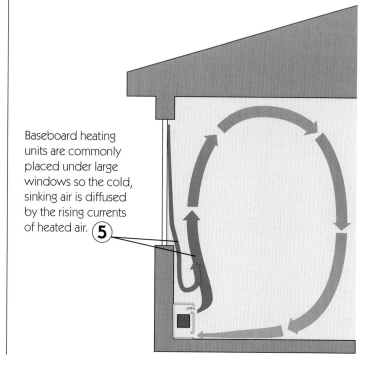

Baseboard heating units are commonly placed under large windows so the cold, sinking air is diffused by the rising currents of heated air. **5**

Before Calling for Help

If your electric baseboard fails to heat even with the thermostat turned to its highest setting, check the pair of circuit breakers for that circuit in the main breaker or fuse panel. Click the breakers all the way off and then on again.

If it still doesn't produce heat, replace it with a similar model of the same length—remembering first to turn the breakers off. Baseboards are inexpensive, and the job is no more complicated than that of replacing a light switch.

Vacuuming the fins annually will remove dust and maximize the flow of warm air.

Warm Air Distribution

How It Works

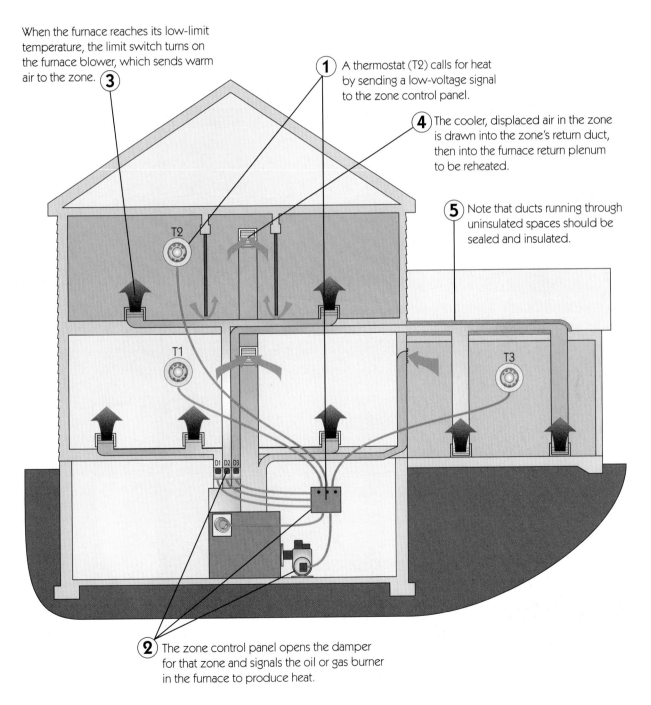

When the furnace reaches its low-limit temperature, the limit switch turns on the furnace blower, which sends warm air to the zone. **3**

1 A thermostat (T2) calls for heat by sending a low-voltage signal to the zone control panel.

4 The cooler, displaced air in the zone is drawn into the zone's return duct, then into the furnace return plenum to be reheated.

5 Note that ducts running through uninsulated spaces should be sealed and insulated.

T2

T1

T3

D1 D2 D3

2 The zone control panel opens the damper for that zone and signals the oil or gas burner in the furnace to produce heat.

How It Works

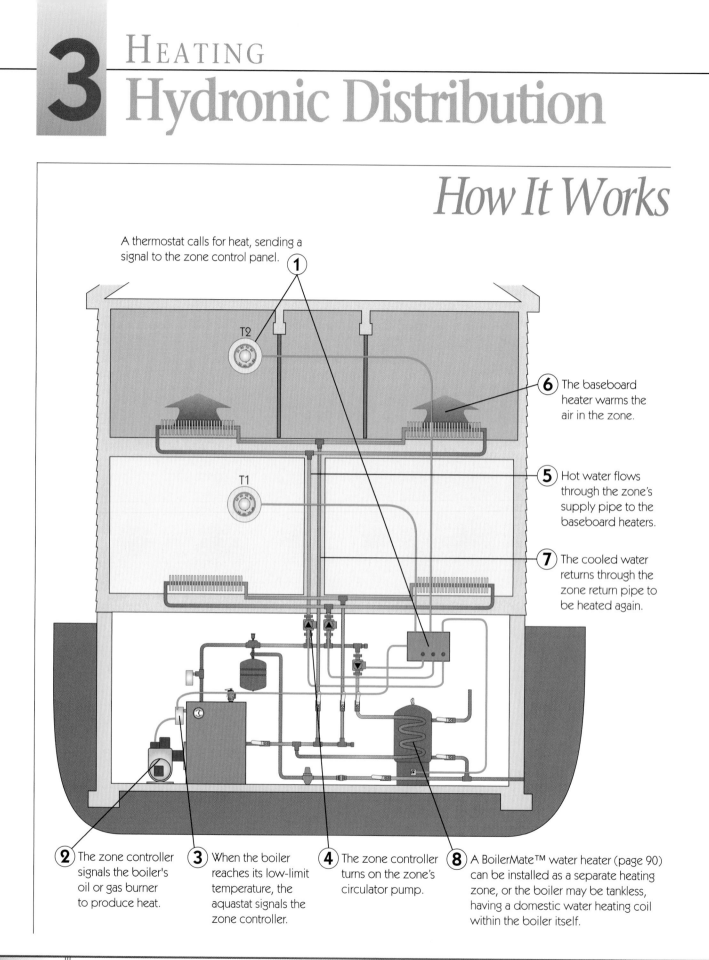

A thermostat calls for heat, sending a signal to the zone control panel. **(1)**

(6) The baseboard heater warms the air in the zone.

(5) Hot water flows through the zone's supply pipe to the baseboard heaters.

(7) The cooled water returns through the zone return pipe to be heated again.

(2) The zone controller signals the boiler's oil or gas burner to produce heat.

(3) When the boiler reaches its low-limit temperature, the aquastat signals the zone controller.

(4) The zone controller turns on the zone's circulator pump.

(8) A BoilerMate™ water heater (page 90) can be installed as a separate heating zone, or the boiler may be tankless, having a domestic water heating coil within the boiler itself.

Hot Water Radiant Heat

How It Works

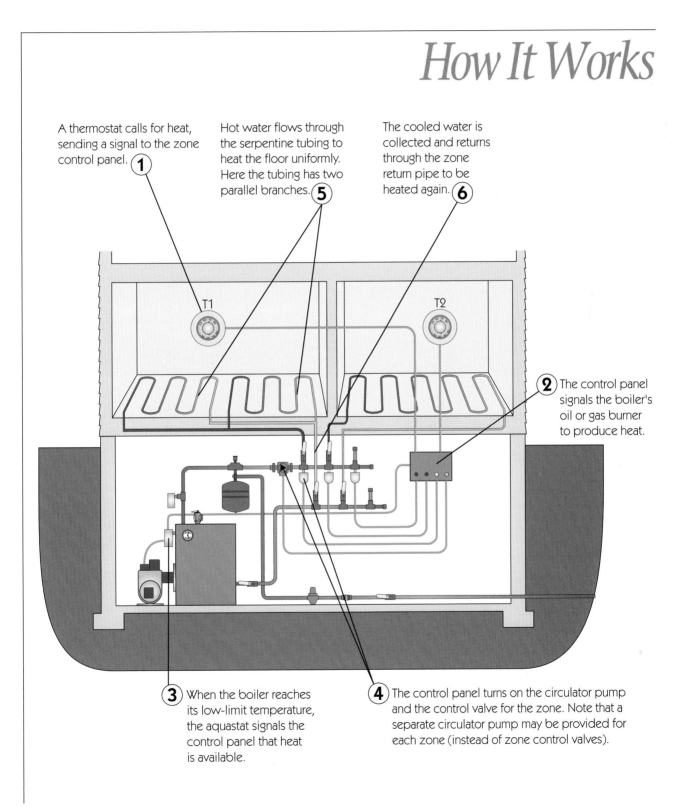

A thermostat calls for heat, sending a signal to the zone control panel. **1**

Hot water flows through the serpentine tubing to heat the floor uniformly. Here the tubing has two parallel branches. **5**

The cooled water is collected and returns through the zone return pipe to be heated again. **6**

T1

T2

2 The control panel signals the boiler's oil or gas burner to produce heat.

3 When the boiler reaches its low-limit temperature, the aquastat signals the control panel that heat is available.

4 The control panel turns on the circulator pump and the control valve for the zone. Note that a separate circulator pump may be provided for each zone (instead of zone control valves).

Bimetallic Thermostat

Mercury Switch

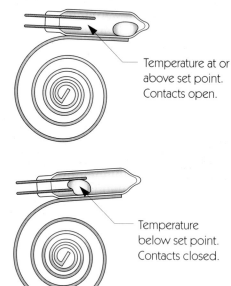

Temperature at or above set point. Contacts open.

Temperature below set point. Contacts closed.

How It Works

Thin strips of dissimilar metals laminated together will bend with temperature change due to differing thermal expansion coefficients. A long strip bent into a coil will evidence significant rotation with just a few degrees of temperature change.

This phenomenon and the electrical conductivity of liquid mercury are used in an electrical switch that turns on and off with temperature, i.e. a thermostat. A glass tube containing a drop of mercury and a pair of contacts at one end is attached to a bimetallic coil. At the desired temperature, the coil is rotated until the mercury moves downhill away from the contacts, opening the switch. If the temperature drops, the coil unwinds and the mercury flows back to again close the contacts.

Thermostat

Current flowing through the anticipator—a variable resistor—produces a small amount of heat inside the thermostat, causing it to turn off before the air temperature reaches the set point. This prevents the excess heat in the furnace or boiler from overshooting the desired temperature.

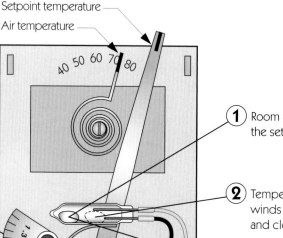

Setpoint temperature

Air temperature

40 50 60 70 80

1 Room air temperature is at or above the set point. Mercury switch is open.

2 Temperature drops; bimetallic coil winds to right; mercury moves to right and closes switch, signaling for heat.

3 Room air temperature rises to the set point. Mercury moves to left, opening switch and turning heat off.

4 COOLING

When the weather is hot, Americans have come to expect that they can be cooled. Unlike our ancestors, who depended on a variety of non-mechanical means to survive the "dog days" and nights of summer, we assume we can turn down a thermostat, and the room (or automobile) will cool. But air conditioning is expensive, and it may not be as necessary as we assume.

This chapter will first explain what determines "thermal comfort." You will find that feeling cool involves several factors other than the temperature shown on a thermometer. In many situations, you can use these variables to achieve cooling without turning on the AC.

But the power of natural cooling is limited, so we will also show how room and central air conditioners work and how to keep them running most efficiently. Like heating systems, air conditioning equipment requires maintenance, such as cleaning vent covers, seasonally cleaning and covering condensers, and replacing air filters.

Prevailing Wind

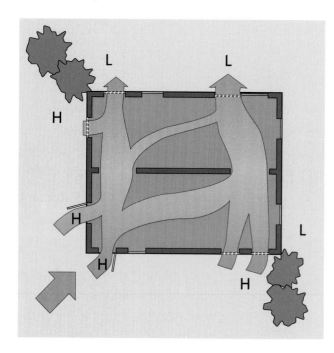

Stack Effect

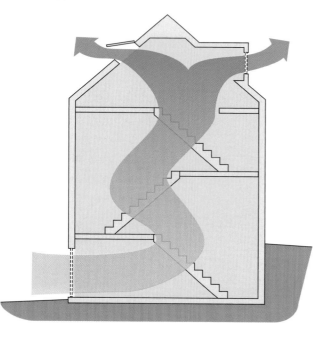

How It Works

Until about 100 years ago, people relied on prevailing winds and the buoyancy of warm air to cool their homes.

In most areas of the world, the prevailing wind directions during the warm months are well known. Coastal areas, for example, experience breezes from sea to land on hot days, with the direction reversing at night.

Orienting the home so that the breeze flows directly through large, openable windows from front to back maximizes the potential benefit.

As the illustration shows, strategically placed casement windows and shrubs can create pressure zones, resulting in air flow from high (H) to low (L) pressure. Keep this in mind when replacing windows and planting shrubs around an existing home.

Smoke stacks that remove smoke from factories without fans work because warm air—like a hot air balloon—is less dense than the surrounding air, so it rises.

The same "stack" effect can be used to ventilate a house, particularly after a hot day, when the house air is still hot, but the outside air has cooled.

Air flow is maximized when inlets and outlets are as low and high as possible. For a given ventilation opening, maximum air exchange is realized if the inlet and outlet areas are equal. However, if maximum air speed through a specific opening (a window next to your bed, for example) is the goal, the total outlet area should be at least double the inlet area.

Ceiling Fan

Moving Air

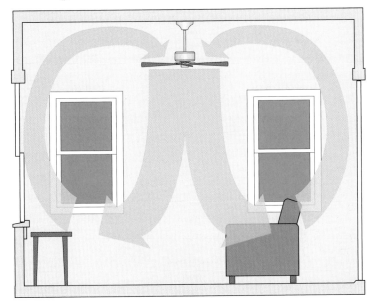

Human Comfort

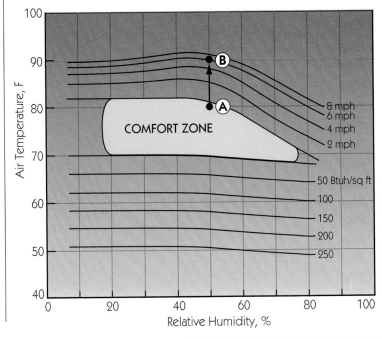

How It Works

While ceiling fans do not lower air temperature, they achieve a remarkable cooling effect simply by moving air in the room. To see how this works, we need to understand the physiology of comfort.

Our bodies maintain constant internal temperature by balancing the heat they generate against heat lost or gained from our surroundings. Heat is transferred by:

- conduction (things we are touching)
- convection (moving air)
- evaporation (of moisture from our skin)
- radiation (from warmer, or to cooler, surrounding surfaces)

Human comfort is the feeling of being neither too warm nor too cool while at rest in ordinary clothing. The chart at left shows the *comfort zone* of the average person. This is a range of air temperature and relative humidity, with no radiation or air movement.

The lower set of curves shows how the entire comfort zone is shifted toward lower air temperatures in the presence of radiation (think sunshine). The upper curves show how the zone is shifted to higher temperatures when a breeze blows across our skin (think wind chill).

Picture sitting in the green chair above. With the fan off, you are comfortable up to a room temperature of 80°F (Point A). Turn the fan on, creating a breeze of 6 mph. You should now feel equally comfortable up to 90°F (Point B).

Whole-House Fan

How It Works

During the summer, ambient air temperature commonly varies 20 F° or more in a 24-hour period, peaking in mid-afternoon and reaching its low point just before sunrise. Using a low-tech, low-energy whole-house fan, you can take advantage of this natural temperature swing to pump heat out of the house.

Here is how it works. As soon as the outside air temperature rises to the indoor temperature, close the house up tight, relying on the building's mass and insulation to slow the interior temperature rise.

After sunset, as soon as the outside temperature drops to the now-higher inside temperature, open screened windows and doors throughout the house, and switch on the powerful whole-house fan.

The volume of air in a typical 2,000-sq. ft. home with 8-foot ceilings is $2,000 \times 8 = 16,000$ cubic feet. A typical $1/2$-horsepower (375-watt) fan removes 4,000 cubic feet of air per minute (cfm). Such a fan would replace the hot inside air with cooler outside air fifteen times per hour.

Note that normal attic ventilation is not sufficient for the large volumes of air a whole house fan moves. The rule of thumb is 1 square foot of net free opening for every 750 cfm of fan rating.

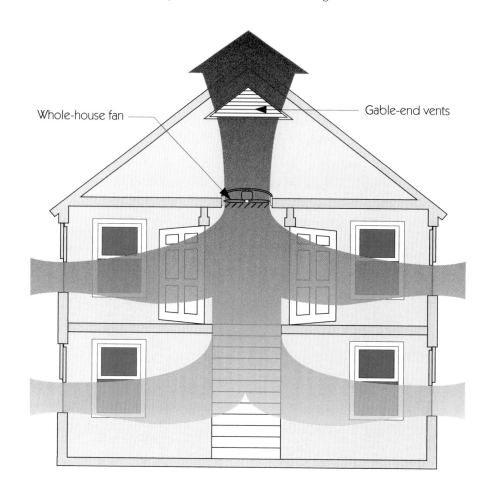

Whole-house fan — Gable-end vents

Window Air Conditioner

How It Works

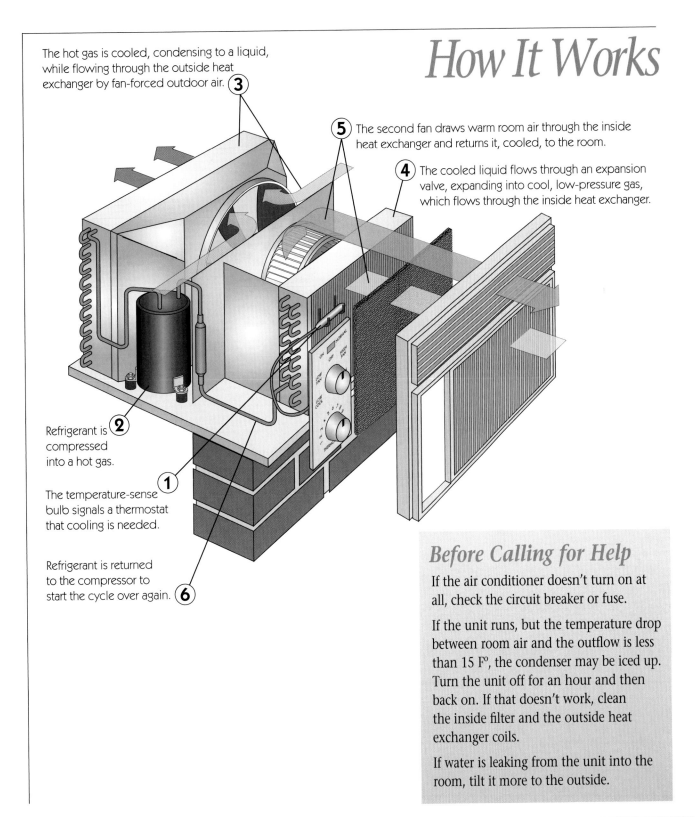

The hot gas is cooled, condensing to a liquid, while flowing through the outside heat exchanger by fan-forced outdoor air. (3)

(5) The second fan draws warm room air through the inside heat exchanger and returns it, cooled, to the room.

(4) The cooled liquid flows through an expansion valve, expanding into cool, low-pressure gas, which flows through the inside heat exchanger.

Refrigerant is (2) compressed into a hot gas.

The temperature-sense bulb signals a thermostat that cooling is needed.

Refrigerant is returned to the compressor to start the cycle over again. (6)

Before Calling for Help

If the air conditioner doesn't turn on at all, check the circuit breaker or fuse.

If the unit runs, but the temperature drop between room air and the outflow is less than 15 F°, the condenser may be iced up. Turn the unit off for an hour and then back on. If that doesn't work, clean the inside filter and the outside heat exchanger coils.

If water is leaking from the unit into the room, tilt it more to the outside.

Central Air Conditioner

How It Works

The furnace blower forces warm house air through the inside heat exchanger (evaporator) and returns it, cooled, to the house through the distribution ducts. **(5)**

The cooled liquid flows through an expansion valve and expands into a cool, low-pressure gas, which flows through the inside heat exchanger. **(4)**

(3) The hot gas gives off heat and condenses to a liquid while flowing through the outside heat exchanger.

(2) Refrigerant vapor is compressed to high pressure and temperature by the compressor.

(6) Refrigerant vapor returns to the compressor for another cycle.

FURNACE

(1) A central air conditioner often shares distribution ductwork with a gas or oil furnace.

Before Calling for Help

If the air conditioner doesn't turn on at all, check all of the heating system's circuit breakers or fuses.

If the breakers are on, turn the heating thermostat to a high temperature. If the furnace doesn't kick on, the thermostat or its wiring is faulty.

If the air conditioner runs, but the temperature drop between room air and the cooled outflow is less than 15 F°, replace the furnace filter and clean both inside and outside heat exchanger coils.

Depending on how dirty they get, furnace filters should be replaced as often as once per month. If you suffer from allergies, try switching to a filter of the same size but of a higher MERV (minimum efficiency reporting value) rating.

Evaporative Cooler

Inside the Cooler

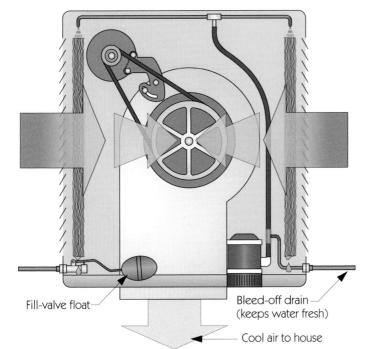

Fill-valve float

Bleed-off drain
(keeps water fresh)

Cool air to house

The Cooling Effect (as shown in a psychrometric chart)

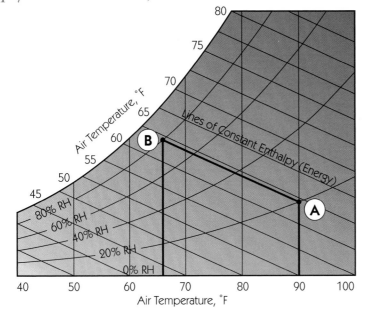

Air Temperature, °F

Lines of Constant Enthalpy (Energy)

80% RH
60% RH
40% RH
20% RH
0% RH

Air Temperature, °F

How It Works

Wet your hand and blow on it. Your skin feels cooler because evaporating water removes heat. With an evaporative ("swamp") cooler, a blower sucks hot, dry outdoor air through fibrous pads that are kept wet by a pump. As the dry air flows through the pads, its relative humidity (RH) increases, but its temperature drops by 20 F° or more.

The psychrometric chart below shows the cooling effect. Point A represents air at 90°F and 20% RH. After passing through the evaporative pads, the air is at Point B, at 67°F and 80% RH.

The drier the outdoor air, the greater the temperature drop, and the more cost-effective the swamp cooler will be. These systems work well in the desert southwest but not at all in the humid southeast.

Before Calling for Help

If the unit stops moving air, check the circuit breaker. If the breaker is OK, check the drive belt, which may be slipping or broken.

If the blower is moving air, but the air is not cooled as much as it should be, the pads may be clogged with mineral deposits. If the water supply contains minerals (hard water), the minerals are left behind during evaporation and can build up on the pad, restricting the flow of air. Fortunately, replacement pads are inexpensive and widely available.

5 AIR QUALITY

We now know that the quality of the air we breathe has a huge effect on our health. The quality of air in the environment is beyond our immediate control, but the quality of the air in our homes is not.

Not only can we warm it and cool it, but we can add or remove moisture. We can also cleanse it of things we don't want in our lungs: dust and dust mites, animal hair and dander, and molds and pathogens.

This chapter shows how this is done, and how to keep the machines that do it working.

Moisture & Mold

How It Works

Heated homes in cold-climates are usually felt to be too dry, not too humid. So why do so many of them experience moisture condensation and mold? The answer can be seen in the psychrometric chart below, which traces what happens when dry outdoor air infiltrates the home, receives additional water vapor from evaporation of water sources inside the home, and then contacts cool building surfaces, such as windows, exterior walls, and attic roofs.

What water sources inside the home? The table at right lists typical amounts of water vapor (in quarts of liquid water evaporated) in a home with four occupants.

The facing page addresses the problem of mold, which often occurs on the condensing surfaces.

Sources of Water Vapor, qt/day

Construction materials, first year	40
Standing water in basement	30
Damp basement or crawl space	25
Clothes dryer vented to inside	13
Respiration and perspiration	4.7
Clothes washing	2.1
Unvented gas range	1.3
Cooking without pot lids	1.0
Houseplants, average number	0.5
Showering/bathing	0.3

Tracking Infiltrating Air in a Humid Home in Winter

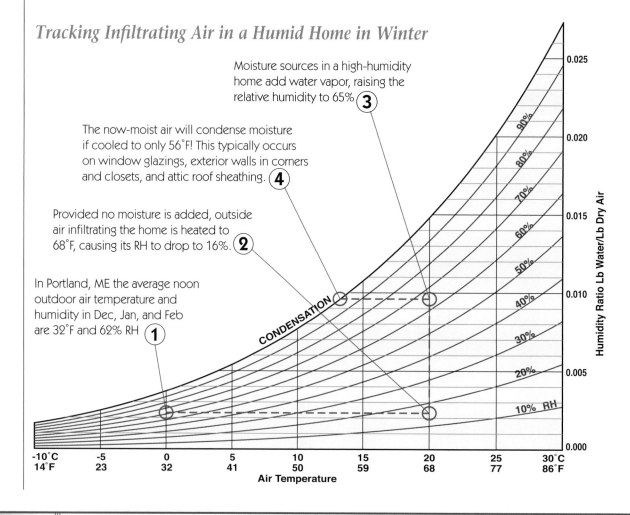

Moisture sources in a high-humidity home add water vapor, raising the relative humidity to 65% ③

The now-moist air will condense moisture if cooled to only 56°F! This typically occurs on window glazings, exterior walls in corners and closets, and attic roof sheathing. ④

Provided no moisture is added, outside air infiltrating the home is heated to 68°F, causing its RH to drop to 16%. ②

In Portland, ME the average noon outdoor air temperature and humidity in Dec, Jan, and Feb are 32°F and 62% RH ①

What Is the Best RH for Health?

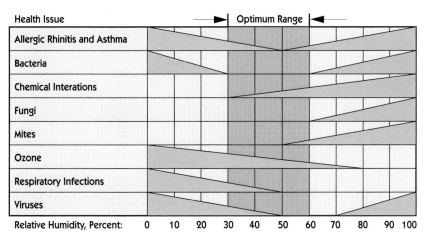

Health Issue	Optimum Range
Allergic Rhinitis and Asthma	
Bacteria	
Chemical Interations	
Fungi	
Mites	
Ozone	
Respiratory Infections	
Viruses	
Relative Humidity, Percent:	0 10 20 30 40 50 60 70 80 90 100

Mold isn't the only health issue affected by relative humidity. As the chart at left shows, there are as many problems exacerbated by too dry air as too moist. The ideal range, minimizing the total of ill effects, is considered 30–60% RH.

If your house is reasonably airtight, this range is easily maintained by either a humidifier (page 102) or a dehumidifier (page 103).

Where You Are Most Likely to Find Mold

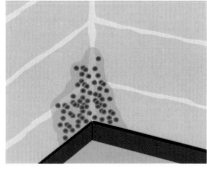

In a damp basement

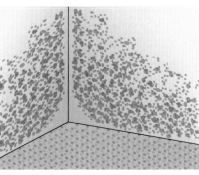

In a corner of an outside wall

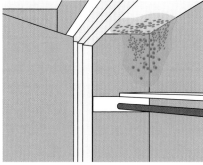

In a closet on an outside wall

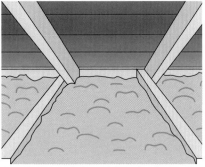

On the roof sheathing in the attic

Finding mold is not difficult once you understand the conditions that promote its growth: temperature over 50°F and relative humidity over 70%.

Since your home is probably heated to at least 65°F, look for interior surfaces most likely to be colder than average: windows (although mold is not a problem on glass), corners where two outside walls join, inside closets or other closed rooms on outside walls, inside kitchen and bathroom cabinets, and in the attic or other space between the roof and ceiling below.

After insulating outside walls (including basement walls), increase air flow by opening doors and by ventilating the attic.

How It Works

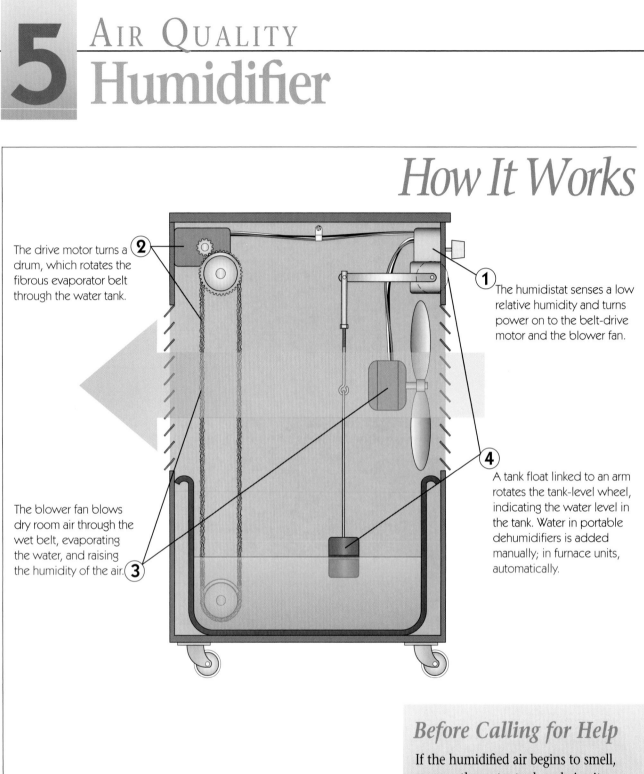

The drive motor turns a drum, which rotates the fibrous evaporator belt through the water tank. **②**

① The humidistat senses a low relative humidity and turns power on to the belt-drive motor and the blower fan.

The blower fan blows dry room air through the wet belt, evaporating the water, and raising the humidity of the air. **③**

④ A tank float linked to an arm rotates the tank-level wheel, indicating the water level in the tank. Water in portable dehumidifiers is added manually; in furnace units, automatically.

Before Calling for Help

If the humidified air begins to smell, remove the water tank and give it a thorough scrubbing to prevent mold, bacteria, etc.

If the volume of air flow decreases, mineral deposits may have built up in the belt. If so, replace the belt or remove it and soak it in vinegar overnight.

Dehumidifier

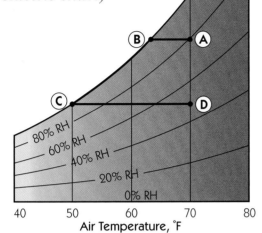

The Cooling Effect (as shown in a psychrometric chart)

80% RH
60% RH
40% RH
20% RH
0% RH

Air Temperature, °F

40   50   60   70   80

How It Works

A dehumidifier is like an air conditioner (pages 97 and 98) that runs entirely inside the house. It removes moisture from the air by cooling it to below its dew point, forcing water vapor to condense out of the air.

In the chart on the left, air at 70°F and 80% RH (Point A) is drawn through the cold evaporator coils. At first (from Point A to Point B), it simply cools. At Point B, the air reaches its dew point. Further cooling (B to C) forces moisture to condense on the evaporator coils and drip into the pan. The air then flows through the condenser, where it is warmed back to 70°F, but at 50% RH (D).

Portable Dehumidifier

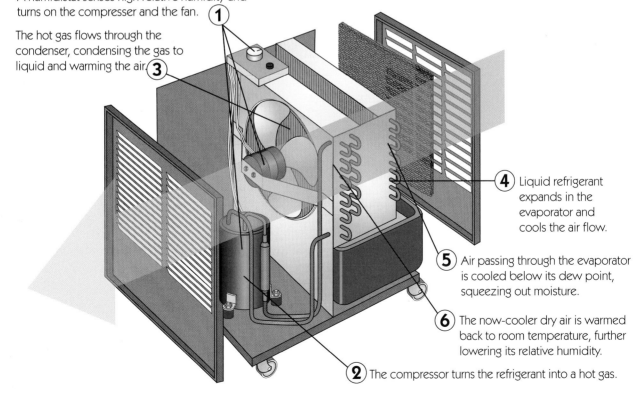

A humidistat senses high relative humidity and turns on the compresser and the fan. **1**

The hot gas flows through the condenser, condensing the gas to liquid and warming the air. **3**

4 Liquid refrigerant expands in the evaporator and cools the air flow.

5 Air passing through the evaporator is cooled below its dew point, squeezing out moisture.

6 The now-cooler dry air is warmed back to room temperature, further lowering its relative humidity.

2 The compressor turns the refrigerant into a hot gas.

Furnace Filter

Mechanical Furnace Filters

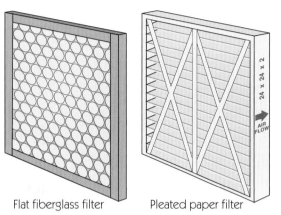

Flat fiberglass filter   Pleated paper filter

24 x 24 x 2
AIR FLOW

Typical Filter Installation

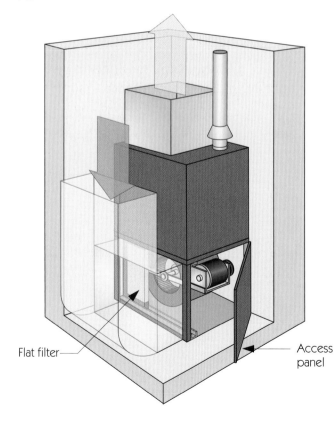

Flat filter

Access panel

How It Works

The common flat furnace filter consists of $1/2$"–1" of low-density fibrous or cellular material in a frame. The filter material may be treated with a viscous coating, but the filter is still so porous that it captures less than 20% of particles in the 1–10 micron range (a human hair = 25–100 microns).

Less-porous pleated paper filters capture nearly 100% of the same particles. Pleats increase the surface area by 10×, so air resistance remains about the same.

Before Calling for Help

If you have noticed slower-than-normal air flow from your heating vents, your furnace filter may be clogged.

Turn off power to the furnace, and locate the access panel, usually at the bottom of the furnace. Open the panel and find the filter. If it is covered with dust and lint, it is retarding air flow.

If the filter has a plastic or metal frame, it can be washed with a garden hose. Dry thoroughly and replace.

If the filter has a cardboard frame, take it to a home center and purchase a replacement of the same size. Buy a half dozen. They are inexpensive and should be replaced several times during the heating season, or monthly with pets.

While the furnace is open, check the blower belt. Replace it if you detect fraying or cracking.

Electronic Air Cleaner

Inside an Electronic Air Cleaner

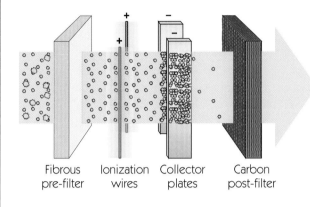

Fibrous pre-filter   Ionization wires   Collector plates   Carbon post-filter

Typical Furnace Air Cleaner

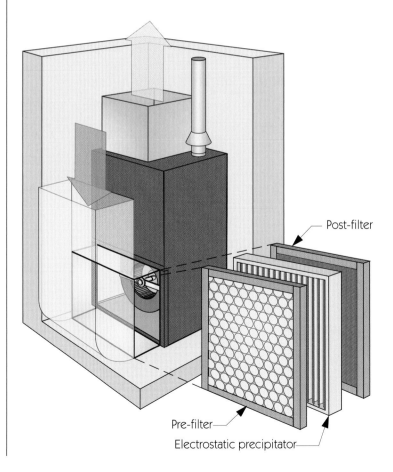

Post-filter

Pre-filter

Electrostatic precipitator

How It Works

In addition to a fibrous pre-filter and activated charcoal post-filter, the most common type of electronic air cleaner employs an electrostatic precipitator.

The two-stage precipitator consists of: 1) a row of high-voltage wires, which charge passing airborne particles, followed by 2) a row of oppositely charged metal plates, which capture the particles.

The plates should be cleaned whenever the dust accumulation is obvious to the eye.

Before Calling for Help

The pre- and post-filters in an electronic air cleaner are cleaned or replaced in the same way as the filters on the facing page. The electrostatic precipitator may be cleaned, but with care.

- First, the cabinet contains high voltage, so wait a minute after turning off the power before opening the access panel.

- Next, soften the deposits with dish detergent, either by soaking in a tub or by spraying with a detergent solution.

- After 15 minutes of soaking, rinse off using a sink or garden hose. Be careful not to bend the thin aluminum collector plates or break the wires.

- Make sure the unit is completely dry before replacing and restoring power.

6 APPLIANCES

Would you discard your 5-year old automobile if it had a flat tire, a broken fan belt, or a blown fuse? Of course not, but that is essentially what many homeowners do with their appliances. They do it because the cost of repair, on average, equals the depreciated value of the appliance.

Appliance repair is expensive for a single reason: instead of you driving the appliance to the repair shop, the repairman has to come to the appliance. As a result, travel accounts for half or more of the time and expense.

The fact is, more than half of all appliance repairs could be made in the home, by the homeowner, with common tools. Many replacement parts are available from the appliance retailer; nearly all of the parts—and much valuable guidance— are available online from sites such as *repairclinic.com*.

This chapter gives you x-ray vision into all of your large appliances, a basic understanding of how they work, and simple things to look for before you have one hauled away or call the repairman.

How It Works

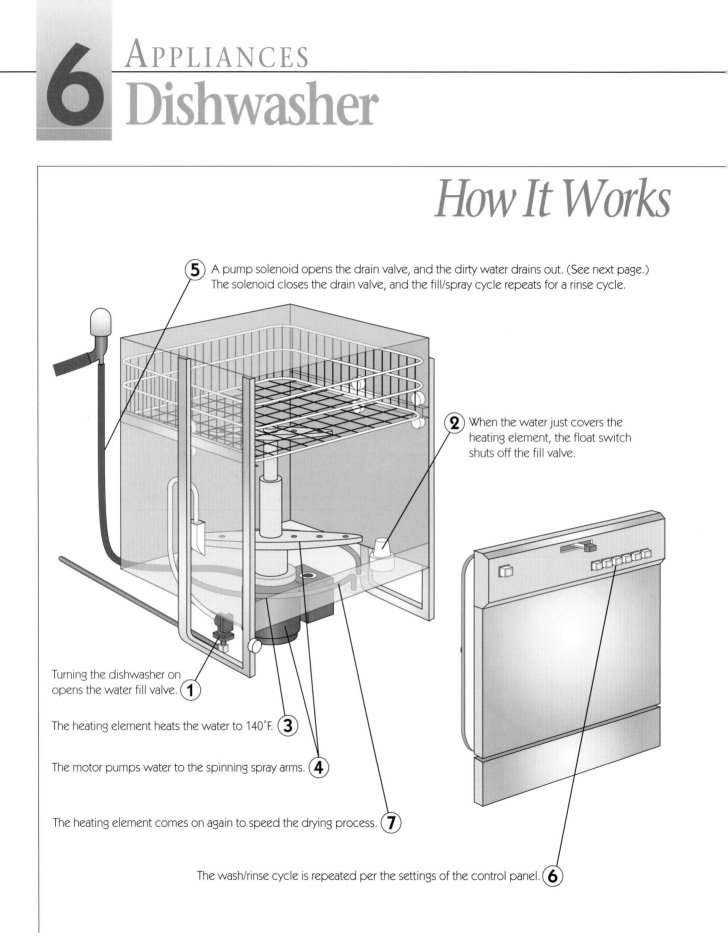

5 A pump solenoid opens the drain valve, and the dirty water drains out. (See next page.) The solenoid closes the drain valve, and the fill/spray cycle repeats for a rinse cycle.

2 When the water just covers the heating element, the float switch shuts off the fill valve.

Turning the dishwasher on opens the water fill valve. **1**

The heating element heats the water to 140°F. **3**

The motor pumps water to the spinning spray arms. **4**

The heating element comes on again to speed the drying process. **7**

The wash/rinse cycle is repeated per the settings of the control panel. **6**

A Double-Duty Pump

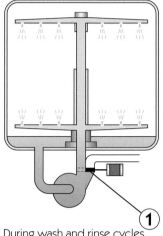

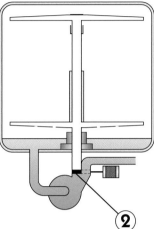

During wash and rinse cycles, the solenoid opens the spray line and closes the drain pipe.

During drain cycles, the solenoid closes the spray line and opens the drain pipe.

Dishwasher Air Gap

Air gaps prevent a possible backflow from a drain into the water supply. They are required by most plumbing codes for dishwashers.

During a drain cycle, the shield deflects water down the drain pipe.

After the drain cycle, air flows into the shield, preventing drainwater from siphoning back into the dishwasher.

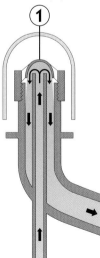

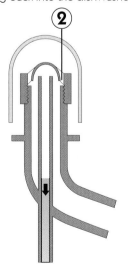

Before Calling for Help

If the dishwasher won't start:

- Check the circuit breaker in the service panel. Flip the breaker off, then on again.

- If the breaker is on, check to see if a separate wall switch is "off" or if the cord has become unplugged.

If the dishes are not coming out clean:

- Make sure you are using *dishwasher* detergent, not *dishwashing* detergent.

- Interrupt a wash and measure the water temperature. It should be 140°F.

- Remove food from plates before washing.

- Interrupt a wash cycle and check the water level. It should be just over the heating element. If not, remove and clean the float switch until it slides up and down freely.

- Remove the spray arm(s), and clean the spray holes. After replacing, make sure the arm spins freely.

If the dishwasher is leaking:

- Make sure you are using the manufacturer-recommended amount of *dishwasher* detergent. Note that *dishwashing* detergent makes too many suds, which will spill out.

- Check the float switch. If stuck in the down position, it will cause the dishwasher to overfill.

- Clean the door gasket with a sponge and detergent until it feels smooth.

How It Works

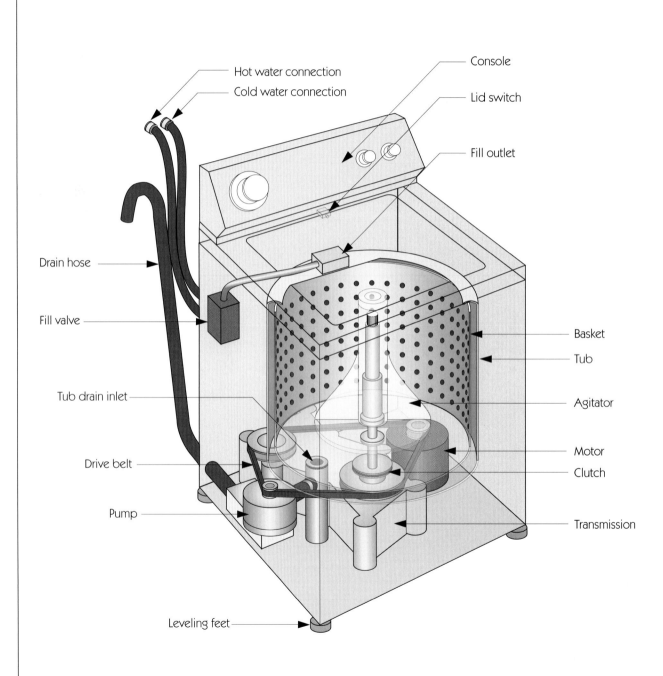

Hot water connection
Cold water connection
Console
Lid switch
Fill outlet
Drain hose
Fill valve
Basket
Tub
Tub drain inlet
Agitator
Drive belt
Motor
Clutch
Pump
Transmission
Leveling feet

Agitate Cycle

The agitate solenoid activates and pushes its cam bar forward. **(3)**

(2) The "wigwag" oscillates back and forth constantly.

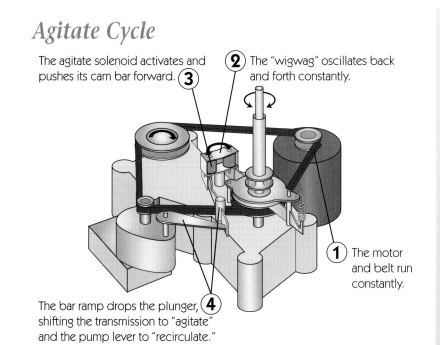

(1) The motor and belt run constantly.

The bar ramp drops the plunger, **(4)** shifting the transmission to "agitate" and the pump lever to "recirculate."

Spin Cycle

At the end of the spin cycle, the spin solenoid releases its cam bar, which moves forward. The cam ramp forces the clutch yoke and shaft back up, releasing the clutch and stopping the basket. **(8)**

The spin solenoid activates and pulls the spin cam bar back. **(5)**

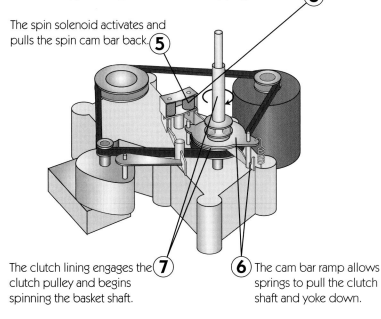

The clutch lining engages the **(7)** clutch pulley and begins spinning the basket shaft.

(6) The cam bar ramp allows springs to pull the clutch shaft and yoke down.

Before Calling for Help

If the washing machine won't start:

- Check the circuit breaker in the service panel. Flip the breaker off, then on again.

- If the breaker is on, check to see if the cord has become unplugged.

- Check the lid switch under the lid. If you have a test meter, unplug the washer, remove the screws at the front of the console, and tilt it back. Disconnect the plug leading to the lid switch, and read the resistance between the contacts as you depress the switch. If the resistance doesn't drop to zero, replace the switch.

If the washer is taking much longer to fill than it used to:

- Check to see if someone has turned off the water supply.

- Remove the fill hoses, one at a time, and check that each has strong flow.

- Check the inlet screens (inside where the hoses connect to the machine) to see if they are clogged. They are easily removed. Brush away loose material with a toothbrush. Mineral deposits can be dissolved by soaking the screens overnight in vinegar.

If the clothes washer is "walking" during a wash, the machine is overloaded, or one of the leveling feet needs to be adjusted. To level, adjust the one not making solid floor contact using an adjustable wrench.

Electric Clothes Dryer

How It Works

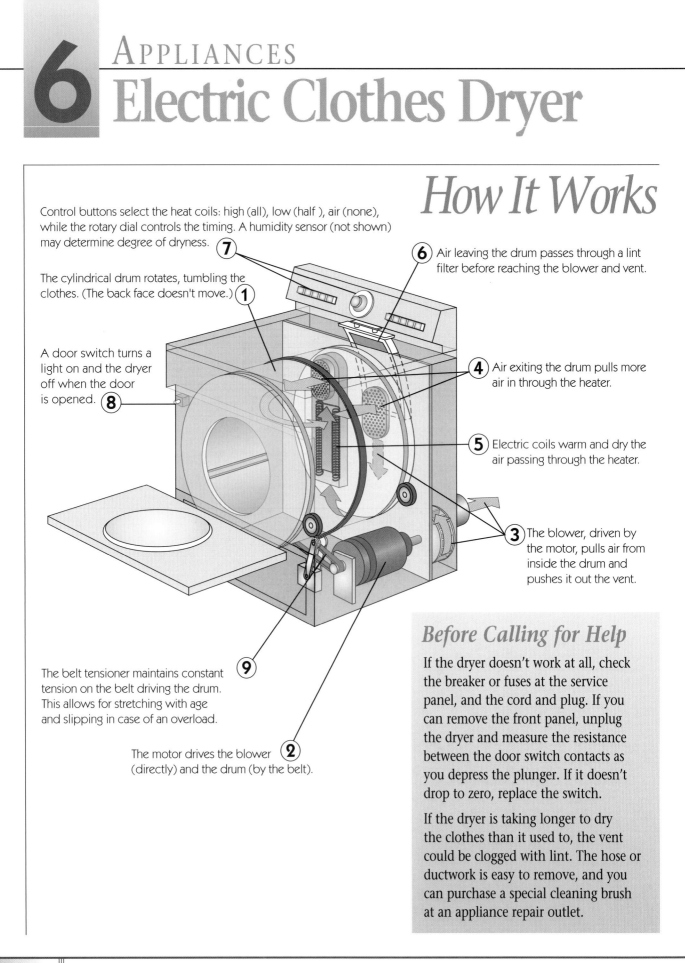

Control buttons select the heat coils: high (all), low (half), air (none), while the rotary dial controls the timing. A humidity sensor (not shown) may determine degree of dryness. **7**

The cylindrical drum rotates, tumbling the clothes. (The back face doesn't move.) **1**

A door switch turns a light on and the dryer off when the door is opened. **8**

6 Air leaving the drum passes through a lint filter before reaching the blower and vent.

4 Air exiting the drum pulls more air in through the heater.

5 Electric coils warm and dry the air passing through the heater.

3 The blower, driven by the motor, pulls air from inside the drum and pushes it out the vent.

The belt tensioner maintains constant tension on the belt driving the drum. This allows for stretching with age and slipping in case of an overload. **9**

The motor drives the blower (directly) and the drum (by the belt). **2**

Before Calling for Help

If the dryer doesn't work at all, check the breaker or fuses at the service panel, and the cord and plug. If you can remove the front panel, unplug the dryer and measure the resistance between the door switch contacts as you depress the plunger. If it doesn't drop to zero, replace the switch.

If the dryer is taking longer to dry the clothes than it used to, the vent could be clogged with lint. The hose or ductwork is easy to remove, and you can purchase a special cleaning brush at an appliance repair outlet.

Gas Clothes Dryer

How It Works

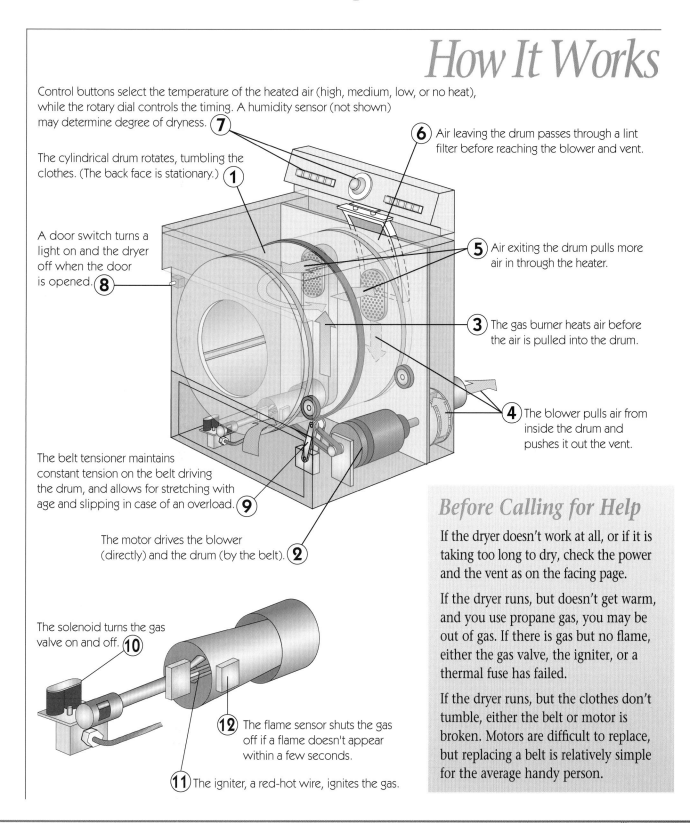

Control buttons select the temperature of the heated air (high, medium, low, or no heat), while the rotary dial controls the timing. A humidity sensor (not shown) may determine degree of dryness. **7**

The cylindrical drum rotates, tumbling the clothes. (The back face is stationary.) **1**

A door switch turns a light on and the dryer off when the door is opened. **8**

6 Air leaving the drum passes through a lint filter before reaching the blower and vent.

5 Air exiting the drum pulls more air in through the heater.

3 The gas burner heats air before the air is pulled into the drum.

4 The blower pulls air from inside the drum and pushes it out the vent.

The belt tensioner maintains constant tension on the belt driving the drum, and allows for stretching with age and slipping in case of an overload. **9**

The motor drives the blower (directly) and the drum (by the belt). **2**

The solenoid turns the gas valve on and off. **10**

12 The flame sensor shuts the gas off if a flame doesn't appear within a few seconds.

11 The igniter, a red-hot wire, ignites the gas.

Before Calling for Help

If the dryer doesn't work at all, or if it is taking too long to dry, check the power and the vent as on the facing page.

If the dryer runs, but doesn't get warm, and you use propane gas, you may be out of gas. If there is gas but no flame, either the gas valve, the igniter, or a thermal fuse has failed.

If the dryer runs, but the clothes don't tumble, either the belt or motor is broken. Motors are difficult to replace, but replacing a belt is relatively simple for the average handy person.

How It Works

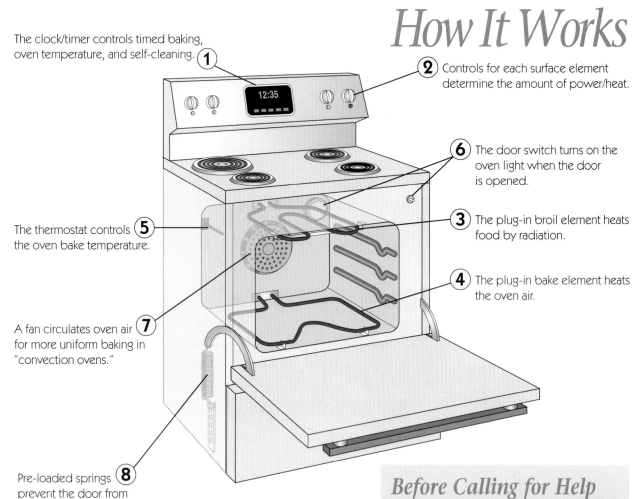

The clock/timer controls timed baking, oven temperature, and self-cleaning. **①**

② Controls for each surface element determine the amount of power/heat.

⑥ The door switch turns on the oven light when the door is opened.

The thermostat controls **⑤** the oven bake temperature.

③ The plug-in broil element heats food by radiation.

④ The plug-in bake element heats the oven air.

A fan circulates oven air **⑦** for more uniform baking in "convection ovens."

Pre-loaded springs **⑧** prevent the door from falling open and allow it to be left ajar for cooling.

12:35

Before Calling for Help

If nothing—not even the clock—works, check the large circuit breakers at the service panel. Also make sure the range plug is firmly seated in its receptacle.

If a surface element won't heat, it is probably burned out. If the oven bakes poorly or not at all, the bake element has failed. Similarly, if the broiler doesn't glow, it, too, needs replacing.

All of these elements simply plug in. You can find replacement surface elements at home centers, and bake and broil elements at appliance repair shops.

Gas Range/Oven

How It Works

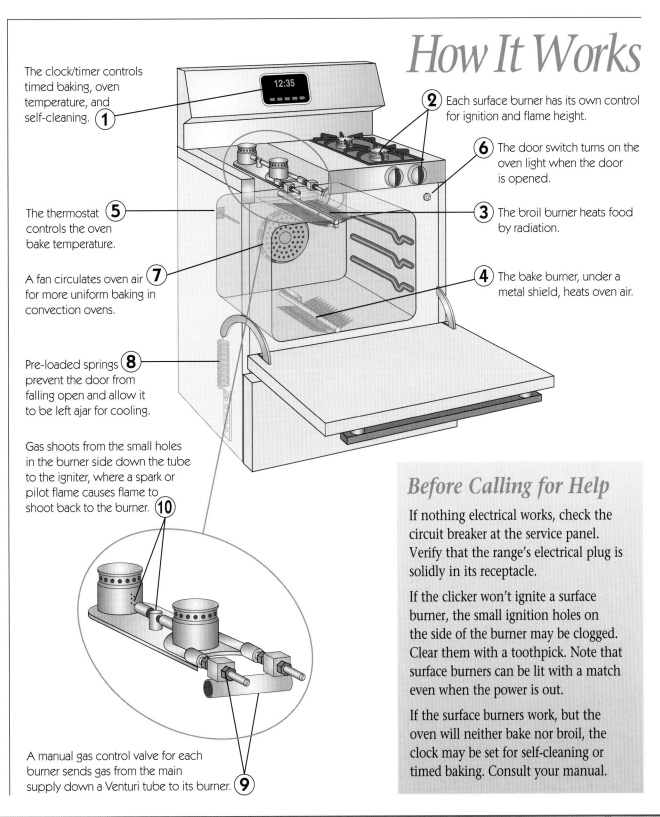

The clock/timer controls timed baking, oven temperature, and self-cleaning. **1**

2 Each surface burner has its own control for ignition and flame height.

6 The door switch turns on the oven light when the door is opened.

The thermostat **5** controls the oven bake temperature.

3 The broil burner heats food by radiation.

A fan circulates oven air **7** for more uniform baking in convection ovens.

4 The bake burner, under a metal shield, heats oven air.

Pre-loaded springs **8** prevent the door from falling open and allow it to be left ajar for cooling.

Gas shoots from the small holes in the burner side down the tube to the igniter, where a spark or pilot flame causes flame to shoot back to the burner. **10**

A manual gas control valve for each burner sends gas from the main supply down a Venturi tube to its burner. **9**

Before Calling for Help

If nothing electrical works, check the circuit breaker at the service panel. Verify that the range's electrical plug is solidly in its receptacle.

If the clicker won't ignite a surface burner, the small ignition holes on the side of the burner may be clogged. Clear them with a toothpick. Note that surface burners can be lit with a match even when the power is out.

If the surface burners work, but the oven will neither bake nor broil, the clock may be set for self-cleaning or timed baking. Consult your manual.

How It Works

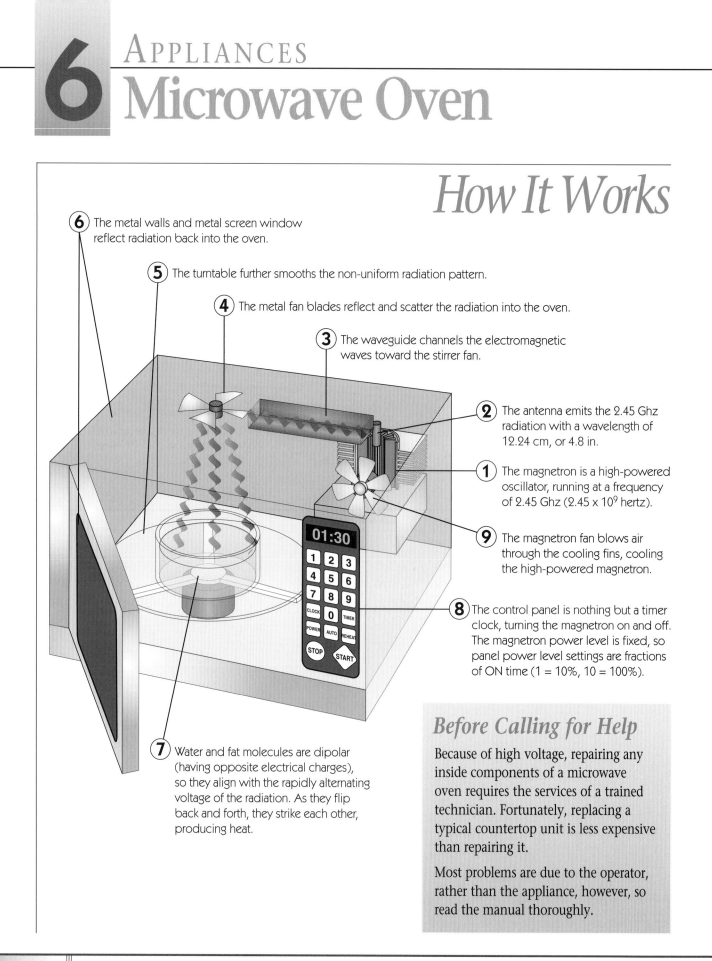

6 The metal walls and metal screen window reflect radiation back into the oven.

5 The turntable further smooths the non-uniform radiation pattern.

4 The metal fan blades reflect and scatter the radiation into the oven.

3 The waveguide channels the electromagnetic waves toward the stirrer fan.

2 The antenna emits the 2.45 Ghz radiation with a wavelength of 12.24 cm, or 4.8 in.

1 The magnetron is a high-powered oscillator, running at a frequency of 2.45 Ghz (2.45×10^9 hertz).

9 The magnetron fan blows air through the cooling fins, cooling the high-powered magnetron.

8 The control panel is nothing but a timer clock, turning the magnetron on and off. The magnetron power level is fixed, so panel power level settings are fractions of ON time (1 = 10%, 10 = 100%).

7 Water and fat molecules are dipolar (having opposite electrical charges), so they align with the rapidly alternating voltage of the radiation. As they flip back and forth, they strike each other, producing heat.

Before Calling for Help

Because of high voltage, repairing any inside components of a microwave oven requires the services of a trained technician. Fortunately, replacing a typical countertop unit is less expensive than repairing it.

Most problems are due to the operator, rather than the appliance, however, so read the manual thoroughly.

Garbage Disposer

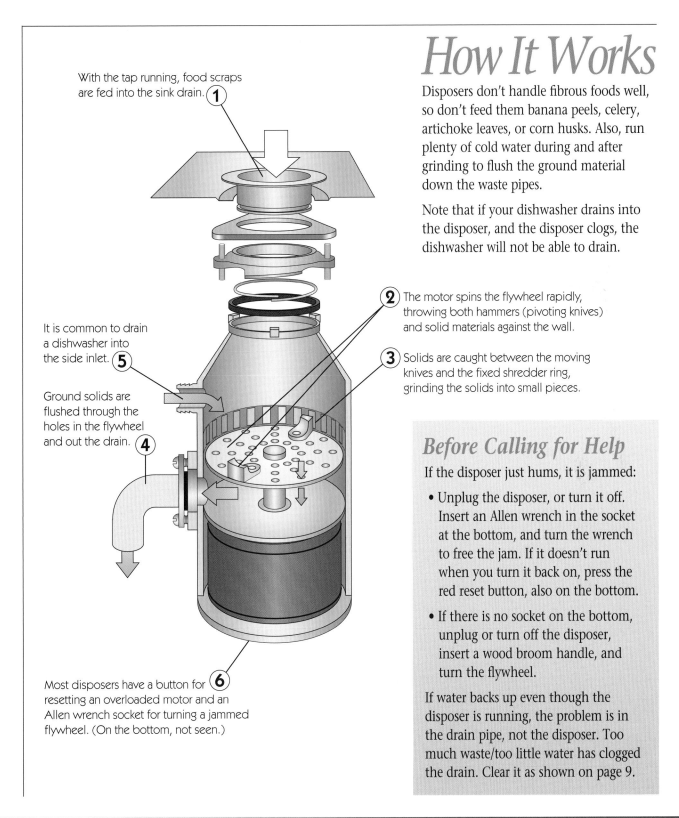

With the tap running, food scraps are fed into the sink drain. **1**

It is common to drain a dishwasher into the side inlet. **5**

Ground solids are flushed through the holes in the flywheel and out the drain. **4**

Most disposers have a button for resetting an overloaded motor and an Allen wrench socket for turning a jammed flywheel. (On the bottom, not seen.) **6**

How It Works

Disposers don't handle fibrous foods well, so don't feed them banana peels, celery, artichoke leaves, or corn husks. Also, run plenty of cold water during and after grinding to flush the ground material down the waste pipes.

Note that if your dishwasher drains into the disposer, and the disposer clogs, the dishwasher will not be able to drain.

2 The motor spins the flywheel rapidly, throwing both hammers (pivoting knives) and solid materials against the wall.

3 Solids are caught between the moving knives and the fixed shredder ring, grinding the solids into small pieces.

Before Calling for Help

If the disposer just hums, it is jammed:

- Unplug the disposer, or turn it off. Insert an Allen wrench in the socket at the bottom, and turn the wrench to free the jam. If it doesn't run when you turn it back on, press the red reset button, also on the bottom.

- If there is no socket on the bottom, unplug or turn off the disposer, insert a wood broom handle, and turn the flywheel.

If water backs up even though the disposer is running, the problem is in the drain pipe, not the disposer. Too much waste/too little water has clogged the drain. Clear it as shown on page 9.

How It Works

Refrigerators, freezers, and air conditioners are all specialized applications of the heat-pump principle, wherein the temperature and pressure relationships of a refrigerant are used to move heat energy from one place to another. (A detailed explanation of heat pumps appears on pages 76–77.)

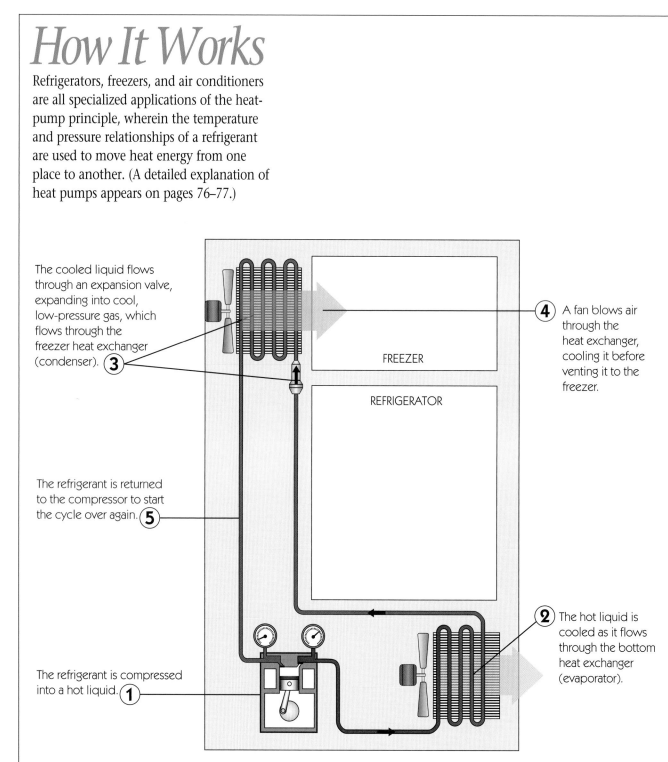

The cooled liquid flows through an expansion valve, expanding into cool, low-pressure gas, which flows through the freezer heat exchanger (condenser). **3**

FREEZER

REFRIGERATOR

4 A fan blows air through the heat exchanger, cooling it before venting it to the freezer.

The refrigerant is returned to the compressor to start the cycle over again. **5**

2 The hot liquid is cooled as it flows through the bottom heat exchanger (evaporator).

The refrigerant is compressed into a hot liquid. **1**

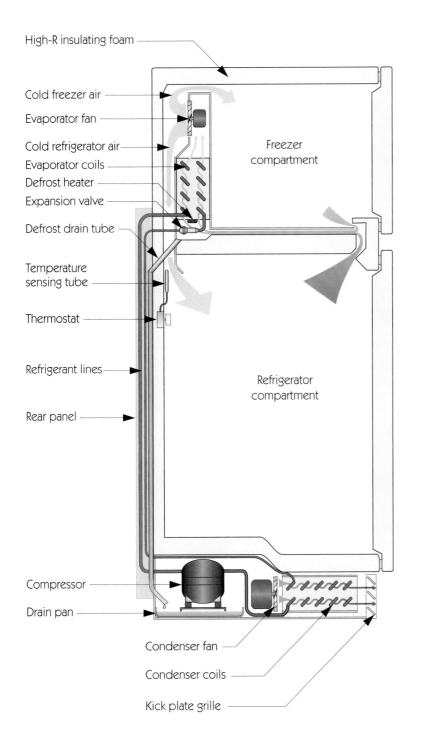

High-R insulating foam

Cold freezer air

Evaporator fan

Cold refrigerator air

Evaporator coils

Defrost heater

Expansion valve

Defrost drain tube

Temperature sensing tube

Thermostat

Refrigerant lines

Rear panel

Freezer compartment

Refrigerator compartment

Compressor

Drain pan

Condenser fan

Condenser coils

Kick plate grille

Before Calling for Help

If the refrigerator seems dead (even the light won't come on), check the breaker for the refrigerator circuit at the service panel. Next, check to make sure the refrigerator's plug hasn't pulled out of the wall receptacle or been damaged.

If there is power to the plug, replace the light bulb with one of the same size and wattage.

If the light now works, try simply turning the thermostat to the maximum cold position. If you don't hear the compressor humming, remove the kick panel at floor level, or pull the refrigerator away from the wall, and put your hand on the compressor. If it is running, you should be able to feel it vibrating, and it should be warm.

If the compressor runs, but cooling is poor, either the evaporator coils are iced up, preventing the fan from circulating cold air to the freezer and refrigerator, or the condenser coils are clogged with dust.

To check for iced-up evaporator coils, empty the refrigerator and turn it off for 24 hours with the freezer door open. If after restarting, it cools properly, the defroster is defective.

To clean the condenser coils, remove the kick panel and use a refrigerator condenser brush (available from appliance repair shops) and the nozzle attachment of your vacuum cleaner.

How It Works

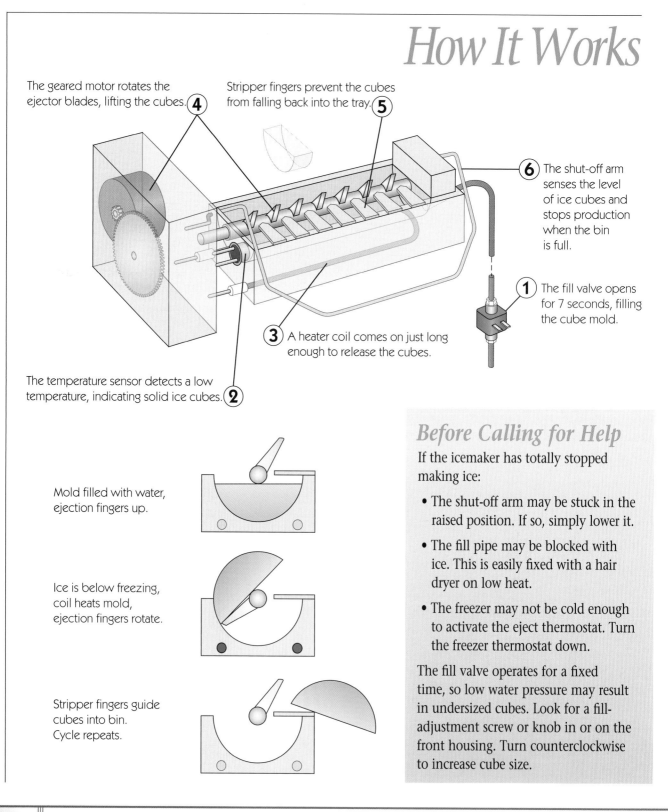

The geared motor rotates the ejector blades, lifting the cubes. **(4)**

Stripper fingers prevent the cubes from falling back into the tray. **(5)**

(6) The shut-off arm senses the level of ice cubes and stops production when the bin is full.

(1) The fill valve opens for 7 seconds, filling the cube mold.

(3) A heater coil comes on just long enough to release the cubes.

The temperature sensor detects a low temperature, indicating solid ice cubes. **(2)**

Mold filled with water, ejection fingers up.

Ice is below freezing, coil heats mold, ejection fingers rotate.

Stripper fingers guide cubes into bin. Cycle repeats.

Before Calling for Help

If the icemaker has totally stopped making ice:

- The shut-off arm may be stuck in the raised position. If so, simply lower it.

- The fill pipe may be blocked with ice. This is easily fixed with a hair dryer on low heat.

- The freezer may not be cold enough to activate the eject thermostat. Turn the freezer thermostat down.

The fill valve operates for a fixed time, so low water pressure may result in undersized cubes. Look for a fill-adjustment screw or knob in or on the front housing. Turn counterclockwise to increase cube size.

Trash Compactor

How It Works

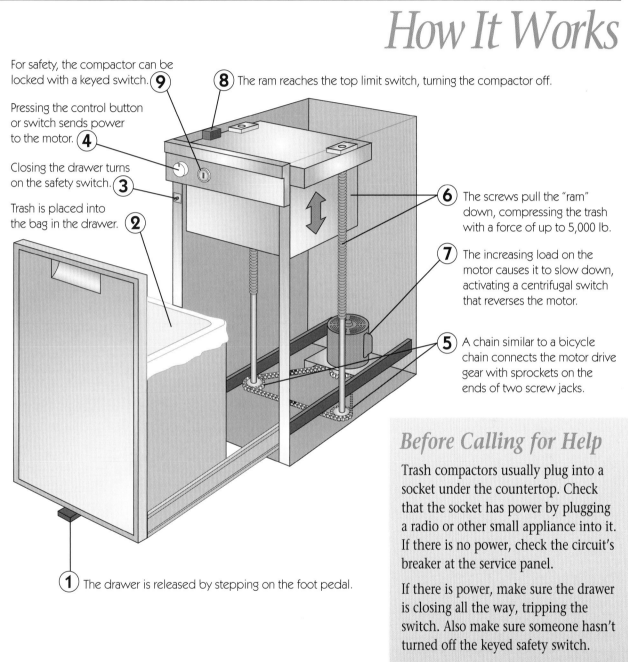

For safety, the compactor can be locked with a keyed switch. **9**

8 The ram reaches the top limit switch, turning the compactor off.

Pressing the control button or switch sends power to the motor. **4**

Closing the drawer turns on the safety switch. **3**

Trash is placed into the bag in the drawer. **2**

6 The screws pull the "ram" down, compressing the trash with a force of up to 5,000 lb.

7 The increasing load on the motor causes it to slow down, activating a centrifugal switch that reverses the motor.

5 A chain similar to a bicycle chain connects the motor drive gear with sprockets on the ends of two screw jacks.

1 The drawer is released by stepping on the foot pedal.

Before Calling for Help

Trash compactors usually plug into a socket under the countertop. Check that the socket has power by plugging a radio or other small appliance into it. If there is no power, check the circuit's breaker at the service panel.

If there is power, make sure the drawer is closing all the way, tripping the switch. Also make sure someone hasn't turned off the keyed safety switch.

If the drawer sticks, food has probably accumulated in the track. Remove the drawer, clean the track and rollers with a toothbrush and detergent, and oil the rollers with general-purpose lubricant.

Vacuum Cleaners

Filtering vs. Centrifuging

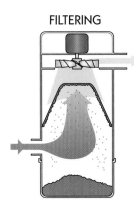

FILTERING

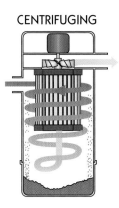

CENTRIFUGING

Portable Vacuums

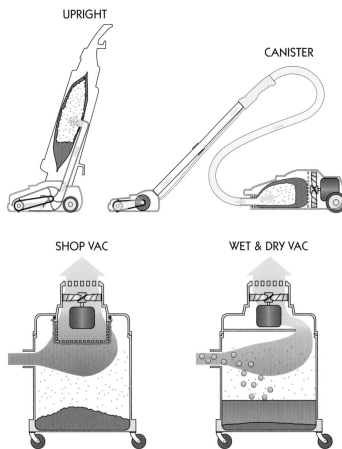

UPRIGHT

CANISTER

SHOP VAC

WET & DRY VAC

How They Work

Vacuum cleaners remove dust and debris by entraining it in rapidly moving air. The greater the air velocity, the greater the density of material they can pick up, so horsepower is an important variable. Vacuums for carpet cleaning also employ rotating "beater bars," which vibrate the carpet to shake loose dirt deep in the pile.

At the other end of the vacuum, the particles must be removed before the air is recirculated to the room. Otherwise, vacuuming would do nothing but redistribute dirt.

The two basic approaches to dirt separation are filtering and centrifuging (see top, left).

Filtering vacuums employ semi-porous paper or cloth bags. The porosity of the filter involves a huge tradeoff: A coarse filter allows for great air speed, but it allows fine dust and microbes to pass through. A fine filter retains more dust, but the dust builds up on the filter and rapidly diminishes suction.

Shop vacuums and wet-and-dry vacuums are intended for coarse materials and liquids. They use minimal filtering, but rely instead on the drop in air speed (and dirt-carrying power) when the air stream enters the much larger canister from the hose.

Centrifuging vacuums use two forces: centrifugal and gravity. Just as you feel centrifugal force when you drive around a curve rapidly, objects following a curved path are thrown to the outside of the curve. Centrifugal, or "cyclonic," vacuums spin air so that dirt, even fine dust, is thrown to the outside of the canister, where gravity causes it to drop into the dust container.

Central Vacuum Systems

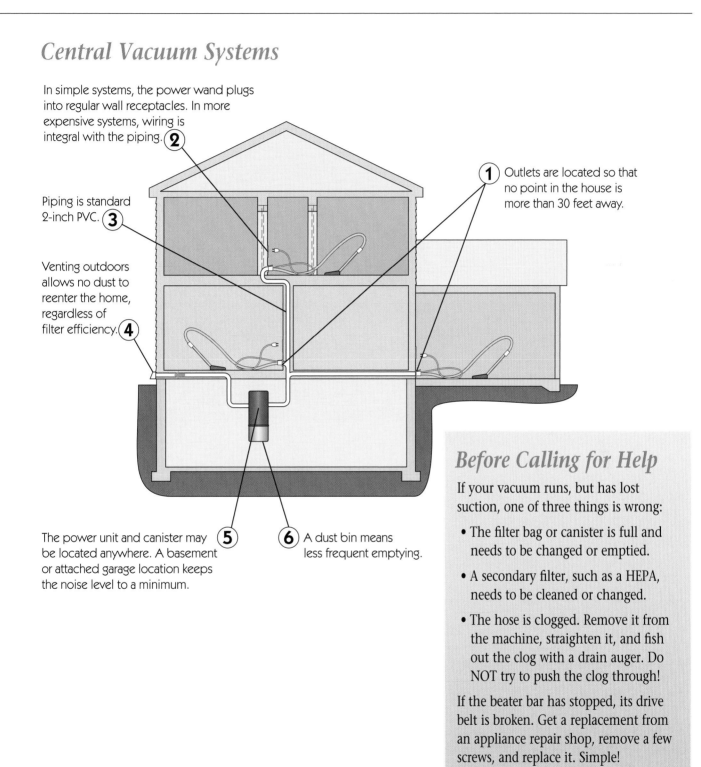

In simple systems, the power wand plugs into regular wall receptacles. In more expensive systems, wiring is integral with the piping. **2**

Piping is standard 2-inch PVC. **3**

Venting outdoors allows no dust to reenter the home, regardless of filter efficiency. **4**

1 Outlets are located so that no point in the house is more than 30 feet away.

The power unit and canister may **5** be located anywhere. A basement or attached garage location keeps the noise level to a minimum.

6 A dust bin means less frequent emptying.

Before Calling for Help

If your vacuum runs, but has lost suction, one of three things is wrong:

- The filter bag or canister is full and needs to be changed or emptied.

- A secondary filter, such as a HEPA, needs to be cleaned or changed.

- The hose is clogged. Remove it from the machine, straighten it, and fish out the clog with a drain auger. Do NOT try to push the clog through!

If the beater bar has stopped, its drive belt is broken. Get a replacement from an appliance repair shop, remove a few screws, and replace it. Simple!

7 WINDOWS & DOORS

What to do is pretty obvious when a window glazing breaks, a screen tears, or the screws in a door hinge fall out. But what if your key no longer opens the door, or the garage door opener disobeys your commands? This is a short chapter, but the technologies covered are fascinating, and the information will be useful to most homeowners.

Before you purchase new or replacement windows, make sure you read the section "Low-E Windows," in Chapter 10.

Older Wood Windows

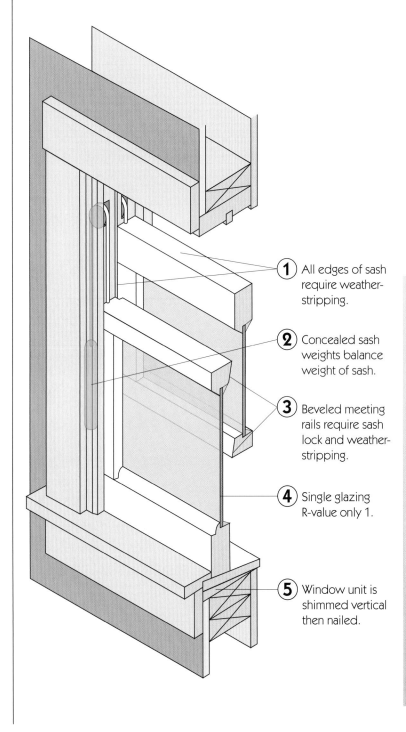

1. All edges of sash require weather-stripping.

2. Concealed sash weights balance weight of sash.

3. Beveled meeting rails require sash lock and weather-stripping.

4. Single glazing R-value only 1.

5. Window unit is shimmed vertical then nailed.

How It Works

Wood windows have been replaced in most new home construction because they are expensive. The new vinyl, aluminum, and even fiberglass windows with double-glazed, low-e glazings are not only less expensive, but are more energy-efficient.

However, if you have wood windows that are in pretty good shape, and you have little money but lots of time, consider stripping, painting, puttying, and weatherstripping the windows and adding the do-it-yourself double-glazed interior insert panels described on pages 182-183.

Before Replacing

If the sash cord has broken and the weights fallen down, consider sealing the pulleys (they are a heat leak). Raise the lower sash to its open position, and drill 1/8-inch holes through the interior sides of the sashes (stiles) into the window frame. Long finish nails inserted through the stiles and frame will hold the sash up.

If the sashes can't be made to lock, nails and holes drilled in the sash-down position make an effective lock.

If a glazing is broken, warm the putty with a heat gun and remove with a putty knife, or chisel. Pull the glazing points and remove the glass. Buy an exact replacement at the hardware store and reinstall. After 24 hours, paint and seal the putty to the glass.

Modern Vinyl or Aluminum Window

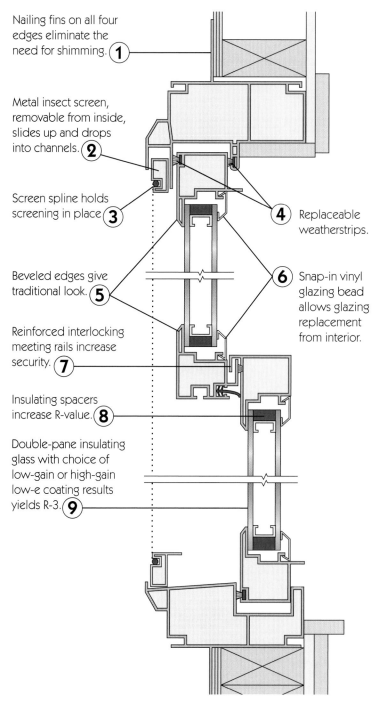

Nailing fins on all four edges eliminate the need for shimming. **(1)**

Metal insect screen, removable from inside, slides up and drops into channels. **(2)**

Screen spline holds screening in place **(3)**

Beveled edges give traditional look. **(5)**

Reinforced interlocking meeting rails increase security. **(7)**

Insulating spacers increase R-value. **(8)**

Double-pane insulating glass with choice of low-gain or high-gain low-e coating results yields R-3. **(9)**

(4) Replaceable weatherstrips.

(6) Snap-in vinyl glazing bead allows glazing replacement from interior.

If your home is less than twenty-five years old, chances are great it has vinyl windows. The reason vinyl has replaced wood—regardless of what architectural preservations say—is it makes a more efficient and low-maintenance window.

If your home is an architectural treasure, then by all means preserve its old wood windows. Otherwise go modern.

Before Replacing

Don't like the color? Just clean the vinyl surfaces with detergent and a scrubby pad, wipe down lightly with acetone, and paint with any semigloss exterior acrylic latex paint.

Is a pane fogged up or cracked? See if you can pry out the vinyl glazing beads that hold the glass in place. If so, remove the old double-glazed unit and take it to your local glass store. They will measure it and make or order an exact replacement. Ask them how to install and seal the new glazing.

Is the insect screen torn? Remove the screen spline and screening. Buy the identical diameter spline and fiberglass screening at a home center or glass store and install with a spline roller.

Is the screen frame damaged? Make your own frame from the aluminum extrusions and corner connectors found at any home center.

Casement Window

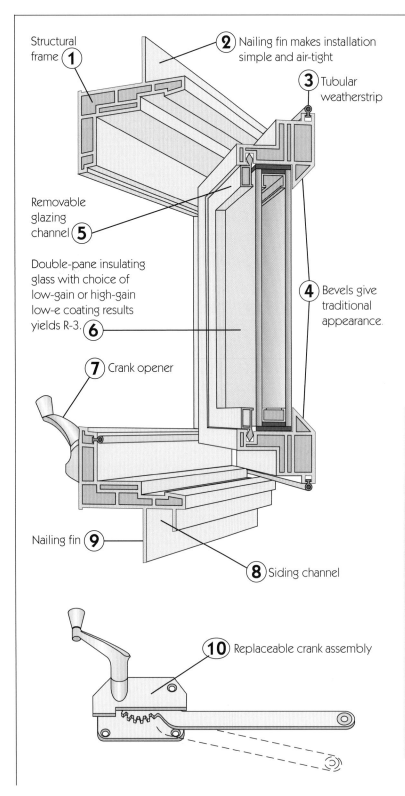

Structural frame ①

② Nailing fin makes installation simple and air-tight

③ Tubular weatherstrip

Removable glazing channel ⑤

Double-pane insulating glass with choice of low-gain or high-gain low-e coating results yields R-3. ⑥

④ Bevels give traditional appearance.

⑦ Crank opener

Nailing fin ⑨

⑧ Siding channel

⑩ Replaceable crank assembly

How It Works

Casement windows resemble small glazed doors, except they are opened and closed by a crank assembly at the bottom.

Casements offer several advanges over double-hung windows: 1) they open nearly all the way, 2) provided the hinges are on the appropriate side, they can scoop cooling breezes into the room.

Disadvantages include: 1) possible damage to the window by forcing the crank when the upper latch is closed, 2) difficulty washing the window from the inside.

As with double-hung windows, instead of replacing sound single-glazed units, consider the do-it-yourself interior insert panels described on pages 182-183.

Before Replacing

Is a double-glazed pane fogged up or cracked? A glass store can remove the interior glazing channel on site and order or make an exact replacement. While you are it, upgrade the unit to R-3 with low-e glazing.

Is the insect screen torn? Remove the screen spline and screening. Buy the identical diameter spline and fiberglass screening at a home center or glass store and install with a spline roller.

Is the screen frame damaged? Make your own frame from the aluminum extrusions and corner connectors found at any home center.

Cylinder Lock

The Cylinder

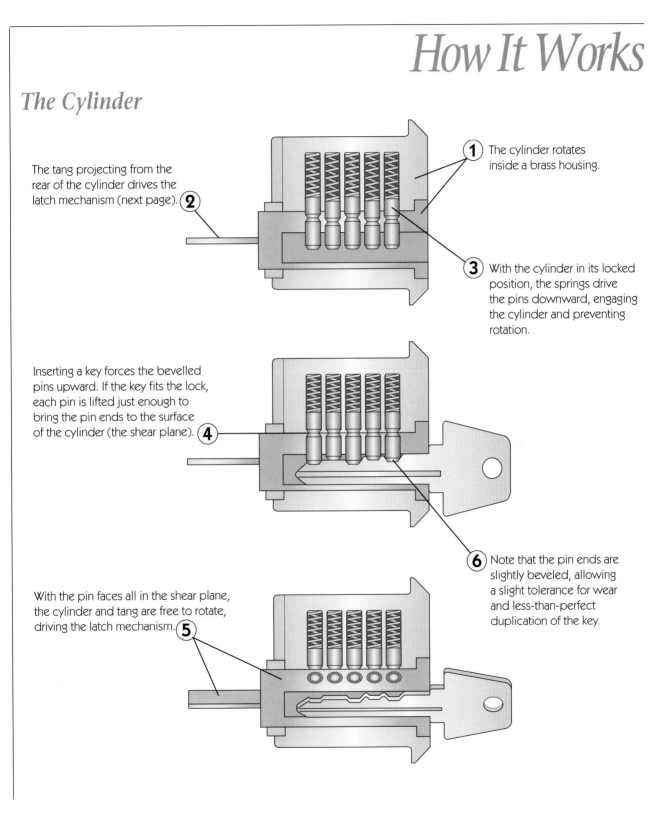

The tang projecting from the rear of the cylinder drives the latch mechanism (next page). **②**

① The cylinder rotates inside a brass housing.

③ With the cylinder in its locked position, the springs drive the pins downward, engaging the cylinder and preventing rotation.

Inserting a key forces the bevelled pins upward. If the key fits the lock, each pin is lifted just enough to bring the pin ends to the surface of the cylinder (the shear plane). **④**

⑥ Note that the pin ends are slightly beveled, allowing a slight tolerance for wear and less-than-perfect duplication of the key.

With the pin faces all in the shear plane, the cylinder and tang are free to rotate, driving the latch mechanism. **⑤**

How They Work

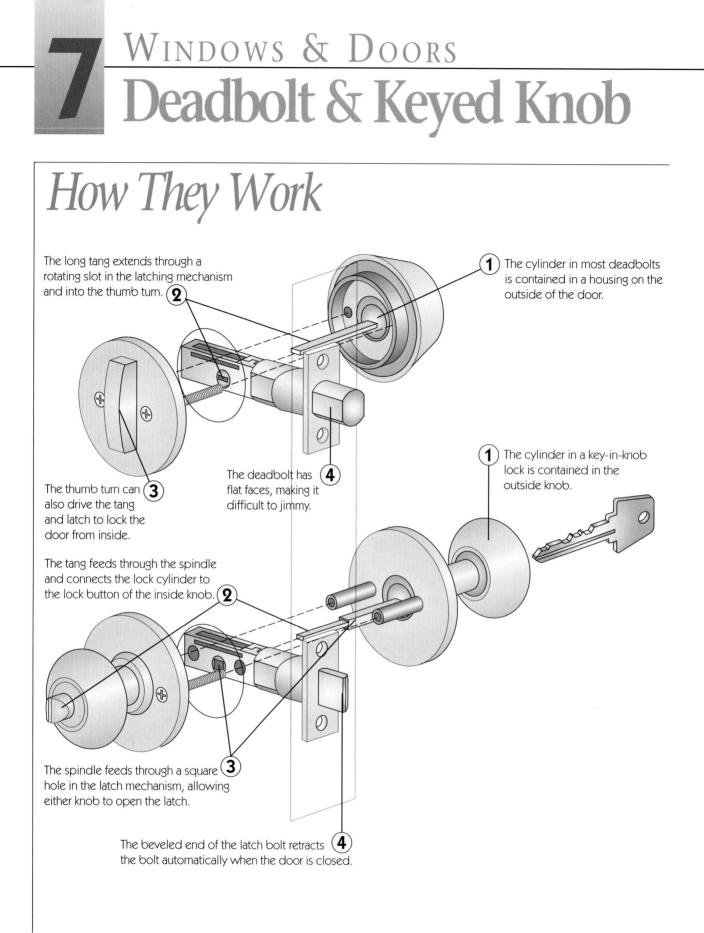

The long tang extends through a rotating slot in the latching mechanism and into the thumb turn. **2**

1 The cylinder in most deadbolts is contained in a housing on the outside of the door.

The thumb turn can also drive the tang and latch to lock the door from inside. **3**

The deadbolt has flat faces, making it difficult to jimmy. **4**

1 The cylinder in a key-in-knob lock is contained in the outside knob.

The tang feeds through the spindle and connects the lock cylinder to the lock button of the inside knob. **2**

The spindle feeds through a square hole in the latch mechanism, allowing either knob to open the latch. **3**

The beveled end of the latch bolt retracts the bolt automatically when the door is closed. **4**

Garage Door Opener

How It Works

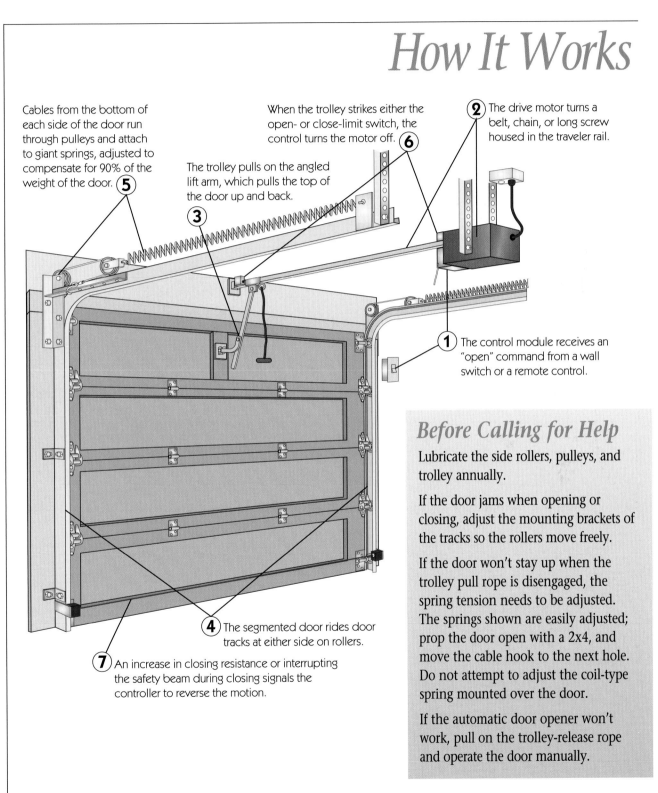

Cables from the bottom of each side of the door run through pulleys and attach to giant springs, adjusted to compensate for 90% of the weight of the door. **5**

The trolley pulls on the angled lift arm, which pulls the top of the door up and back. **3**

When the trolley strikes either the open- or close-limit switch, the control turns the motor off. **6**

2 The drive motor turns a belt, chain, or long screw housed in the traveler rail.

1 The control module receives an "open" command from a wall switch or a remote control.

4 The segmented door rides door tracks at either side on rollers.

7 An increase in closing resistance or interrupting the safety beam during closing signals the controller to reverse the motion.

Before Calling for Help

Lubricate the side rollers, pulleys, and trolley annually.

If the door jams when opening or closing, adjust the mounting brackets of the tracks so the rollers move freely.

If the door won't stay up when the trolley pull rope is disengaged, the spring tension needs to be adjusted. The springs shown are easily adjusted; prop the door open with a 2x4, and move the cable hook to the next hole. Do not attempt to adjust the coil-type spring mounted over the door.

If the automatic door opener won't work, pull on the trolley-release rope and operate the door manually.

8 Foundation & Frame

A wise builder once told me, "A basement is a well we pray water will never enter." Those with basements will say, "Amen." According to the National Association of Home Builders, the #1 reason for builder callbacks is foundations.

A properly designed and constructed foundation will never cause a problem; improperly constructed, it will never cease to be a problem.

This chapter shows the proper design of foundations—designs that will never heave, settle, flood, or collect radon.

Framing is rarely an issue for homeowners until they wish to cut into it, or they're planning a new house or remodeling project. Since the primary function of a building's frame is supporting weight, great forces are involved, and great care should be taken in making any changes. This chapter will illustrate how framing has evolved, from the settler's post-and-beam to today's advanced, engineered frame. Knowing how the frame works will allow you to answer that classic DIY question, "I wonder what this wall is holding up?"

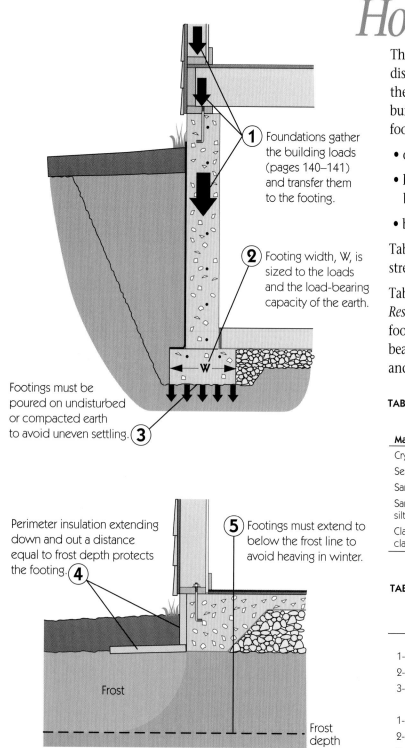

① Foundations gather the building loads (pages 140–141) and transfer them to the footing.

② Footing width, W, is sized to the loads and the load-bearing capacity of the earth.

Footings must be poured on undisturbed or compacted earth to avoid uneven settling. ③

Perimeter insulation extending down and out a distance equal to frost depth protects the footing. ④

⑤ Footings must extend to below the frost line to avoid heaving in winter.

Frost

Frost depth

How They Work

The sole function of the footing is to distribute building loads (weights) to the earth in a manner guaranteeing the building will never move. To do so, a footing must be:

• on undisturbed or compacted soil

• large enough to not exceed the load-bearing strength of the soil

• below the maximum depth of frost

Table 1 lists the assumed load-bearing strengths of different soil types.

Table 2, excerpted from the *International Residential Code*, shows minimum required footing width as a function of soil load-bearing strength, style of construction, and number of stories.

TABLE 1. LOAD-BEARING STRENGTHS OF SOIL TYPES

Material	Load-bearing Strength, pounds per square foot
Crystalline bedrock	12,000
Sedimentary bedrock	4,000
Sandy gravel and gravel	3,000
Sand, silty sand, clayey sand, silty gravel, clayey gravel	2,000
Clay, sandy clay, silty clay, clayey silt	1,500

TABLE 2. WIDTH OF CONCRETE FOOTINGS, INCHES

	Load-bearing Strength of Soil, psf			
	1,500	2,000	3,000	4,000
Light frame construction				
1-story	12	12	12	12
2-story	15	12	12	12
3-story	23	17	12	12
Brick veneer over wood or 8-inch hollow block				
1-story	12	12	12	12
2-story	21	16	12	12
3-story	32	24	16	12

Drainage

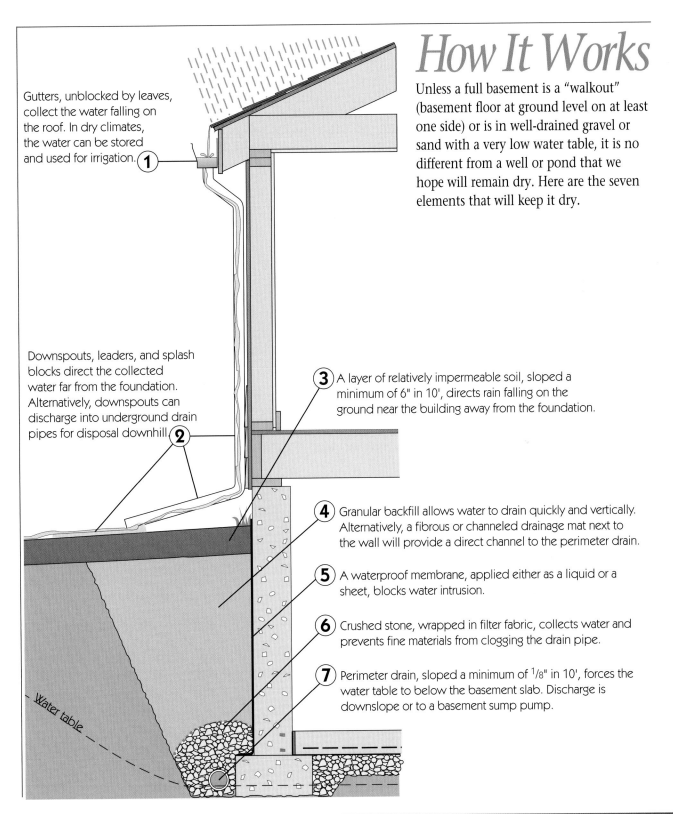

How It Works

Unless a full basement is a "walkout" (basement floor at ground level on at least one side) or is in well-drained gravel or sand with a very low water table, it is no different from a well or pond that we hope will remain dry. Here are the seven elements that will keep it dry.

Gutters, unblocked by leaves, collect the water falling on the roof. In dry climates, the water can be stored and used for irrigation. **1**

Downspouts, leaders, and splash blocks direct the collected water far from the foundation. Alternatively, downspouts can discharge into underground drain pipes for disposal downhill. **2**

3 A layer of relatively impermeable soil, sloped a minimum of 6" in 10', directs rain falling on the ground near the building away from the foundation.

4 Granular backfill allows water to drain quickly and vertically. Alternatively, a fibrous or channeled drainage mat next to the wall will provide a direct channel to the perimeter drain.

5 A waterproof membrane, applied either as a liquid or a sheet, blocks water intrusion.

6 Crushed stone, wrapped in filter fabric, collects water and prevents fine materials from clogging the drain pipe.

7 Perimeter drain, sloped a minimum of $1/8$" in 10', forces the water table to below the basement slab. Discharge is downslope or to a basement sump pump.

Water table

8 Radon Abatement

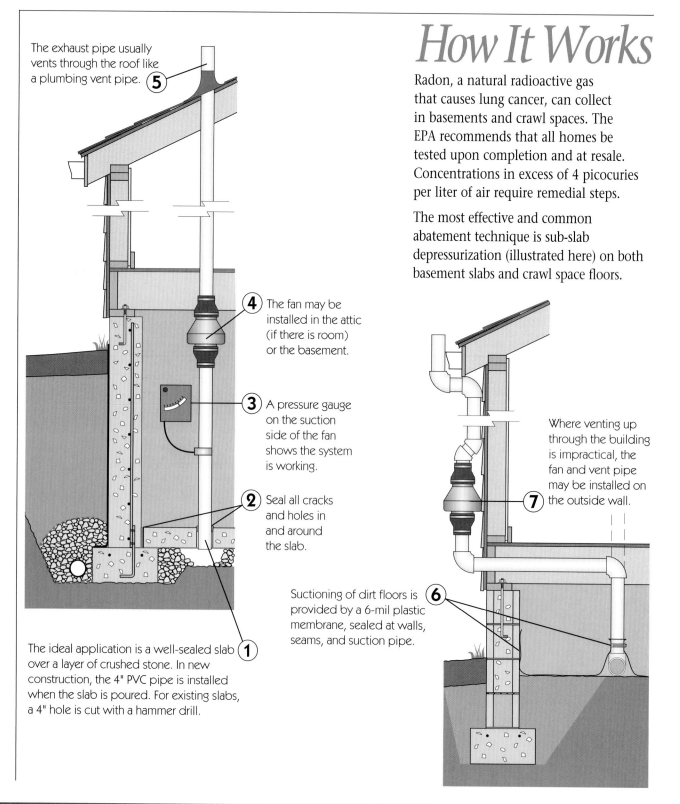

The exhaust pipe usually vents through the roof like a plumbing vent pipe. **(5)**

(4) The fan may be installed in the attic (if there is room) or the basement.

(3) A pressure gauge on the suction side of the fan shows the system is working.

(2) Seal all cracks and holes in and around the slab.

The ideal application is a well-sealed slab **(1)** over a layer of crushed stone. In new construction, the 4" PVC pipe is installed when the slab is poured. For existing slabs, a 4" hole is cut with a hammer drill.

Suctioning of dirt floors is provided by a 6-mil plastic membrane, sealed at walls, seams, and suction pipe. **(6)**

How It Works

Radon, a natural radioactive gas that causes lung cancer, can collect in basements and crawl spaces. The EPA recommends that all homes be tested upon completion and at resale. Concentrations in excess of 4 picocuries per liter of air require remedial steps.

The most effective and common abatement technique is sub-slab depressurization (illustrated here) on both basement slabs and crawl space floors.

Where venting up through the building is impractical, the fan and vent pipe may be installed on **(7)** the outside wall.

Pier Foundation

How It Works

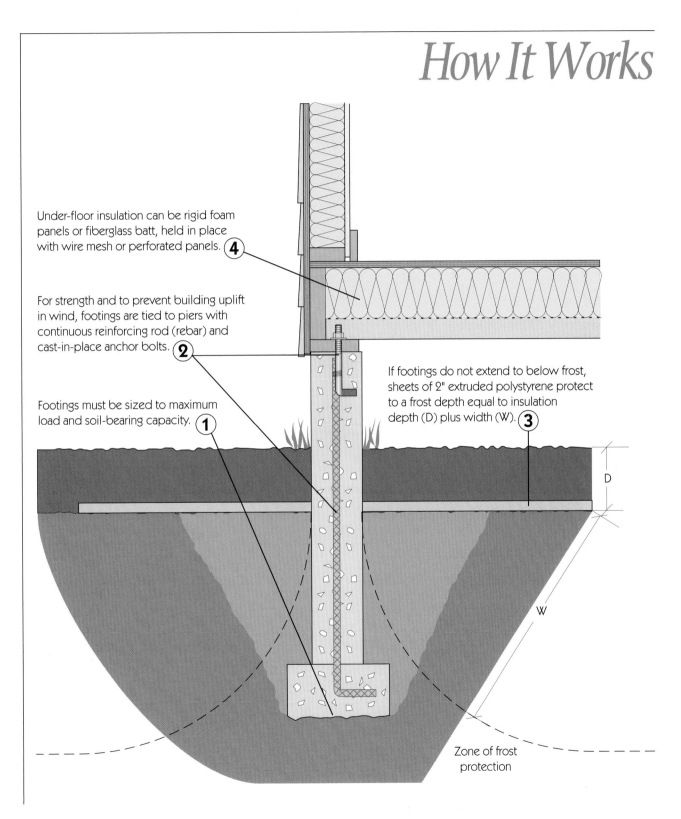

Under-floor insulation can be rigid foam panels or fiberglass batt, held in place with wire mesh or perforated panels. **4**

For strength and to prevent building uplift in wind, footings are tied to piers with continuous reinforcing rod (rebar) and cast-in-place anchor bolts. **2**

Footings must be sized to maximum load and soil-bearing capacity. **1**

If footings do not extend to below frost, sheets of 2" extruded polystyrene protect to a frost depth equal to insulation depth (D) plus width (W). **3**

D

W

Zone of frost protection

How It Works

Heated Building

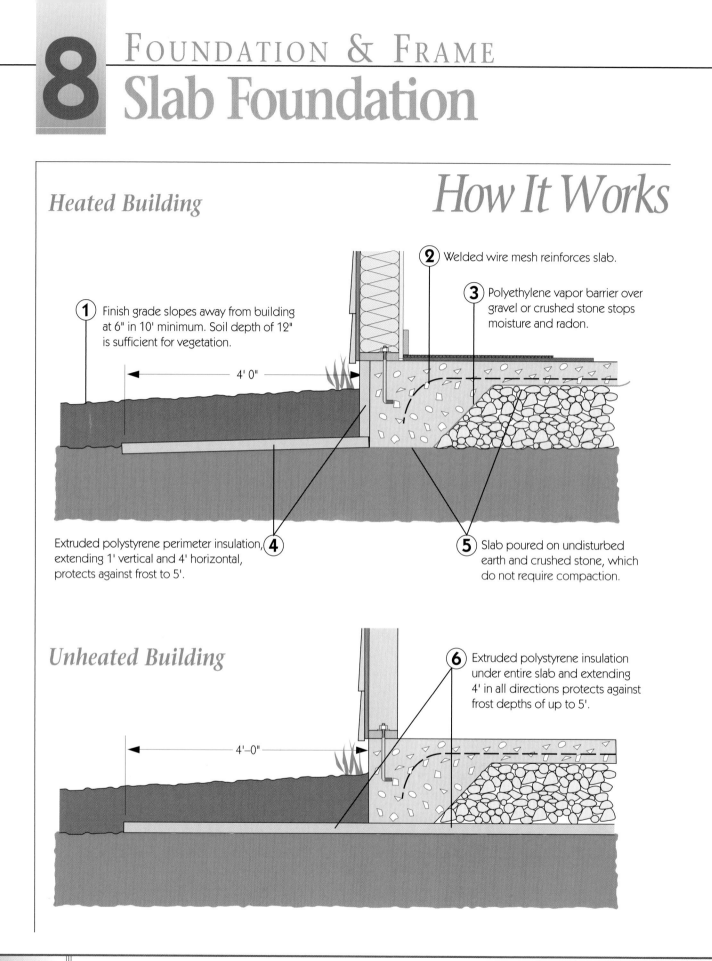

1 Finish grade slopes away from building at 6" in 10' minimum. Soil depth of 12" is sufficient for vegetation.

2 Welded wire mesh reinforces slab.

3 Polyethylene vapor barrier over gravel or crushed stone stops moisture and radon.

4' 0"

Extruded polystyrene perimeter insulation, extending 1' vertical and 4' horizontal, protects against frost to 5'. **4**

5 Slab poured on undisturbed earth and crushed stone, which do not require compaction.

Unheated Building

6 Extruded polystyrene insulation under entire slab and extending 4' in all directions protects against frost depths of up to 5'.

4'–0"

Full Foundation

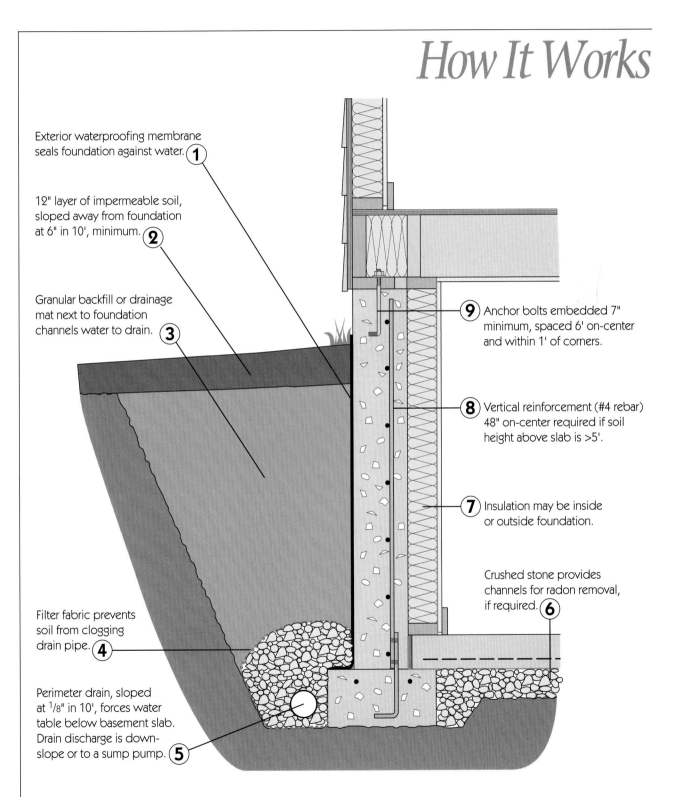

Exterior waterproofing membrane seals foundation against water. **(1)**

12" layer of impermeable soil, sloped away from foundation at 6" in 10', minimum. **(2)**

Granular backfill or drainage mat next to foundation channels water to drain. **(3)**

Filter fabric prevents soil from clogging drain pipe. **(4)**

Perimeter drain, sloped at $1/8$" in 10', forces water table below basement slab. Drain discharge is down-slope or to a sump pump. **(5)**

(9) Anchor bolts embedded 7" minimum, spaced 6' on-center and within 1' of corners.

(8) Vertical reinforcement (#4 rebar) 48" on-center required if soil height above slab is >5'.

(7) Insulation may be inside or outside foundation.

Crushed stone provides channels for radon removal, if required. **(6)**

How It Works

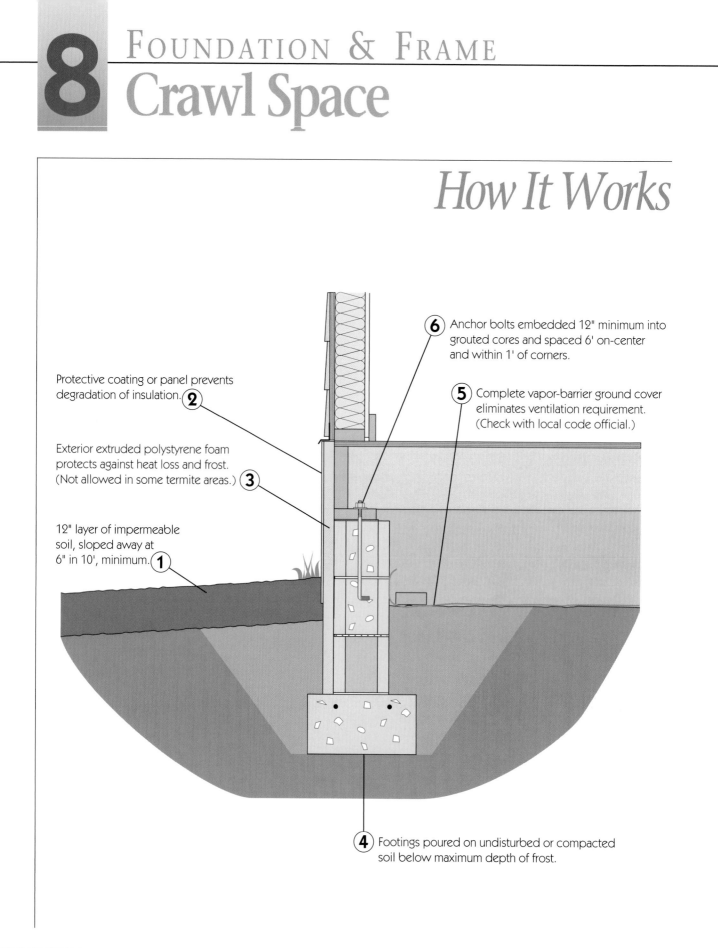

Protective coating or panel prevents degradation of insulation. **(2)**

Exterior extruded polystyrene foam protects against heat loss and frost. (Not allowed in some termite areas.) **(3)**

12" layer of impermeable soil, sloped away at 6" in 10', minimum. **(1)**

(6) Anchor bolts embedded 12" minimum into grouted cores and spaced 6' on-center and within 1' of corners.

(5) Complete vapor-barrier ground cover eliminates ventilation requirement. (Check with local code official.)

(4) Footings poured on undisturbed or compacted soil below maximum depth of frost.

Grade Beam

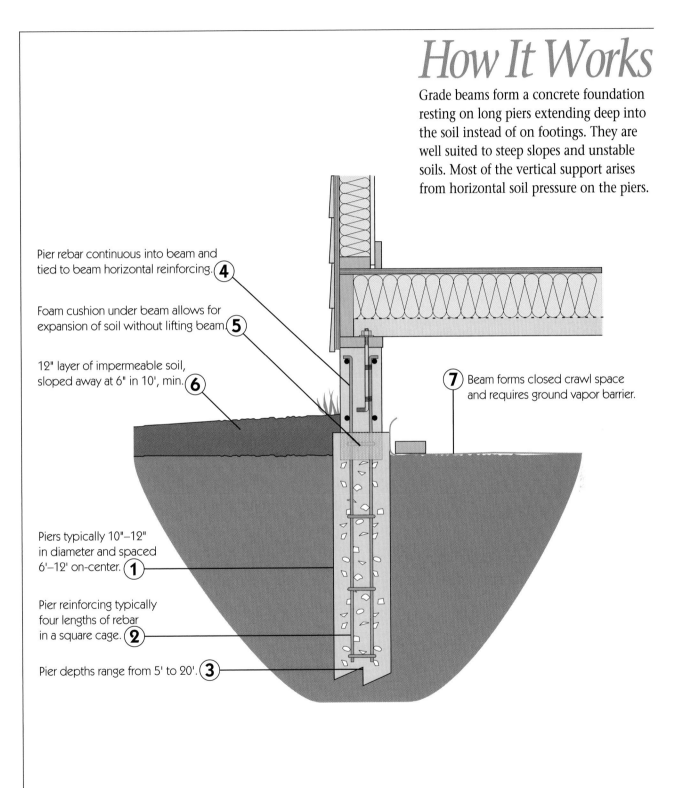

How It Works

Grade beams form a concrete foundation resting on long piers extending deep into the soil instead of on footings. They are well suited to steep slopes and unstable soils. Most of the vertical support arises from horizontal soil pressure on the piers.

Pier rebar continuous into beam and tied to beam horizontal reinforcing. **(4)**

Foam cushion under beam allows for expansion of soil without lifting beam. **(5)**

12" layer of impermeable soil, sloped away at 6" in 10', min. **(6)**

(7) Beam forms closed crawl space and requires ground vapor barrier.

Piers typically 10"–12" in diameter and spaced 6'–12' on-center. **(1)**

Pier reinforcing typically four lengths of rebar in a square cage. **(2)**

Pier depths range from 5' to 20'. **(3)**

What They Are

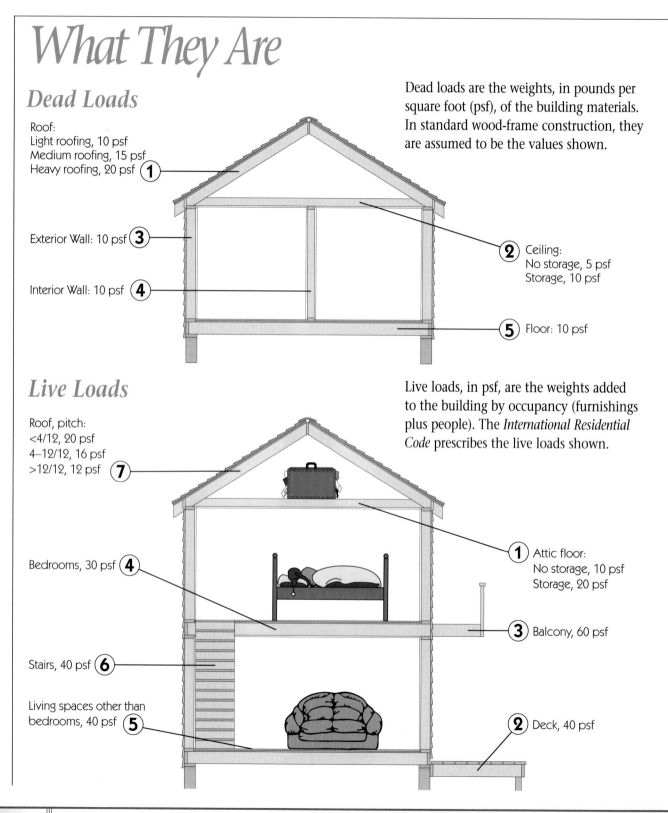

Dead Loads

Roof:
Light roofing, 10 psf
Medium roofing, 15 psf
Heavy roofing, 20 psf **1**

Exterior Wall: 10 psf **3**

Interior Wall: 10 psf **4**

Dead loads are the weights, in pounds per square foot (psf), of the building materials. In standard wood-frame construction, they are assumed to be the values shown.

2 Ceiling:
No storage, 5 psf
Storage, 10 psf

5 Floor: 10 psf

Live Loads

Roof, pitch:
<4/12, 20 psf
4–12/12, 16 psf
>12/12, 12 psf **7**

Bedrooms, 30 psf **4**

Stairs, 40 psf **6**

Living spaces other than bedrooms, 40 psf **5**

Live loads, in psf, are the weights added to the building by occupancy (furnishings plus people). The *International Residential Code* prescribes the live loads shown.

1 Attic floor:
No storage, 10 psf
Storage, 20 psf

3 Balcony, 60 psf

2 Deck, 40 psf

Snow Load

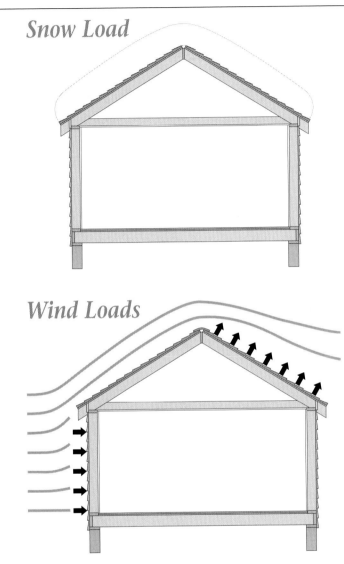

Snow load is the maximum weight of snow, in psf, expected on a horizontal surface once in 50 years.

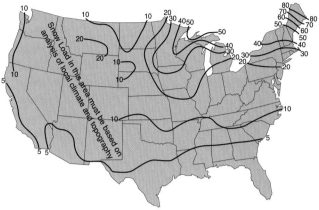

Wind Loads

Wind loads are defined based on the pressure against an upwind wall and uplift on a downwind roof due to the maximum sustained wind expected once in 50 years.

The pressures shown in the table below left depend on a basic wind speed (see map below), height of the building, and exposure class:

- Class C—open terrain with scattered obstructions of height <30'.

- Class D—flat, unobstructed areas exposed to wind over large bodies of water up to 1,500' inland.

Wind Pressures on Walls & Roofs, psf

Exposure Class	Basic Wind Speed, mph	One Story		Two Story	
		Walls	Roof Uplift	Walls	Roof Uplift
C	80	—	20	—	22
	90	—	26	—	28
	100	—	32	32	35
	110	35	38	38	42
D	70	—	20	—	22
	80	—	27	—	28
	90	32	37	36	40
	100	42	46	44	49
	110	50	55	54	59

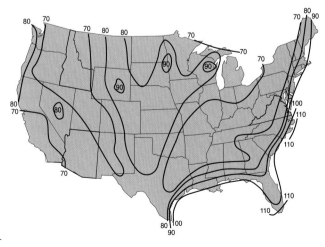

8 Beams in Bending

How They Work

Deflection

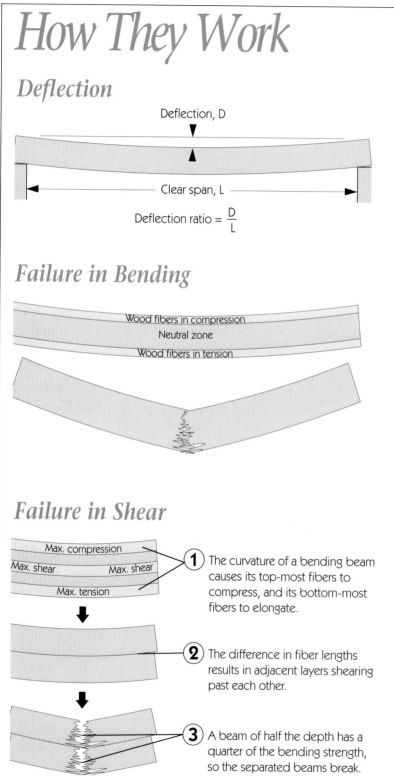

When a load is placed on a beam, the beam bends or deflects. The amount of deflection under full load, D, is not as important as the deflection ratio, D/L, where L is the unsupported span.

The *International Residential Code* specifies maximum deflection ratios of 1/360 for floor joists, 1/240 for ceiling joists, and 1/180 for rafters without attached ceilings.

Failure in Bending

In a bending beam, the bottom-most fibers are in tension, while the top fibers are in compression.

The most common failure in a long beam is due to the bottom fibers pulling apart and the beam breaking, as shown. This explains why many joist and rafter tables show maximum allowed span as a function of extreme fiber stress in bending, f_b.

Failure in Shear

① The curvature of a bending beam causes its top-most fibers to compress, and its bottom-most fibers to elongate.

② The difference in fiber lengths results in adjacent layers shearing past each other.

③ A beam of half the depth has a quarter of the bending strength, so the separated beams break.

Individual wood fibers are long and extremely strong. This gives a beam great strength in both tension and compression in the direction of the fibers (lengthwise). The "glue" (lignin) that holds the fibers together is not very strong, however.

As a beam bends, the top layers compress, while the bottom layers stretch. The combined forces thus conspire to shear the beam into several thinner beams. Because the set of thinner beams is not as strong in bending as the original beam, the end result is most often failure in bending.

The I-Joist

Wood fibers in compression
Shear zone
Wood fibers in tension

Top chord (2x4)
Web (structural panel)
Bottom chord (2x4)

I-joists are wood versions of steel I-beams. Capitalizing on wood's strength in tension and compression and a structural panel's strength in shear (see below), the I-joist achieves greater strength than a solid beam of the same weight by gluing a structural panel between two 2x4s.

Laminated Beams

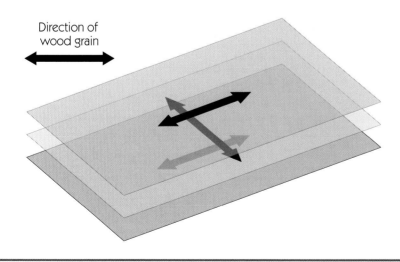

Since most of the tension in a beam is concentrated in its bottom-most layers, sawing a solid beam into thin strips, rearranging the strips with the strongest on the top and bottom, then gluing the whole pile together results in a much stronger beam. Glue-laminated beams are known collectively as "engineered beams."

Structural Panels

Direction of wood grain

Structural panels, including plywood and oriented strand board (OSB), represent the ultimate in re-engineering natural wood.

Plywood consists of thin veneers, with the highest quality (strength, appearance, or both) veneers on the top and bottom faces. The direction of the wood fibers in the veneers alternate, giving the panels nearly uniform strength in all directions, though it is greatest in the direction of the face veneers.

With high shear strength, structural panels are used for wall bracing, as well as floor, wall, and roof sheathing.

How They Work

Joists

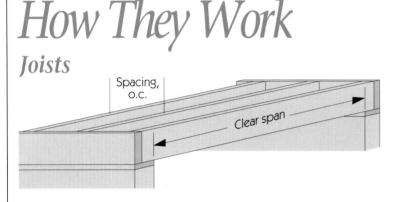

Spacing, o.c.

Clear span

Floor Joists: 40 PSF Live, 10 PSF Dead

Maximum Allowable Span (feet-inches)

Species Group	Spacing in.,oc	2 x 6			2 x 8			2 x 10		
		Sel Str	No.1	No.2	Sel Str	No.1	No.2	Sel Str	No.1	No.2
Douglas fir-larch	12	11-4	10-11	10-9	15-0	14-5	14-2	19-1	18-5	18-0
	16	10-4	9-11	9-9	13-7	13-1	12-9	17-4	16-5	15-7
	24	9-0	8-8	8-3	11-11	11-0	10-5	15-2	13-5	12-9
Hem-fir	12	10-9	10-6	10-0	14-2	13-10	13-2	18-0	17-8	16-10
	16	9-9	9-6	9-1	12-10	12-7	12-0	16-5	16-0	15-2
	24	8-6	8-4	7-11	11-3	10-10	10-2	14-4	13-3	12-5

Notes: Sel Str = lumber grade Select Structural, oc = on-center

As discussed on page 142, floor and ceiling joists must pass three tests:

- bending under dead plus live loads
- shear under dead plus live loads
- deflection under live load

Building codes, such as the *International Residential Code,* reference span tables like the table at left for floor joists for living areas other than sleeping rooms and attics. The table shows the maximum allowed clear span for repetitive joists spaced 12", 16", and 24" on-center (oc), as functions of wood species and grade.

Similar span tables are published by manufacturers of I-Joists.

Beams

Total uniformly distributed load

Solid wood beam

Span, feet

Maximum Uniform Load for Wood Beams, lbs

Nom. Size b x d, in.	Allowable Fiber Stress in Bending, psi								
	900	1000	1100	1200	1300	1400	1500	1600	1800
4 x 6	882	980	1078	1176	1274	1372	1470	1568	1764
4 x 8	1533	1703	1873	2044	2214	2384	2555	2725	3066
4 x 10	2495	2772	3050	3327	3604	3882	4159	4436	4991
4 x 12	3691	4101	4511	4921	5332	5742	6152	6562	7382
6 x 6	1386	1540	1694	1848	2002	2156	2310	2464	2772
6 x 8	2578	2864	3151	3437	3723	4010	4296	4583	5156
6 x 10	4136	4596	5055	5515	5974	6434	6894	7353	8272
6 x 12	6061	6734	7408	8081	8755	9428	10102	10775	12122

Notes: b = breadth (width), d = depth

Beams must pass the same three tests as floor joists, except that beams are used to support other framing members, such as joists, rafters, and studs. Examples are the main girder in a basement that divides the floor span in two, and a header beam over a wide window, which supports the floor joists and wall studs above.

Since beams usually support more than three other members, the load is considered uniformly distributed.

The table at left shows the maximum loads allowed on single beams of clear span 12'.

Similar span tables are published by manufacturers of engineered beams.

Rafters

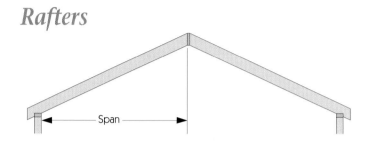

Rafters: No Attic, 40 PSF Live, 10 PSF Dead

Maximum Allowable Span (feet-inches)

Species Group	Spacing in.,oc	2 x 6 Sel Str	No.1	No.2	2 x 8 Sel Str	No.1	No.2	2 x 10 Sel Str	No.1	No.2
Douglas fir-larch	12	13-0	12-6	12-3	17-2	16-6	15-10	21-10	20-4	19-4
	16	11-10	11-5	10-10	15-7	14-5	13-8	19-10	17-8	16-9
	24	10-4	9-4	8-10	13-7	11-9	11-2	17-4	14-5	13-8
Hem-fir	12	12-3	12-0	11-5	16-2	15-10	15-1	20-8	19-10	18-9
	16	11-2	10-11	10-5	14-8	14-1	13-4	18-9	17-2	16-3
	24	9-9	9-1	8-7	12-10	11-6	1-010	16-5	14-0	13-3

Rafters are similar to joists, except the live loads they carry are more likely to be accumulations of snow, rather than furnishings and people.

As with floor joists, the building codes reference span tables for roof rafters. The example partial table at left lists the maximum allowed clear span for repetitive rafters spaced 12", 16", and 24" on-center, based on wood species and grade.

It is important to note that snow loads in mountainous areas are subject to extreme variation. Regardless of where you live, consult your building code official or local structural engineer for your snow load.

Trusses

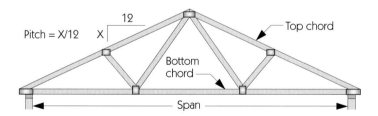

Pitch = X/12

Top chord

Bottom chord

Span

Fink Truss: 24" Spacing, 30 PSF Live, 7 PSF Dead

Species Group	Grade	3/12 Slope Top Chord 2x4	2x6	Bottom Chord 2x4	2x6	5/12 Slope Top Chord 2x4	2x6	Bottom Chord 2x4	2x6
Douglas fir-larch	Sel. Str.	28-2	41-10	33-2	41-10	32-8	43-2	33-2	43-2
	#1	25-8	38-1	27-5	39-1	29-8	43-2	28-3	40-3
	#2	24-6	36-4	24-10	35-1	28-5	41-10	25-7	38-8
Hem-fir	Sel. Str.	26-11	39-9	30-9	39-9	30-0	39-9	30-9	39-9
	#1	24-9	36-7	25-10	36-5	28-9	39-9	26-10	37-11
	#2	23-8	34-10	23-0	32-5	27-5	39-9	24-5	35-2

A triangle is the only construction that, by its geometry, is perfectly rigid. If a great weight were placed on the peak of the truss at left, the only forces in the truss would be compression in the top chords (rafters) and tension in the bottom chord (ceiling joist). Since lumber has high strength in both compression and tension, the truss could span great distances using only 2x4s for its chords.

Roof loads are not concentrated at the peak, but are spread across the rafters. By breaking the truss into a number of smaller triangles, however, the spans of the rafter segments are reduced.

Compare the allowable spans in the table at left to those in the rafter table above.

8 Post & Beam Frame

How It Works

Before the advent of modern sawmills and steel mills, hand-hewn beams and wood pegs were less expensive than hand-sawn lumber and forged nails. Building frames were hand-crafted from large timbers, hewn from whole trees.

The careful craftsmanship and avoidance of rust-prone fasteners gave these frames great strength and resilience.

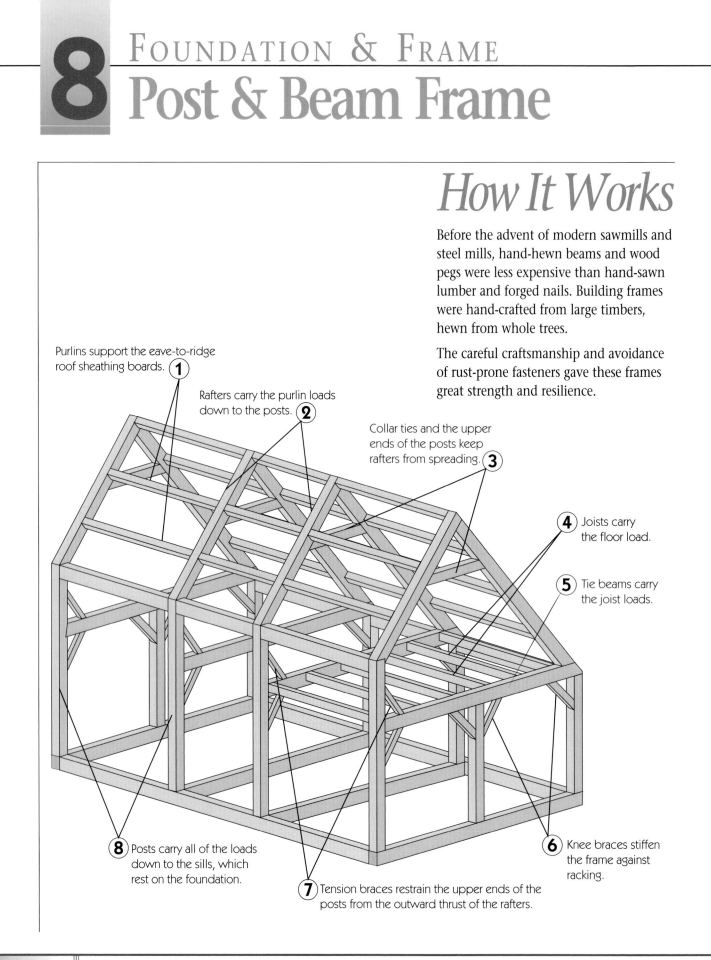

Purlins support the eave-to-ridge roof sheathing boards. **(1)**

Rafters carry the purlin loads down to the posts. **(2)**

Collar ties and the upper ends of the posts keep rafters from spreading. **(3)**

(4) Joists carry the floor load.

(5) Tie beams carry the joist loads.

(6) Knee braces stiffen the frame against racking.

(8) Posts carry all of the loads down to the sills, which rest on the foundation.

(7) Tension braces restrain the upper ends of the posts from the outward thrust of the rafters.

Plank & Beam Frame

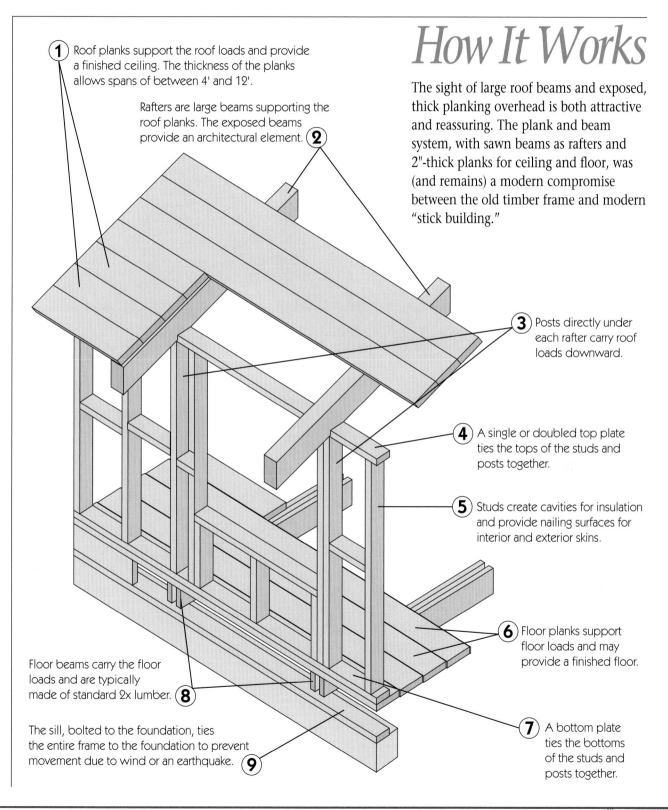

① Roof planks support the roof loads and provide a finished ceiling. The thickness of the planks allows spans of between 4' and 12'.

Rafters are large beams supporting the roof planks. The exposed beams provide an architectural element. ②

How It Works

The sight of large roof beams and exposed, thick planking overhead is both attractive and reassuring. The plank and beam system, with sawn beams as rafters and 2"-thick planks for ceiling and floor, was (and remains) a modern compromise between the old timber frame and modern "stick building."

③ Posts directly under each rafter carry roof loads downward.

④ A single or doubled top plate ties the tops of the studs and posts together.

⑤ Studs create cavities for insulation and provide nailing surfaces for interior and exterior skins.

⑥ Floor planks support floor loads and may provide a finished floor.

Floor beams carry the floor loads and are typically made of standard 2x lumber. ⑧

The sill, bolted to the foundation, ties the entire frame to the foundation to prevent movement due to wind or an earthquake. ⑨

⑦ A bottom plate ties the bottoms of the studs and posts together.

Balloon Frame

How It Works

Thinking the thin 2x4 wall framing so light it might blow away in the wind, the carpenters of the first building of its type coined the name, "balloon frame," in 1833.

While capitalizing on the new, less-expensive sawn lumber and wire nails, the tall, unblocked wall cavities spread fire rapidly. This led to its being banned in the early 1900s.

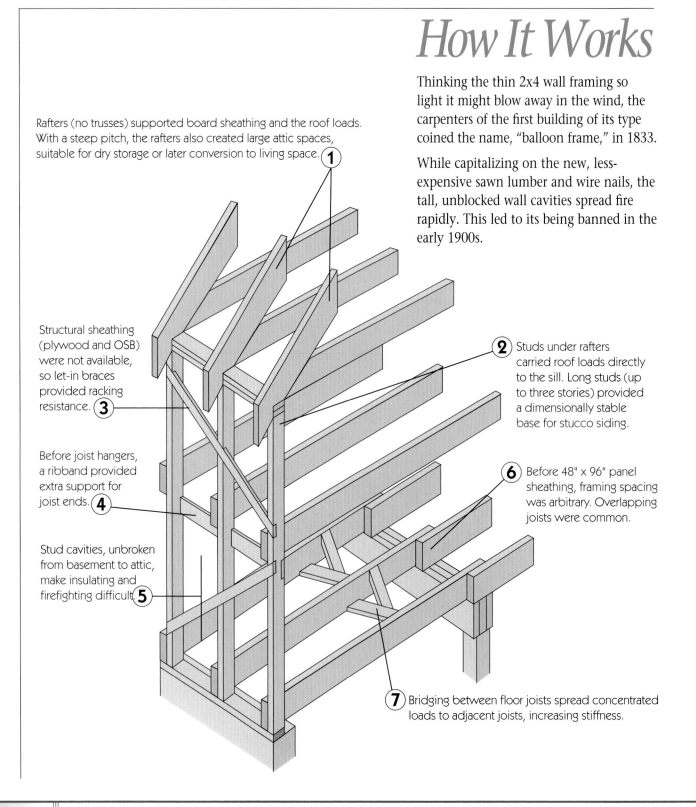

Rafters (no trusses) supported board sheathing and the roof loads. With a steep pitch, the rafters also created large attic spaces, suitable for dry storage or later conversion to living space. **1**

Structural sheathing (plywood and OSB) were not available, so let-in braces provided racking resistance. **3**

Before joist hangers, a ribband provided extra support for joist ends. **4**

Stud cavities, unbroken from basement to attic, make insulating and firefighting difficult. **5**

2 Studs under rafters carried roof loads directly to the sill. Long studs (up to three stories) provided a dimensionally stable base for stucco siding.

6 Before 48" x 96" panel sheathing, framing spacing was arbitrary. Overlapping joists were common.

7 Bridging between floor joists spread concentrated loads to adjacent joists, increasing stiffness.

Platform Frame

In pursuit of lower labor costs, builders sought ways to simplify and standardize all aspects of building. The platform-framed building, developed in the late 1940s, with 4' x 8' plywood floor, wall, and roof sheathing and 12"-, 16"-, and 24"-on-center framing, was the solution.

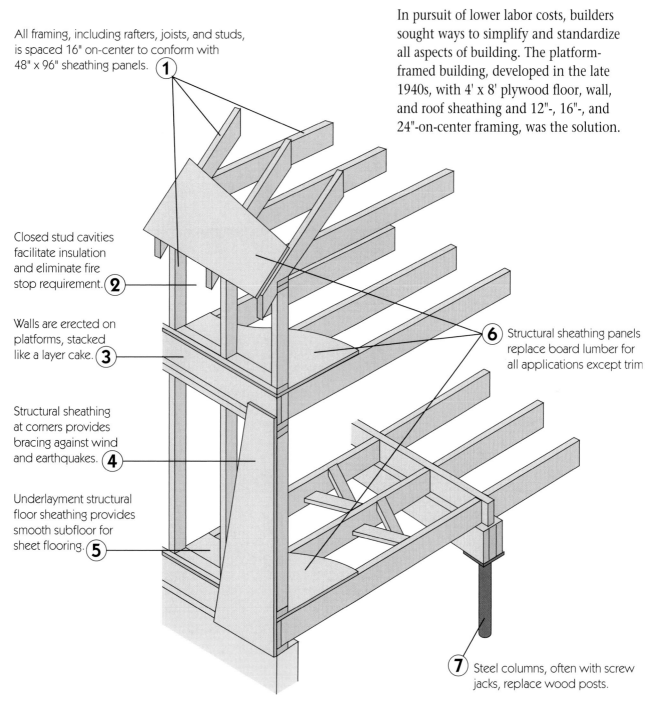

All framing, including rafters, joists, and studs, is spaced 16" on-center to conform with 48" x 96" sheathing panels. **(1)**

Closed stud cavities facilitate insulation and eliminate fire stop requirement. **(2)**

Walls are erected on platforms, stacked like a layer cake. **(3)**

Structural sheathing at corners provides bracing against wind and earthquakes. **(4)**

Underlayment structural floor sheathing provides smooth subfloor for sheet flooring. **(5)**

(6) Structural sheathing panels replace board lumber for all applications except trim

(7) Steel columns, often with screw jacks, replace wood posts.

How It Works

In 1977, the U.S. Department of Housing and Urban Development commissioned the National Association of Home Builders to analyze framing practices in an effort to lower housing costs. The study resulted in an approach to building they termed "Optimum Value Engineering" (OVE).

The approach might be described as, "Why use two sticks when one will do, and why use 2x lumber when 1x will do?"

Framing savings compared to platform framing are estimated to be 25%.

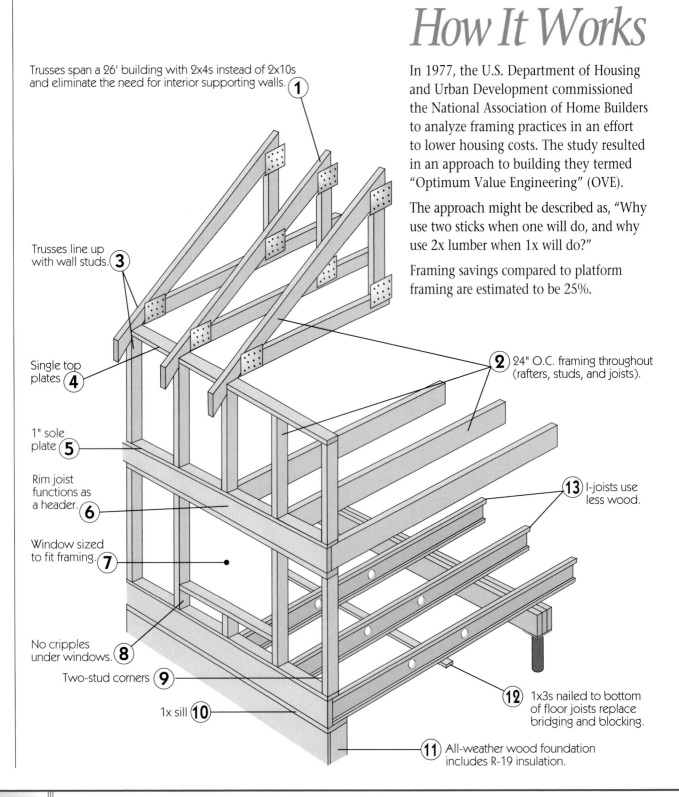

Trusses span a 26' building with 2x4s instead of 2x10s and eliminate the need for interior supporting walls. (1)

Trusses line up with wall studs. (3)

Single top plates (4)

1" sole plate (5)

Rim joist functions as a header. (6)

Window sized to fit framing. (7)

No cripples under windows. (8)

Two-stud corners (9)

1x sill (10)

(2) 24" O.C. framing throughout (rafters, studs, and joists).

(13) I-joists use less wood.

(12) 1x3s nailed to bottom of floor joists replace bridging and blocking.

(11) All-weather wood foundation includes R-19 insulation.

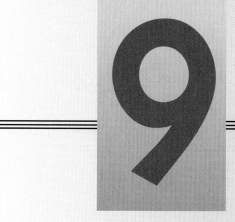

9 OUTDOORS

Our kitchens have been revolutionized, from great-grandmother's woodstove, pitcher pump, and icebox to gas and electric appliances for every aspect of food preparation. Likewise, the tools for maintaining our yards have gone from shovel, rake, and axe to self-propelled lawnmower, string trimmer, and chainsaw.

How It Works

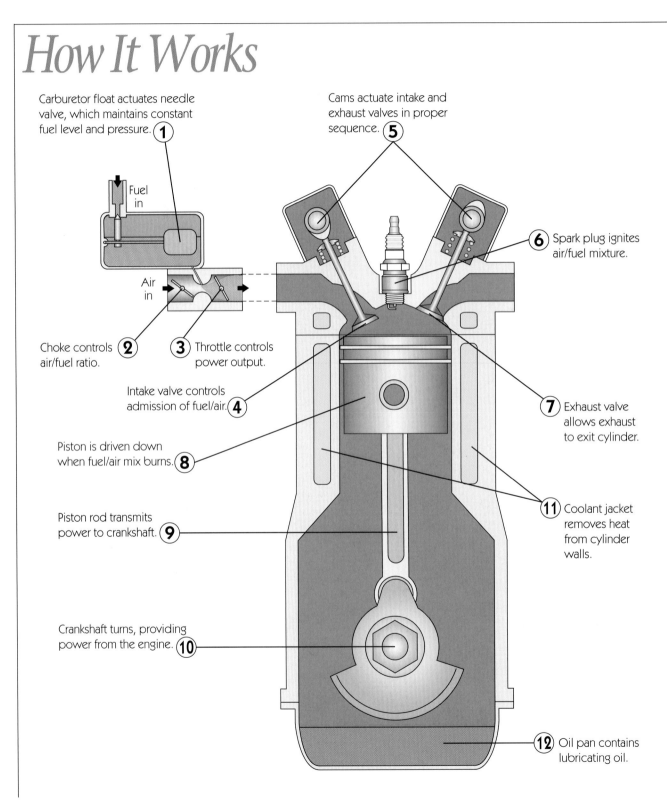

Carburetor float actuates needle valve, which maintains constant fuel level and pressure. **(1)**

Fuel in

Air in

Choke controls air/fuel ratio. **(2)**

(3) Throttle controls power output.

Intake valve controls admission of fuel/air. **(4)**

Piston is driven down when fuel/air mix burns. **(8)**

Piston rod transmits power to crankshaft. **(9)**

Crankshaft turns, providing power from the engine. **(10)**

Cams actuate intake and exhaust valves in proper sequence. **(5)**

(6) Spark plug ignites air/fuel mixture.

(7) Exhaust valve allows exhaust to exit cylinder.

(11) Coolant jacket removes heat from cylinder walls.

(12) Oil pan contains lubricating oil.

See It Run

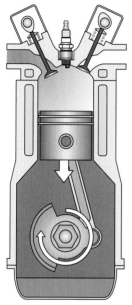

1. INTAKE STROKE
Fuel/air mixture is drawn through open intake valve.

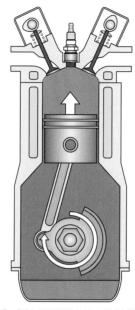

2. COMPRESSION STROKE
Fuel/air mixture is compressed almost 10:1 prior to ignition.

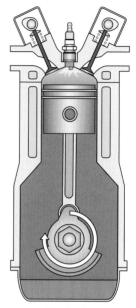

IGNITION
Spark plug arcs, igniting the explosive fuel/air mixture.

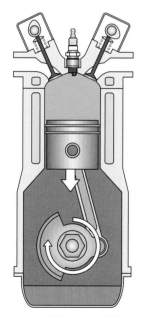

3. POWER STROKE
Burning fuel/air mixture expands. driving the piston down.

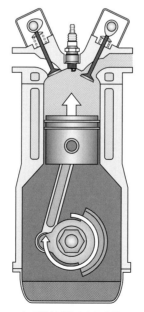

4. EXHAUST STROKE
Piston rises, driving exhaust gases out through open exhaust valve.

Before Calling a Mechanic

If the engine won't start:

- Is the fuel tank empty? Fill with fresh fuel (*not the oil reservoir!*).

- Is the fuel more than two months old? Gasoline with 10% ethanol goes bad quickly. Empty the old fuel into your car (it will run fine) and replace with new.

- Do you smell gasoline? If so, the engine is flooded. Remove the spark plug, dry with a paper towel, pull the starter cord a few time, and replace the plug.

- Are the plug tips worn? Replace with the same or equivalent plug.

2-Cycle Gasoline Engine

How It Works

Compared to four-stroke engines, 2-cycle engines are less complicated (no valves, cams, or timing belts), lighter (nearly twice the horsepower per weight), and will operate in nearly any orientation. These characteristics make them popular for chainsaws (pages 158-159), lawnmowers (pages 160-161), and string trimmers (page 162).

Instead of a separate reservoir of lubricating oil, special 2-cycle oil is mixed with the fuel. The engine is lubricated by the mist of fuel/oil/air in the crankcase and cylinder.

On the down side, less lubrication leads to a shorter life, some of the fuel air mixture is blown out with the exhaust, and the oil in the fuel produces a blue smoke. Because of the pollution, the EPA is slowly banning 2-cycle engines where 4-cycle engines are practical.

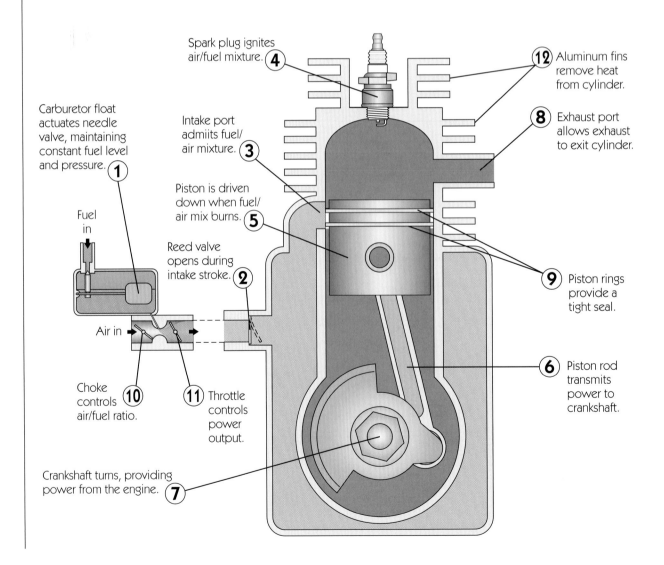

Spark plug ignites air/fuel mixture. **4**

12 Aluminum fins remove heat from cylinder.

Carburetor float actuates needle valve, maintaining constant fuel level and pressure. **1**

Intake port admiits fuel/air mixture. **3**

8 Exhaust port allows exhaust to exit cylinder.

Fuel in

Piston is driven down when fuel/air mix burns. **5**

Reed valve opens during intake stroke. **2**

9 Piston rings provide a tight seal.

Air in

Choke controls air/fuel ratio. **10**

11 Throttle controls power output.

6 Piston rod transmits power to crankshaft.

Crankshaft turns, providing power from the engine. **7**

See It Run

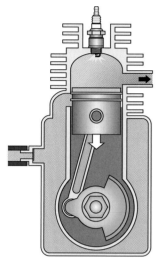

IGNITION
A compressed mixture of fuel and air burns rapidly , almost explosively, when the spark plug fires at the top of the piston stroke. As the exhaust port is uncovered, most of the exhaust exits.

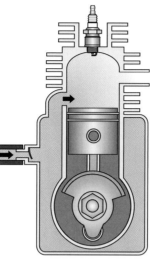

1. INTAKE STROKE
The piston continues downward and uncoveres the inlet port. The vacuum draws fresh fuel/air mixture into the cylinder past the reed valve. At the bottom of the stroke the reed valve closes again.

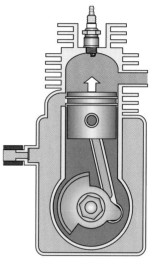

2. COMPRESSION STROKE
As the piston travels upward it first blows some fuel/air out the exhaust port, but then compresses the remaining fuel/air mixture, to be ignited by the sparkplug at the top of the stroke.

The Carburetor in Action

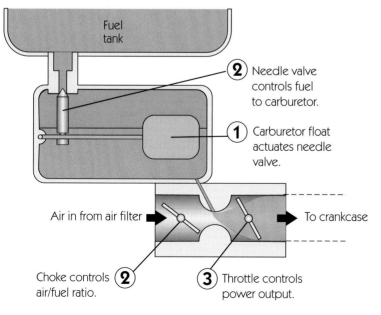

Fuel tank

② Needle valve controls fuel to carburetor.

① Carburetor float actuates needle valve.

Air in from air filter → To crankcase

Choke controls ② air/fuel ratio.

③ Throttle controls power output.

Before Calling a Mechanic

If the engine won't start:

- Is the fuel tank empty? Fill it with a 50:1 gas/2-cycle oil mix.

- Is the fuel more than two months old? Empty the old fuel into your car (it will run fine) and replace with new.

- Do you smell gasoline? If so, you may have flooded the engine. Remove the spark plug, dry with a paper towel, pull the starter cord a few times, and replace the plug.

- Are the plug tips worn? Replace with the same or equivalent plug.

Chain Saw

How It Works

Shown here is a typical chainsaw made by Stihl. Other vary in detail, but the principles remain the same.

Chainsaws utilize 2-cycle gasoline engines (pages 156-157), primarily for their high power-to-weight ratio and their ability to operate in any position.

A chain of precisely ground cutting and clearing teeth run in a lubricated guide bar. Both bar and chain come in a number of lengths.

When idling, the chain doesn't move. When the throttle is pressed, a centrifugal clutch engages the drive sprocket, driving the chain.

Chain saws "kick back" if the nose of the bar engages the wood. To protect the operator a shutoff guard, operating on the principle of inertia, stops the chain.

Chainsaw owner's manuals detail how to fell trees safely. Read yours before playing lumberjack.

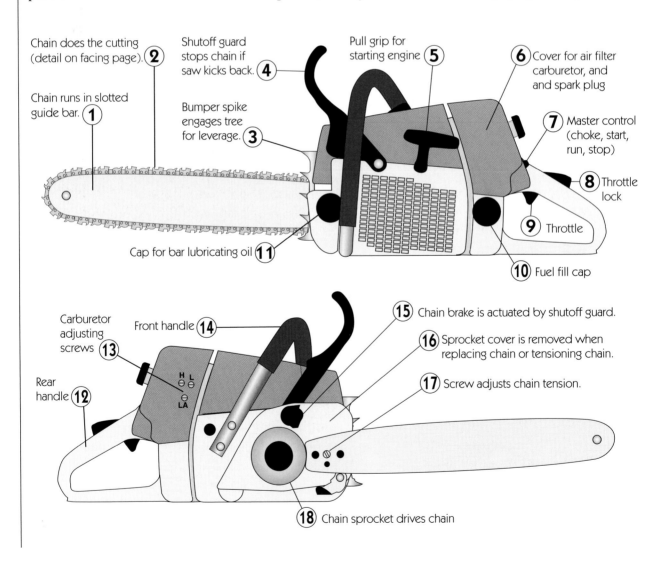

Chain does the cutting (detail on facing page). **2**

Chain runs in slotted guide bar. **1**

Shutoff guard stops chain if saw kicks back. **4**

Bumper spike engages tree for leverage. **3**

Pull grip for starting engine **5**

6 Cover for air filter carburetor, and and spark plug

7 Master control (choke, start, run, stop)

8 Throttle lock

9 Throttle

10 Fuel fill cap

Cap for bar lubricating oil **11**

15 Chain brake is actuated by shutoff guard.

16 Sprocket cover is removed when replacing chain or tensioning chain.

17 Screw adjusts chain tension.

Carburetor adjusting screws **13**

Front handle **14**

Rear handle **12**

18 Chain sprocket drives chain

Starting the Saw

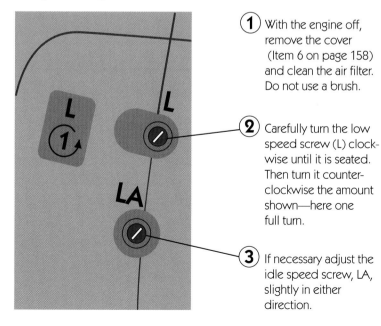

4 Turn off engine by moving lever up to Off position.

3 Release (pull back) shutoff guard, move lever to Run position, and rev engine.

2 Pull starting grip until engine kicks once. Then move lever to Warm Start position.

1 Pressing throttle lock and squeezing throttle at the same time, move master control lever to Cold Start position.

Adjusting the Carburetor

1 With the engine off, remove the cover (Item 6 on page 158) and clean the air filter. Do not use a brush.

2 Carefully turn the low speed screw (L) clockwise until it is seated. Then turn it counterclockwise the amount shown—here one full turn.

3 If necessary adjust the idle speed screw, LA, slightly in either direction.

Before Calling for Repair

If your fuel is more than three months old, dump it into your automobile's tank (it won't mind) and replace with a fresh 50:1 gasoline/2-cycle oil mix.

If the engine still won't start following the procedure at left, "Starting the Saw," remove the spark plug, dry the plug, pull the starting grip a few times with the control lever in the Off position to clear the cylinder of fuel, replace the plug, and repeat the starting procedure.

If it still won't start, adjust the carburetor to its nominal settings as shown at bottom, left, and try again.

If the engine starts, but then stops while idling, reset the low-speed screw, L (Step 2 at bottom, left). Turn the idle-speed screw, LA, clockwise until the chain starts running, then back it off one quarter turn.

If the chain runs while the engine is idling, reset the low-speed screw, L (Step 2 at bottom, left). Then turn the idle-speed screw, LA, counterclockwise until the chain stops running. Then turn the screw one quarter more turn in the same (CCW) direction.

If the saw accelerates poorly, reset the low-speed screw, L (Step 2 at bottom, left). Then turn the low-speed screw, L, counterclockwise until the saw runs and accelerates smoothly. Adjust the idle-speed screw, LA, if necessary.

9 Lawn Mower

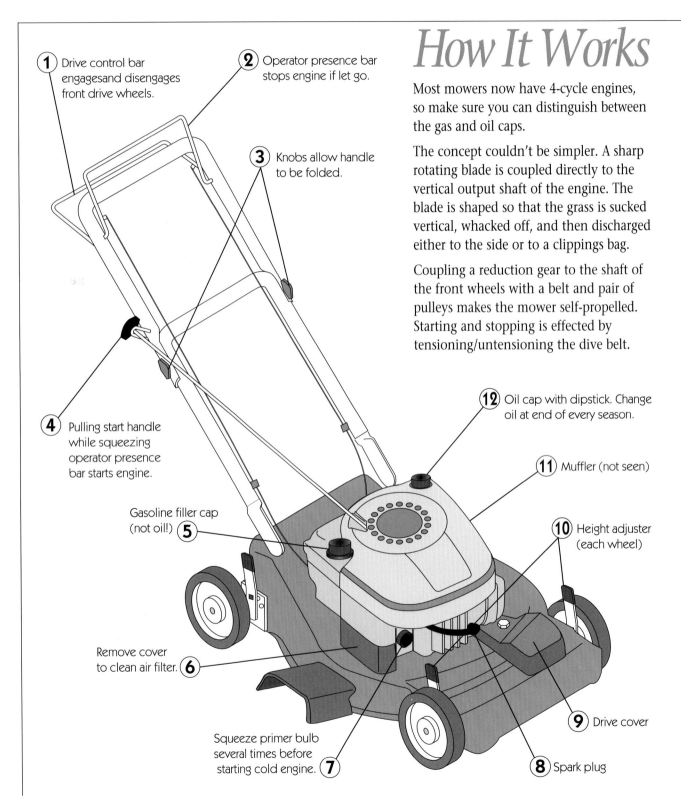

1 Drive control bar engages and disengages front drive wheels.

2 Operator presence bar stops engine if let go.

3 Knobs allow handle to be folded.

4 Pulling start handle while squeezing operator presence bar starts engine.

Gasoline filler cap (not oil!) **5**

Remove cover to clean air filter. **6**

Squeeze primer bulb several times before starting cold engine. **7**

8 Spark plug

9 Drive cover

10 Height adjuster (each wheel)

11 Muffler (not seen)

12 Oil cap with dipstick. Change oil at end of every season.

How It Works

Most mowers now have 4-cycle engines, so make sure you can distinguish between the gas and oil caps.

The concept couldn't be simpler. A sharp rotating blade is coupled directly to the vertical output shaft of the engine. The blade is shaped so that the grass is sucked vertical, whacked off, and then discharged either to the side or to a clippings bag.

Coupling a reduction gear to the shaft of the front wheels with a belt and pair of pulleys makes the mower self-propelled. Starting and stopping is effected by tensioning/untensioning the dive belt.

Replacing the Mower Blade

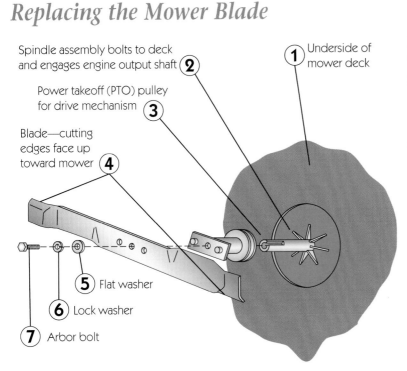

Spindle assembly bolts to deck and engages engine output shaft ②

Power takeoff (PTO) pulley for drive mechanism ③

Blade—cutting edges face up toward mower ④

① Underside of mower deck

⑤ Flat washer

⑥ Lock washer

⑦ Arbor bolt

If your mower begins to cut poorly, or if it vibrates due to a bent blade, it is time to replace the blade.

For safety and cleanliness, disconnect the sparkplug and drain both gasoline and oil.

Tip the mower on its side, and jam a piece of wood between the blade and the housing to keep the blade from turning.

Using a socket wrench, turn the arbor bolt counterclockwise and remove the blade.

Purchase a replacement blade with one having the same length and hole geometry.

Install the blade with the cutting edges up toward the underside of the mower. To tighten the arbor bolt, move the wood jam block to the other side.

The Drive Belt

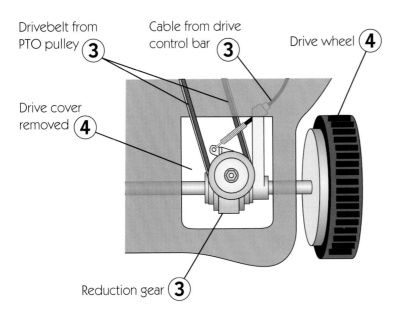

Drivebelt from PTO pulley ③

Cable from drive control bar ③

Drive wheel ④

Drive cover removed ④

Reduction gear ③

If your self-propelled mower refuses to go uphill, it is time to replace the drive belt.

Disconnect the sparkplug and drain both gasoline and oil. Remove the drive cover. Turn the mower on its side. If you don't see the drive belt, remove the access plate.

Remove the belt. If there is a tensioner pulley, loosen it first. Take the belt or the part number printed on the belt to the dealer or to a mower repair shop and purchase a replacement belt.

Slip the new belt over the pulleys, and tighten the tensioner, if there is one. There should be no more than $1/2$-inch "give" in the new belt.

Gas String Trimmer

Replacing the String

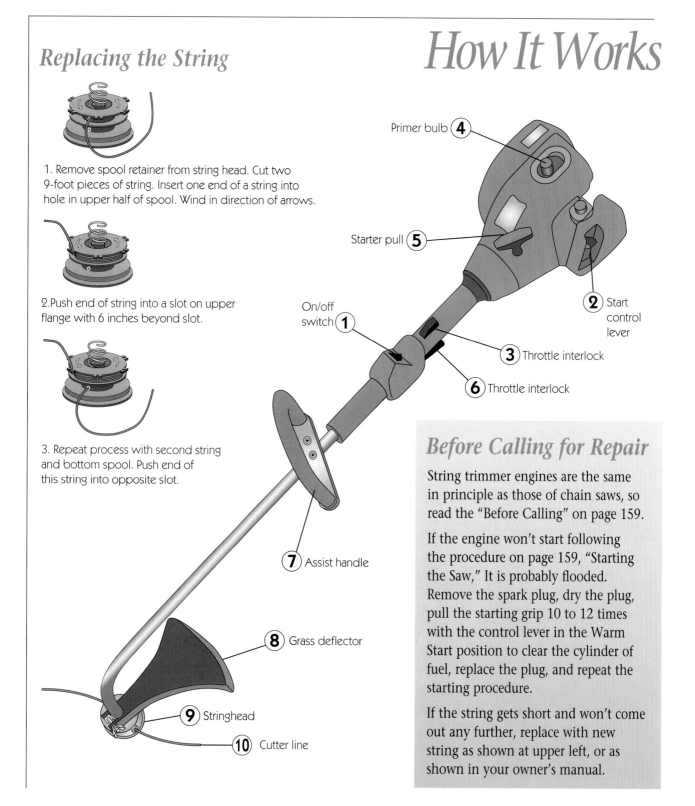

1. Remove spool retainer from string head. Cut two 9-foot pieces of string. Insert one end of a string into hole in upper half of spool. Wind in direction of arrows.

2. Push end of string into a slot on upper flange with 6 inches beyond slot.

3. Repeat process with second string and bottom spool. Push end of this string into opposite slot.

How It Works

Primer bulb **4**

Starter pull **5**

On/off switch **1**

2 Start control lever

3 Throttle interlock

6 Throttle interlock

7 Assist handle

8 Grass deflector

9 Stringhead

10 Cutter line

Before Calling for Repair

String trimmer engines are the same in principle as those of chain saws, so read the "Before Calling" on page 159.

If the engine won't start following the procedure on page 159, "Starting the Saw," It is probably flooded. Remove the spark plug, dry the plug, pull the starting grip 10 to 12 times with the control lever in the Warm Start position to clear the cylinder of fuel, replace the plug, and repeat the starting procedure.

If the string gets short and won't come out any further, replace with new string as shown at upper left, or as shown in your owner's manual.

Pool Pump & Filter

How It Works

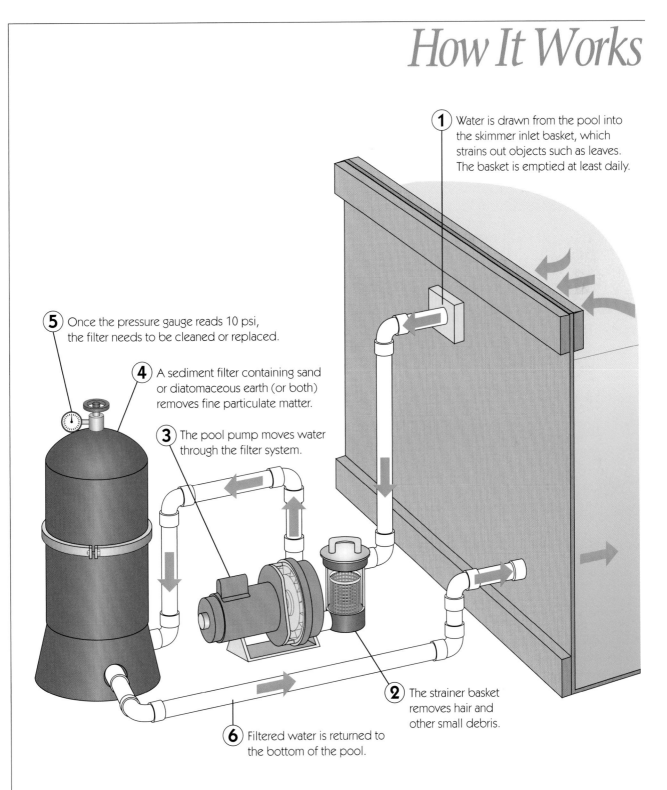

1 Water is drawn from the pool into the skimmer inlet basket, which strains out objects such as leaves. The basket is emptied at least daily.

5 Once the pressure gauge reads 10 psi, the filter needs to be cleaned or replaced.

4 A sediment filter containing sand or diatomaceous earth (or both) removes fine particulate matter.

3 The pool pump moves water through the filter system.

2 The strainer basket removes hair and other small debris.

6 Filtered water is returned to the bottom of the pool.

Lawn Sprinkler System

How It Works

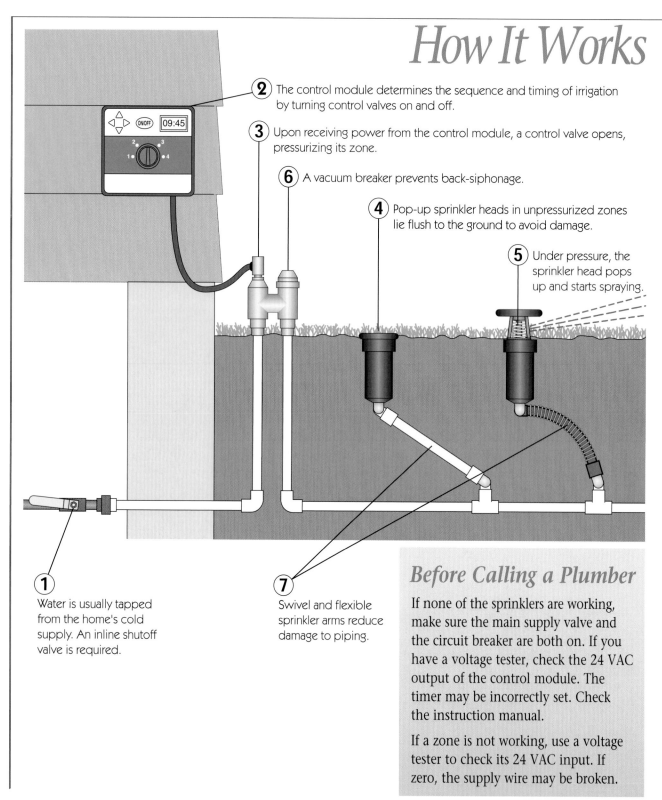

② The control module determines the sequence and timing of irrigation by turning control valves on and off.

③ Upon receiving power from the control module, a control valve opens, pressurizing its zone.

⑥ A vacuum breaker prevents back-siphonage.

④ Pop-up sprinkler heads in unpressurized zones lie flush to the ground to avoid damage.

⑤ Under pressure, the sprinkler head pops up and starts spraying.

① Water is usually tapped from the home's cold supply. An inline shutoff valve is required.

⑦ Swivel and flexible sprinkler arms reduce damage to piping.

Before Calling a Plumber

If none of the sprinklers are working, make sure the main supply valve and the circuit breaker are both on. If you have a voltage tester, check the 24 VAC output of the control module. The timer may be incorrectly set. Check the instruction manual.

If a zone is not working, use a voltage tester to check its 24 VAC input. If zero, the supply wire may be broken.

Spray Patterns and Placement

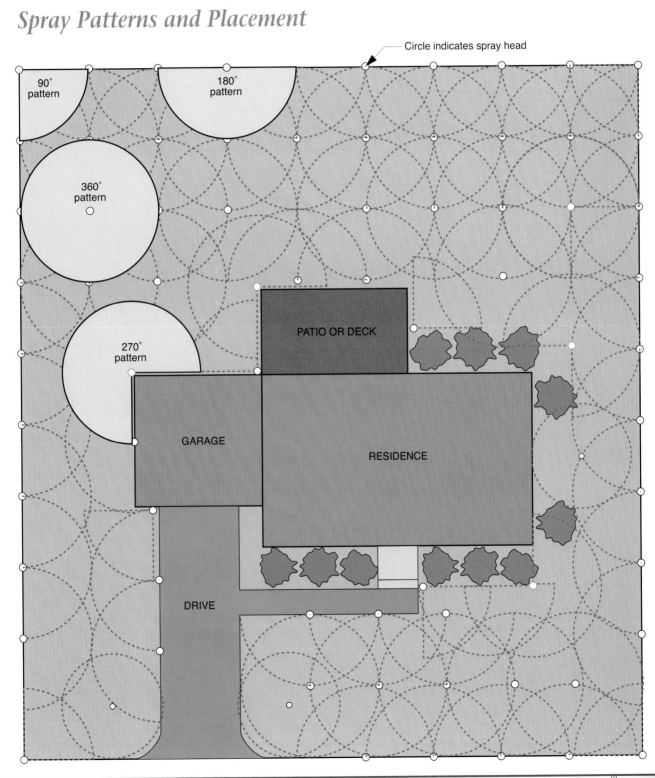

Circle indicates spray head

90°
pattern

180°
pattern

360°
pattern

270°
pattern

PATIO OR DECK

GARAGE

RESIDENCE

DRIVE

How It Works

Drain Field Downslope

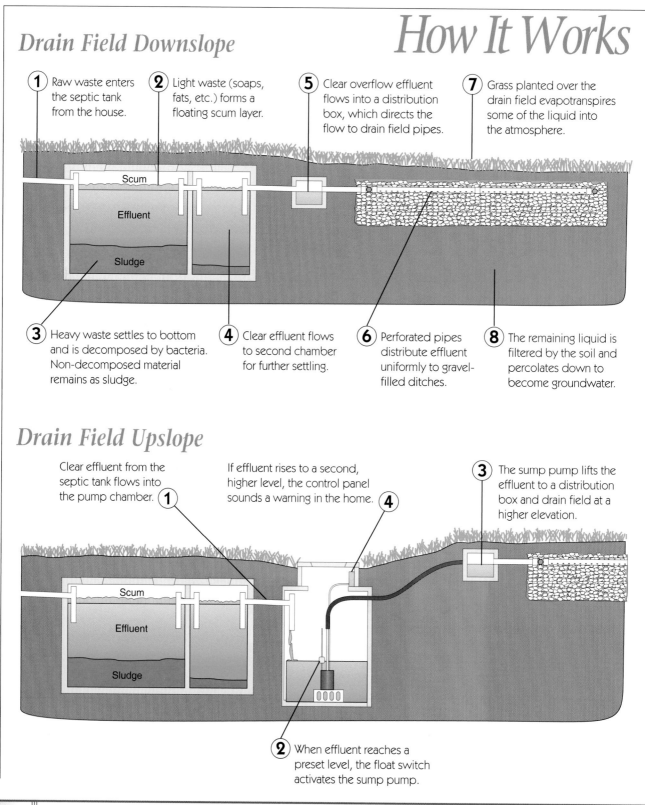

1 Raw waste enters the septic tank from the house.

2 Light waste (soaps, fats, etc.) forms a floating scum layer.

5 Clear overflow effluent flows into a distribution box, which directs the flow to drain field pipes.

7 Grass planted over the drain field evapotranspires some of the liquid into the atmosphere.

3 Heavy waste settles to bottom and is decomposed by bacteria. Non-decomposed material remains as sludge.

4 Clear effluent flows to second chamber for further settling.

6 Perforated pipes distribute effluent uniformly to gravel-filled ditches.

8 The remaining liquid is filtered by the soil and percolates down to become groundwater.

Scum

Effluent

Sludge

Drain Field Upslope

Clear effluent from the septic tank flows into the pump chamber. **1**

If effluent rises to a second, higher level, the control panel sounds a warning in the home. **4**

3 The sump pump lifts the effluent to a distribution box and drain field at a higher elevation.

Scum

Effluent

Sludge

2 When effluent reaches a preset level, the float switch activates the sump pump.

Keeping It Working

If too much sludge accumulates in the septic tank, solid waste may flow straight through and reach the pipes in the drain field. It will then clog the pipes and the gravel trenches, rendering the drain field ineffective.

Your system is failing if you observe one or more of the following:

- slow drains throughout the house

- a persistent wet area over, or next to, the drain field

- sewage seeping through the foundation.

Most jurisdictions will require a fouled system to be replaced in its entirety—a very expensive job. To prevent this from happening and to maximize your system's useful life, here are lists of do's and don'ts.

Do:

- Spread automatic washer use over the week.

- Record and keep in a safe place the location of the septic tank and distribution box.

- Have your septic tank checked every two years for a family of four, and four years for a family of two.

- Keep a log of pump-outs.

- Practice water conservation.

- Keep trees with large root systems far from the drain field.

- Plant grass over the drain field.

- Compost kitchen waste or dispose of it in your garbage.

- Use only RV antifreeze if winterizing your plumbing.

Don't:

- Drain a basement sump pump to the septic system.

- Drain backwash from water treatment equipment to the system.

- Use septic tank additives, in spite of manufacturers' claims.

- Use garbage disposers.

- Drive or park on the drain field.

- Plant anything but grass over the drain field.

- Flush paints, varnish, fats, grease, waste oil, or chemicals.

- Flush paper towels, sanitary napkins, tampons, disposable diapers, dental floss, condoms, kitty litter, cigarettes, or pesticides.

10 TOWARD SUSTAINABILITY

The party is coming to an end. After a century of consumption limited only by our incomes, we are waking to the fact that the earth's resources are finite. If we and the billions of humans in just developing nations wish to enjoy stable and secure lives, we must learn to live on less.

This chapter explains the technologies already available to make your home more energy and resource efficient.

Typical Clock Thermostat

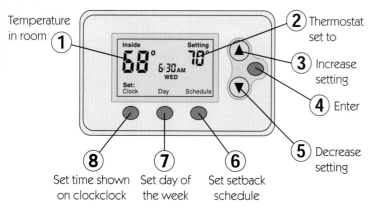

Temperature in room ① — Inside 68° 6:30 AM WED — Setting 70°

② Thermostat set to
③ Increase setting
④ Enter
⑤ Decrease setting

Set: Clock — Day — Schedule

⑧ Set time shown on clockclock
⑦ Set day of the week
⑥ Set setback schedule

Recommended Setbacks

EnergyStar Settings for Maximum Heating/Cooling Savings, °F				
Time of Day	Heat (M-F)	Cool (M-F)	Heat (S-S)	Cool (S-S)
Wake (6AM)	70°	65°	70°	75°
Leave (8AM)	62°	83°	62°	83°
Return (6PM)	70°	75°	70°	75°
Sleep (10PM)	62°	83°	62°	83°

How It Works

The rate at which your house loses heat (or cool) is proportional to the difference in temperatures inside and outside. In the case of heating, lowering the thermostat while no one is in the house and while you are sleeping reduces the temperature difference and, thus, the heating bill.

As rules of thumb, lowering a thermostat permanently reduces heating bills by about 3% per F°, while lowering it overnight only saves about 1% per F°.

Recommended clock thermostat settings for the average home are shown in the table at left. The beauty of a clock thermostat is that you can set it to meet your own needs.

The illustration below graphically depicts the typical savings (here 15%) from the recommended setback schedule.

Fuel Savings From Recommended Temperature Setbacks

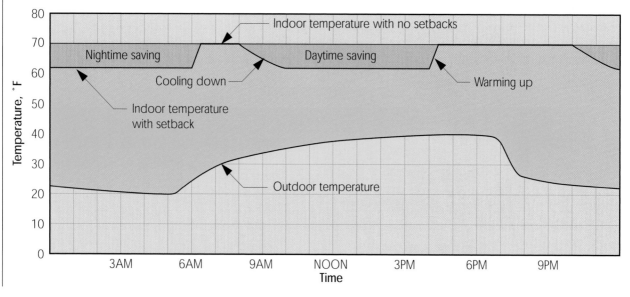

Indoor temperature with no setbacks
Nighttime saving
Daytime saving
Cooling down
Warming up
Indoor temperature with setback
Outdoor temperature

Air-Tight Wood Stove

How It Works

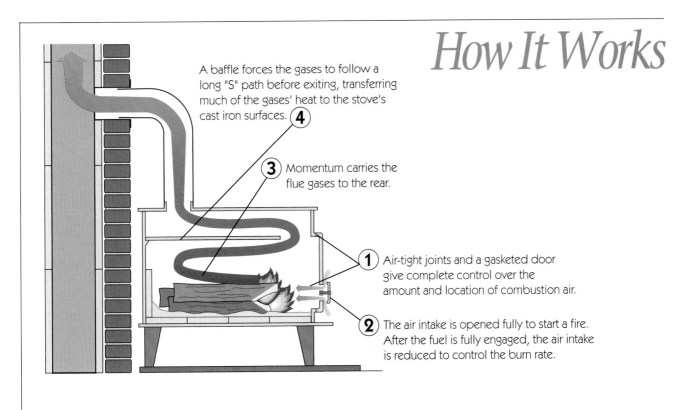

A baffle forces the gases to follow a long "S" path before exiting, transferring much of the gases' heat to the stove's cast iron surfaces. **4**

3 Momentum carries the flue gases to the rear.

1 Air-tight joints and a gasketed door give complete control over the amount and location of combustion air.

2 The air intake is opened fully to start a fire. After the fuel is fully engaged, the air intake is reduced to control the burn rate.

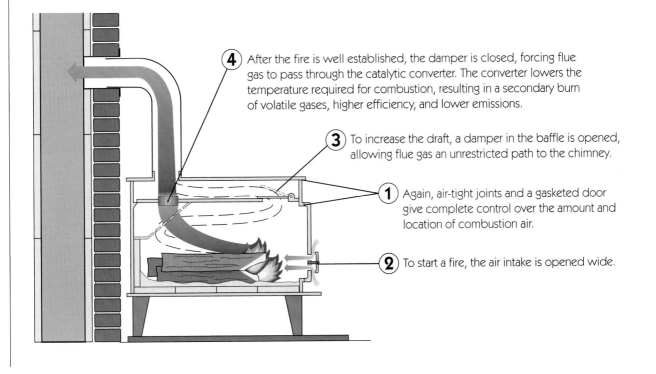

4 After the fire is well established, the damper is closed, forcing flue gas to pass through the catalytic converter. The converter lowers the temperature required for combustion, resulting in a secondary burn of volatile gases, higher efficiency, and lower emissions.

3 To increase the draft, a damper in the baffle is opened, allowing flue gas an unrestricted path to the chimney.

1 Again, air-tight joints and a gasketed door give complete control over the amount and location of combustion air.

2 To start a fire, the air intake is opened wide.

How It Works

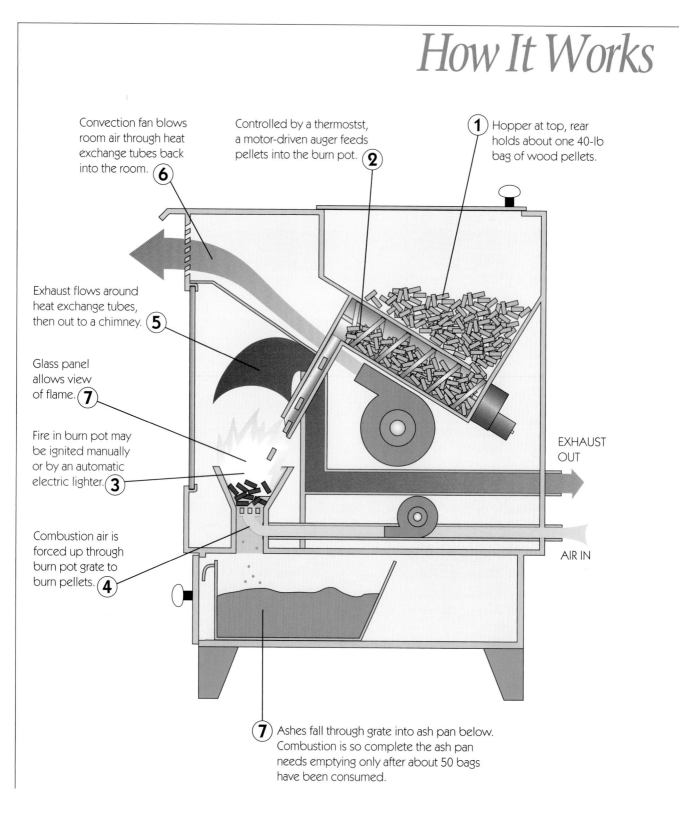

Convection fan blows room air through heat exchange tubes back into the room. **6**

Controlled by a thermostst, a motor-driven auger feeds pellets into the burn pot. **2**

1 Hopper at top, rear holds about one 40-lb bag of wood pellets.

Exhaust flows around heat exchange tubes, then out to a chimney. **5**

Glass panel allows view of flame. **7**

Fire in burn pot may be ignited manually or by an automatic electric lighter. **3**

Combustion air is forced up through burn pot grate to burn pellets. **4**

EXHAUST OUT

AIR IN

7 Ashes fall through grate into ash pan below. Combustion is so complete the ash pan needs emptying only after about 50 bags have been consumed.

Venting a Pellet Stove

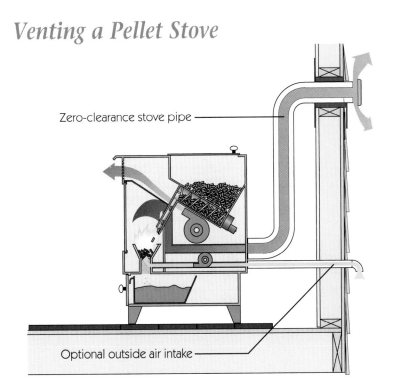

Zero-clearance stove pipe

Optional outside air intake

The air intake and exhaust of a pellet stove are both forced by a combustion blower. Because the exhaust doesn't depend on the creation of a natural draft, the exhaust pipe can be small (3 or 4 inches in diameter) and horizontal (although a vertical rise is desirable in case of power failure).

Pellet Vent pipe (L-Vent pipe) is the best because it is rated "zero clearance," and it will last as long as the stove.

Manufactured woodstove pipe (Class A pipe) in 6, 7, and 8 inch diameters is acceptable. However, it is very expensive, and the large diameters are not required.

Masonry chimneys with clay liners are also acceptable. Pellet vent pipe can vent directly into Class A lined chimneys.

Heat Content and Relative Pollution

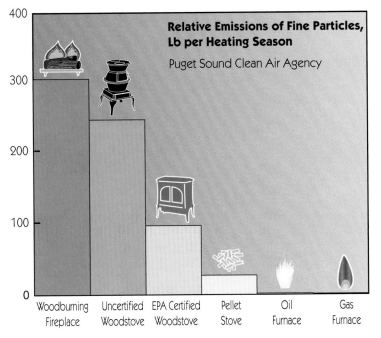

Relative Emissions of Fine Particles, Lb per Heating Season

Puget Sound Clean Air Agency

400 — 300 — 200 — 100 — 0

Woodburning Fireplace · Uncertified Woodstove · EPA Certified Woodstove · Pellet Stove · Oil Furnace · Gas Furnace

Wood pellets contain approximately 8,000 Btu/lb. Assuming 100% combustion efficiency (you factor in the actual efficiencies), a ton (2,000 lb) of pellets is equivalent to 0.64 cord of red oak or sugar maple, 114 gallons of fuel oil, 160 ccf of natural gas, and 4,700 kWh of electricity.

Wood pellets consist of wood fiber, so one should be concerned about the smoke typically produced when burning wood. However, pellets contain 5–10% moisture compared to 20% for air-dried firewood, and the controlled conditions in a pellet stove achieve greater burn efficiency. As a result, and as shown in the graph at left, fine particle emissions (smoke) from a pellet stove are much lower than those for any other solid fuel burner.

Vertical Loops

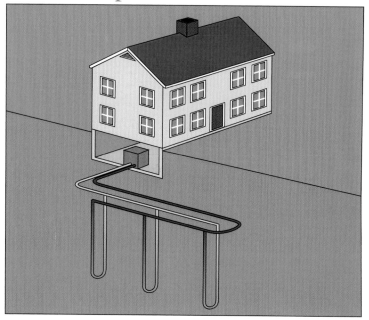

Slinky Loops

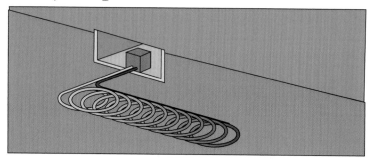

Horizontal Loops

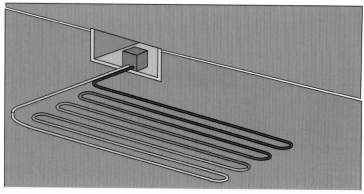

How It Works

Air source heat pumps were described on pages 80-81. Ground-source heat pumps differ only in that they exchange heat with the ground instead of outside air.

Due to the immense thermal capacity of the earth, while the temperature of outdoor air ranges from over 100°F down to -30°F, the temperature of the earth at depths of 20 feet or more is the annual average air temperature for the location. Except for the most southern states, this temperature ranges between 45°F and 60°F.

Heat pump efficiency is strongly dependent on source temperature, so in the coldest months ground source heat pump efficiencies are much greater than those of air source heat pumps. In the northernmost states, Heating Season Performance Factors (HSPF), the amount of heat energy moved divided by the electrical energy consumed, varies from 250 to 350%. Excepting areas with very low gas costs or very high electricity costs, the ground source heat pump is the most economical HVAC system to operate.

High thermal efficiency comes at a cost, however. Installation costs are up to five times those of gas or oil systems. Most of the difference is due to the added cost of the underground piping (ground loop). The three most common loops are shown at left. The "slinky" is lowest in cost and lowest in efficiency. The horizontal loop is the most efficient where there is sufficient land available. Vertical loops are used where lot size prohibits the other two.

Winter Heating Mode

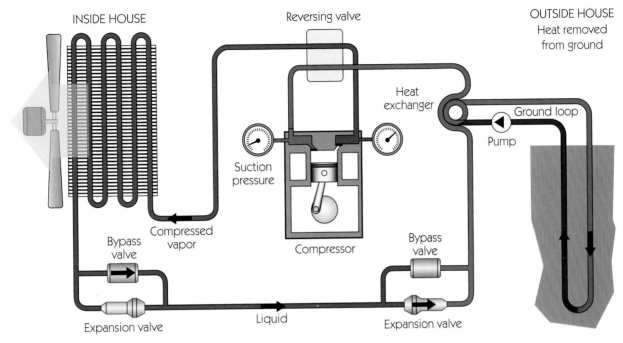

INSIDE HOUSE

Reversing valve

OUTSIDE HOUSE
Heat removed
from ground

Heat
exchanger

Ground loop

Pump

Suction
pressure

Compressor

Bypass
valve

Compressed
vapor

Bypass
valve

Expansion valve

Liquid

Expansion valve

Summer Cooling Mode

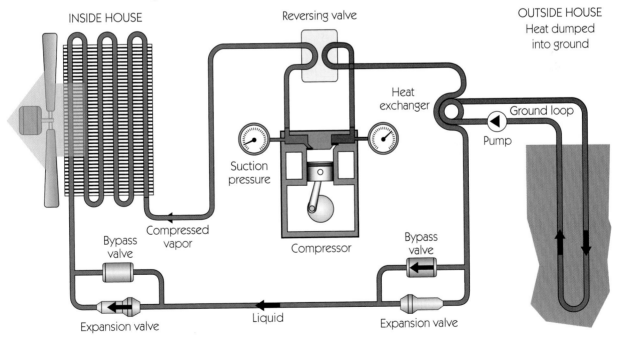

INSIDE HOUSE

Reversing valve

OUTSIDE HOUSE
Heat dumped
into ground

Heat
exchanger

Ground loop

Pump

Suction
pressure

Compressor

Bypass
valve

Compressed
vapor

Bypass
valve

Expansion valve

Liquid

Expansion valve

How It Works

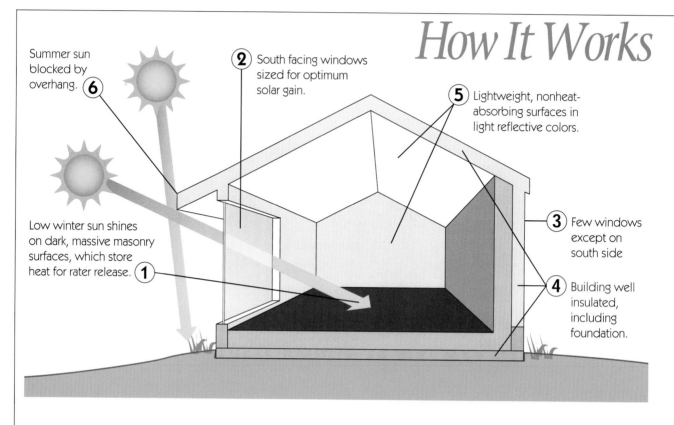

Summer sun blocked by overhang. **6**

2 South facing windows sized for optimum solar gain.

5 Lightweight, nonheat-absorbing surfaces in light reflective colors.

3 Few windows except on south side

Low winter sun shines on dark, massive masonry surfaces, which store heat for rater release. **1**

4 Building well insulated, including foundation.

Target Percentage Solar Contribution to Heating

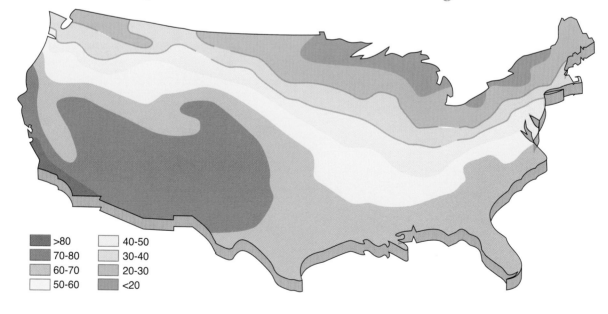

- >80
- 70-80
- 60-70
- 50-60
- 40-50
- 30-40
- 20-30
- <20

Required Areas of Thermal Mass

If a building has too little ability to absorb incoming solar radiation, it will overheat, windows will be opened, and the excess solar gain will be wasted. The illustrations and tables below show the required areas of different mass materials, thicknesses, and placements per square foot of south facing window to avoid overheating. For example, 4 square feet of 4-inch thick concrete floor are required per square foot of south glazing.

Mass types and locations may be combined.

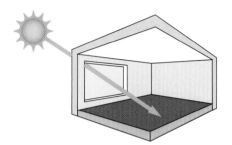

FLOORS AND WALLS IN DIRECT SUN

Mass Thickness	Sq Ft of Mass per Sq Ft of Glazing				
	Concrete	Brick	Drywall	Oak	Pine
½"	—	—	76	—	—
1"	14	17	38	17	21
2"	7	8	20	10	12
4"	4	5	—	11	12

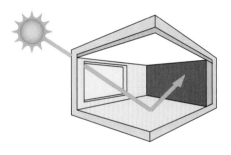

FLOOR, WALL, OR CEILING IN INDIRECT SUN

Mass Thickness	Sq Ft of Mass per Sq Ft of Glazing				
	Concrete	Brick	Drywall	Oak	Pine
½"	—	—	114	—	—
1"	25	30	57	28	36
2"	12	15	31	17	21
4"	7	9	—	19	21

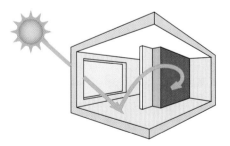

FLOOR, WALL, OR CEILING REMOTE FROM SUN

Mass Thickness	Sq Ft of Mass per Sq Ft of Glazing				
	Concrete	Brick	Drywall	Oak	Pine
½"	—	—	114	—	—
1"	27	32	57	32	39
2"	17	20	35	24	27
4"	14	17	—	24	30

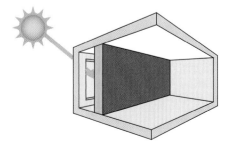

MASS WALL OR WATER WALL IN DIRECT SUN

Material and Thickness	Sq Ft of Mass Surface per Sq Ft of Glazing
8" thick brick	1
12" thick brick	1
8" thick water wall	1

Natural Ventilation

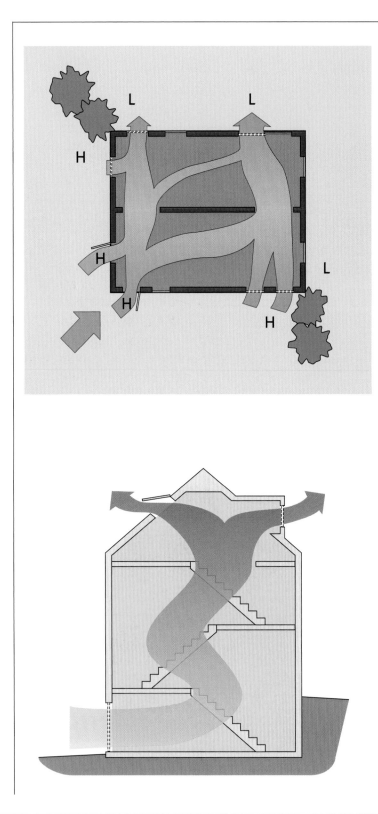

How It Works

Until about 100 years ago, people relied on prevailing winds and the buoyancy of warm air to cool their homes.

In most areas of the world, the prevailing wind directions during the warm months are well known. Coastal areas, for example, experience breezes from sea to land on hot days, with the direction reversing at night.

Orienting the home so that the breeze flows directly through large, openable windows from front to back maximizes the potential benefit.

As the illustration shows, strategically placed casement windows and shrubs can create pressure zones, resulting in air flow from high (H) to low (L) pressure. Keep this in mind when replacing windows and planting shrubs around an existing home.

Smoke stacks that remove smoke from factories without fans work because warm air—like a hot air balloon—is less dense than the surrounding air, so it rises.

The same "stack" effect can be used to ventilate a house, particularly after a hot day, when the house air is still hot, but the outside air has cooled.

Air flow is maximized when inlets and outlets are as low and high as possible. For a given ventilation opening, maximum air exchange is realized if the inlet and outlet areas are equal. However, if maximum air speed through a specific opening (a window next to your bed, for example) is the goal, the total outlet area should be at least double the inlet area.

Air-to-Air Heat Exchanger

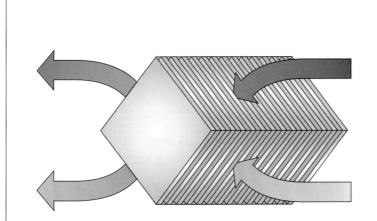

How It Works

In the quest to save heating and cooling energy, you can add as much insulation as will properly fit to reduce conductive heat loss. However, there are limits on how much air infiltration can be reduced in an attempt to reduce energy losses. The code-mandated ventilation minimum is 7.5 cfm per occupant, plus 1 cfm per 100 square feet of living space.

The air-to-air heat exchanger offers a simple solution. Stale inside air and fresh outdoor air are forced to pass through a honeycomb of thin ducts separated only by thin sheets of metal. In the passage, about 80% of the heat energy is recovered. Such units are increasingly found in energy-efficient construction.

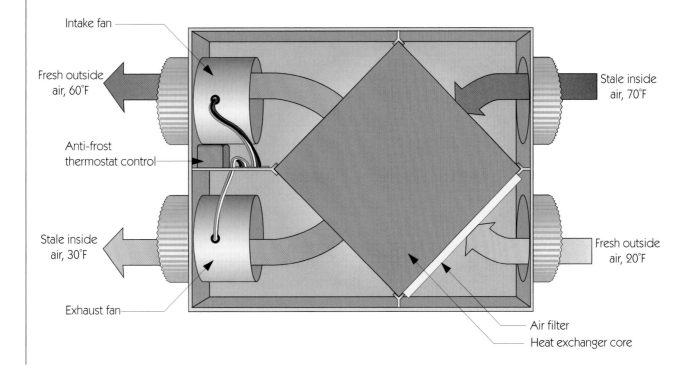

Intake fan

Fresh outside air, 60°F

Anti-frost thermostat control

Stale inside air, 30°F

Exhaust fan

Stale inside air, 70°F

Fresh outside air, 20°F

Air filter

Heat exchanger core

How They Work

Radiation

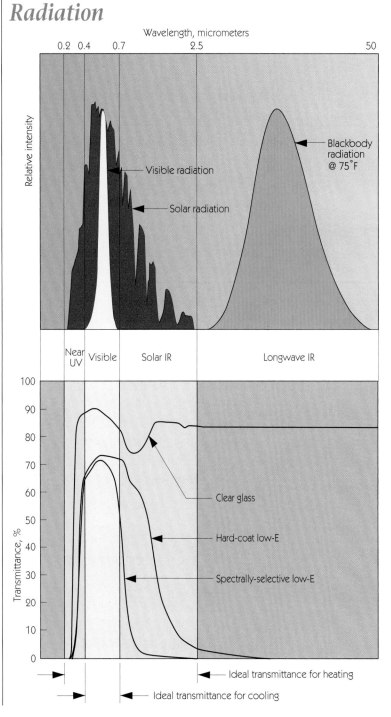

Wavelength, micrometers

0.2 0.4   0.7   2.5   50

Relative intensity

Visible radiation

Solar radiation

Blackbody radiation @ 75°F

Near UV | Visible | Solar IR | Longwave IR

100
90
80
70
60
50
40
30
20
10
0

Transmittance, %

Clear glass

Hard-coat low-E

Spectrally-selective low-E

Ideal transmittance for heating

Ideal transmittance for cooling

Radiation is everywhere. Some of it we see, such as sunlight and candle light. Some of it we cannot see, but can feel, such as the energy radiating from a warm object. Most of it we can neither see nor feel, such as radio waves and the UV rays that fade our rugs and burn our skin. All of this radiation is in the form of electromagnetic waves that travel through space.

The graph at top left shows the intensity of radiation from the sun at different wavelengths. The central yellow area is the range of wavelengths we can see, the red area to the left is the shorter-wavelength UV radiation, and the red area to the right is the longer-wave infrared portion. Most people are surprised at the small fraction of solar radiation we can "see."

They are also surprised to hear that all objects, including the walls and furnishings of their homes, emit radiation, the only difference being much longer wavelengths. The gray area shows the radiation emitted by the interior of a home at 75°F.

Why should radiation be of interest to a homeowner? Because radiation is energy, and energy is expensive—expensive to add when heating, and expensive to remove when cooling.

A window is an imperfect energy valve. We want "sunshine" to brighten the interior, but we don't want UV to fade the drapes. We want "solar heat" to warm us on cold winter days, but we don't want heat to leak back out at night. And on a hot day, we want to keep out the same radiation we welcomed on the cold winter day.

Energy Transmissions Compared

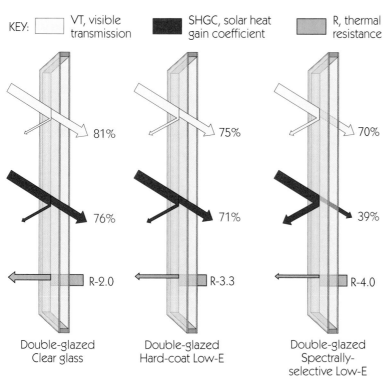

KEY:
- VT, visible transmission
- SHGC, solar heat gain coefficient
- R, thermal resistance

Double-glazed Clear glass — 81%, 76%, R-2.0

Double-glazed Hard-coat Low-E — 75%, 71%, R-3.3

Double-glazed Spectrally-selective Low-E — 70%, 39%, R-4.0

The bottom half of the graph on the facing page shows transmission curves (percentage of radiant energy transmitted) of three types of window glass:

- standard clear
- hard-coat low-E treated
- spectrally-selective low-E

Standard glass is seen to pass 90% of visible energy, about 80% of all infrared energy, and a portion of solar UV energy. In contrast, the low-E treated glass blocks longwave infrared energy. This is the heat energy we would like to keep inside the house in winter.

But note the difference between the low-E glazings. Hardcoat low-E passes nearly all solar energy, while spectrally-selective low-E passes only the visible radiation.

The significance of this difference is seen in the bar graphs to the left. The heights of the bars show annual costs for heating (red) and cooling (blue) identical 2,000-square-foot homes in three different climates with the three glazing alternatives.

In the heating climate (Madison, WI), the lowest total bill is achieved with hardcoat low-E. This is because winter solar gain reduces the predominant heating bill.

In the cooling climate (Miami, FL), solar gain adds to the cooling load, so spectrally selective glazing lowers the bill. In areas where heating and cooling bills are more nearly equal (Oklahoma City), the effects of solar gain balance out, making the choice of glazing less important.

Impact on Energy Bills

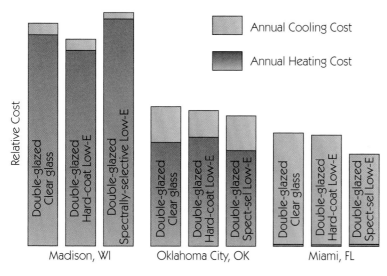

Relative Cost

- Annual Cooling Cost
- Annual Heating Cost

Madison, WI — Double-glazed Clear glass, Double-glazed Hard-coat Low-E, Double-glazed Spectrally-selective Low-E

Oklahoma City, OK — Double-glazed Clear glass, Double-glazed Hard-coat Low-E, Double-glazed Spect-sel Low-E

Miami, FL — Double-glazed Clear glass, Double-glazed Hard-coat Low-E, Double-glazed Spect-sel Low-E

How It Works

Here is a DIY R-2 window panel that increases the R-value of single-glazed windows from 1 to 3, and the R-value of double-glazed windows from 2 to 4. Since heat loss is inversely proportional to R, corresponding heat loss is reduced by 67% and 50% respectively.

See Annual Heating Savings at right for the calculated dollar savings for an average 30" x 60" window.

All of the required materials are readily available at home centers.

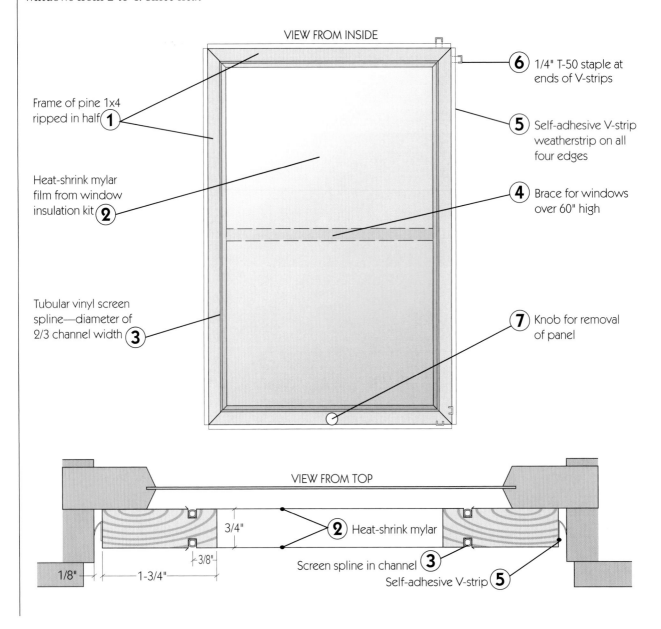

VIEW FROM INSIDE

Frame of pine 1x4 ripped in half **1**

Heat-shrink mylar film from window insulation kit **2**

Tubular vinyl screen spline—diameter of 2/3 channel width **3**

6 1/4" T-50 staple at ends of V-strips

5 Self-adhesive V-strip weatherstrip on all four edges

4 Brace for windows over 60" high

7 Knob for removal of panel

VIEW FROM TOP

3/4"

3/8"

1/8" 1-3/4"

2 Heat-shrink mylar

Screen spline in channel **3**

Self-adhesive V-strip **5**

Annual Heating Savings

COST OF HEAT PER YEAR FOR ONE 30" X 60" WINDOW
Assuming Portland, ME, and Natural Gas @$14/1,000 cf, 70% eff = $2.00/100,000 BTU

☐ Fuel cost due to net heat loss
☐ Fuel saving due to net heat gain

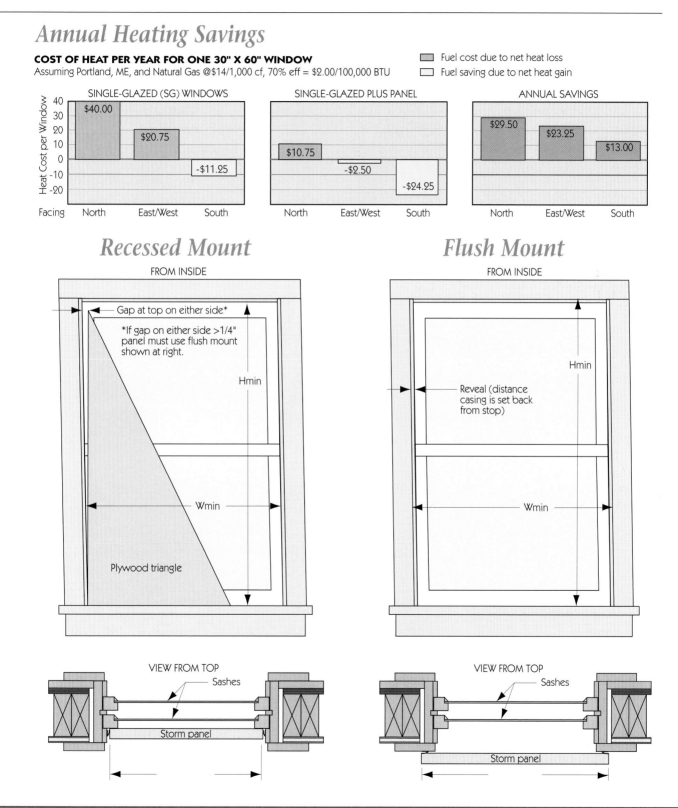

SINGLE-GLAZED (SG) WINDOWS

Heat Cost per Window
- $40.00 (North)
- $20.75 (East/West)
- -$11.25 (South)

Facing: North, East/West, South

SINGLE-GLAZED PLUS PANEL

- $10.75 (North)
- -$2.50 (East/West)
- -$24.25 (South)

North, East/West, South

ANNUAL SAVINGS

- $29.50 (North)
- $23.25 (East/West)
- $13.00 (South)

North, East/West, South

Recessed Mount

FROM INSIDE

Gap at top on either side*

*If gap on either side >1/4" panel must use flush mount shown at right.

Hmin

Wmin

Plywood triangle

VIEW FROM TOP

Sashes

Storm panel

Flush Mount

FROM INSIDE

Hmin

Reveal (distance casing is set back from stop)

Wmin

VIEW FROM TOP

Sashes

Storm panel

Window Insulating Panel ‖ **183**

Motion-Activated Switch

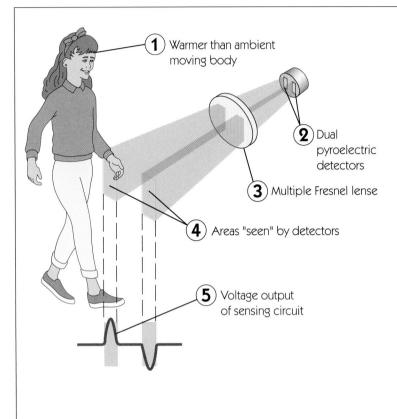

① Warmer than ambient moving body

② Dual pyroelectric detectors

③ Multiple Fresnel lense

④ Areas "seen" by detectors

⑤ Voltage output of sensing circuit

Area Detected

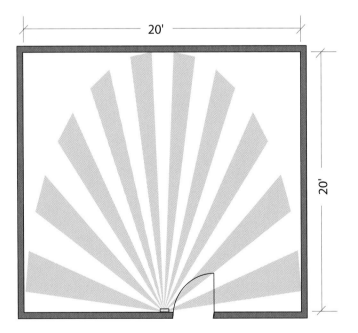

20'

20'

How It Works

Older motion sensors, used in security alarms and automatic door openers, use beams of light, radar, or ultrasonic detectors. All three types are "active"in that they send out signals.

Most new motion senses are "passive infrared" (PIR) sensors. They sense the infrared energy of wavelength 8 to 12 micrometers radiated by the human body. To be useful they need to discriminate between: 1) a moving body and a body sitting or standing still, and 2) a room or objects in a room that are simply warming up to body temperature.

They do this by means of two electronic tricks. First, they look, not at the voltage output of an infrared sensor, but at its *rate of change*. Second, they employ, not one, but a pair of sensors and monitor the *difference in voltage* between the two sensor outputs.

In the illustration at left the girl is passing through two adjacent zones "seen" by the pair of sensors. The voltage output of the first sensor rises and falls as she passes through its zone, but the inverted output of the second sensor does just the opposite as she passes through the second zone. A rise in temperature of the entire room, a stationary person, or a sudden flash of light would produce coincidental cancelling signals and not trigger the device.

The illustration at bottom left shows the importance of placing the sensor where it can monitor the entire room.

Controlling a Room Light

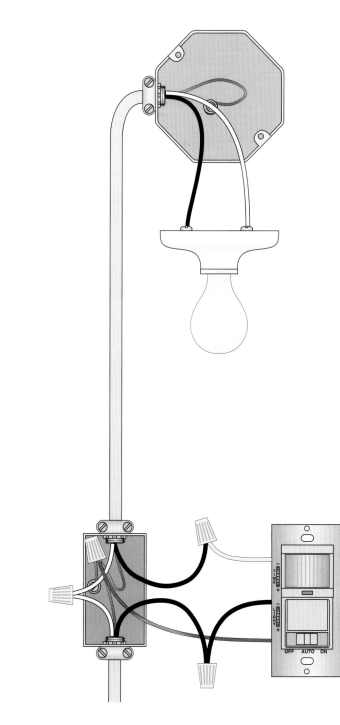

Typical Controls

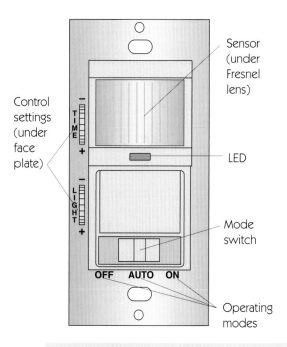

Sensor (under Fresnel lens)

Control settings (under face plate)

LED

Mode switch

OFF   AUTO   ON

Operating modes

Before Calling Electrician

If the light won't come on in either AUTO or ON mode, replace the bulb. If it still won't light, check the circuit breaker for that lighting circuit.

If the light remains always on, make sure the mode switch is set to AUTO and that no one is in the room.

If the light doesn't come on when someone enters the room, make sure the mode switch is set to AUTO.

If the light still won't come on, remove the cover plate and adjust the LIGHT control setting up or down.

If that doesn't work, replace the device.

How It Works

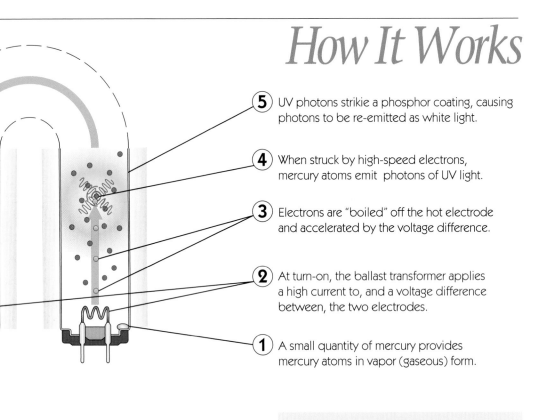

5 UV photons strikie a phosphor coating, causing photons to be re-emitted as white light.

4 When struck by high-speed electrons, mercury atoms emit photons of UV light.

3 Electrons are "boiled" off the hot electrode and accelerated by the voltage difference.

2 At turn-on, the ballast transformer applies a high current to, and a voltage difference between, the two electrodes.

1 A small quantity of mercury provides mercury atoms in vapor (gaseous) form.

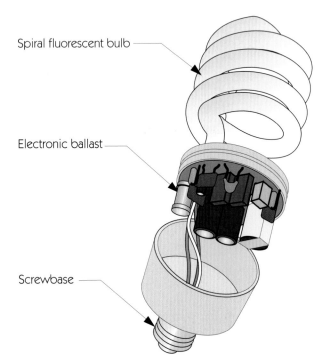

Spiral fluorescent bulb

Electronic ballast

Screwbase

Before Calling Electrician

If the lamp doesn't light, try replacing it with a new bulb.

If the new bulb doesn't light, reset the circuit breaker controlling the lighting circuit or outlet.

If the bulb is in a floor or table lamp, plug the lamp into a different outlet. If it still doesn't light, the lamp is broken (see page 68 to repair).

If the bulb is in a fixture controlled by a wall switch, with the power off, bend up the center tab in the lamp socket.

If the bulb in the fixture still doesn't light, replace the wall switch (see page 58 for repair).

LED Lamp

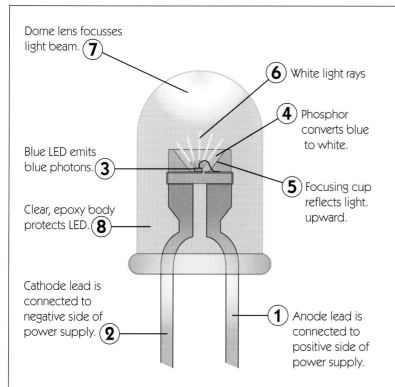

Dome lens focusses light beam. **7**

6 White light rays

4 Phosphor converts blue to white.

Blue LED emits blue photons. **3**

5 Focusing cup reflects light. upward.

Clear, epoxy body protects LED. **8**

Cathode lead is connected to negative side of power supply. **2**

1 Anode lead is connected to positive side of power supply.

How It Works

Light-emitting diodes (LEDs) are tiny sandwiches of semiconducting material. When a voltage is applied across an LED, current will flow from the anode (positive lead) to the cathode (negative lead) but not in the reverse direction. Electrons flowing across the semiconductor junction fall from a higher to a lower energy state, emitting photons (light) of energy.

Depending on the semiconducting materials, the photons may be red, green, or blue. A white LED can be made by combining red, green, and blue LEDS or, as shown at left, by coating a blue LED with a yellow phosphor which converts the blue light to white light.

A Typical LED Replacement Lamp

Individual LEDs behind array of lenses **11**

AC/DC rectifier inside bulb makes DC to power LEDs. **10**

Screwbase **9**

Before Calling Electrician

If the lamp doesn't light, try replacing it with a new bulb.

If the new bulb doesn't light, reset the circuit breaker controlling the lighting circuit or outlet.

If the bulb is in a floor or table lamp, plug the lamp into a different outlet. If it still doesn't light, the lamp is broken (see page 68 to repair).

If the bulb is in a fixture controlled by a wall switch, with the power off, bend up the center tab in the lamp socket.

If the bulb in the fixture still doesn't light, replace the wall switch (see page 58 for repair).

10 Solar Pool Heater

How It Works

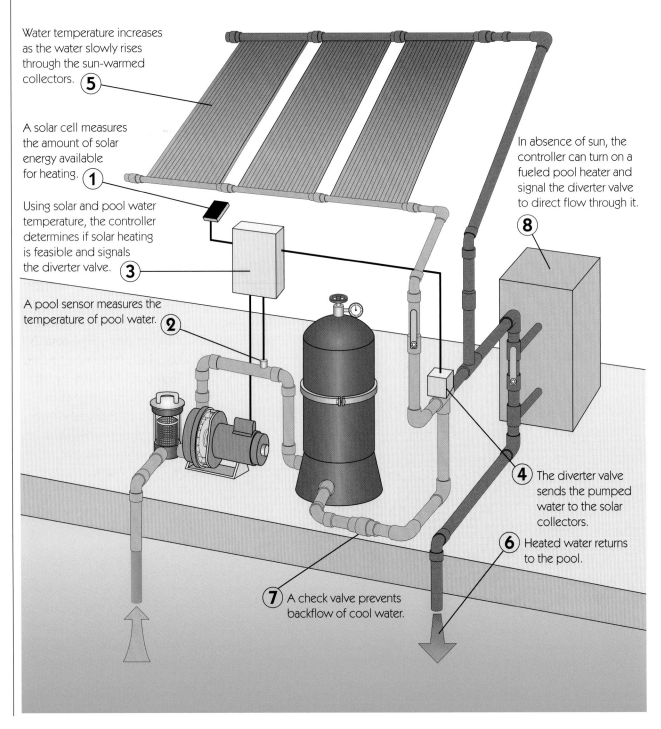

Water temperature increases as the water slowly rises through the sun-warmed collectors. **5**

A solar cell measures the amount of solar energy available for heating. **1**

Using solar and pool water temperature, the controller determines if solar heating is feasible and signals the diverter valve. **3**

A pool sensor measures the temperature of pool water. **2**

In absence of sun, the controller can turn on a fueled pool heater and signal the diverter valve to direct flow through it. **8**

4 The diverter valve sends the pumped water to the solar collectors.

6 Heated water returns to the pool.

7 A check valve prevents backflow of cool water.

Pool Cover

In-Ground Pool Heat Loss

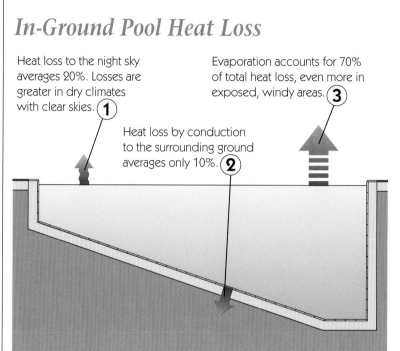

Heat loss to the night sky averages 20%. Losses are greater in dry climates with clear skies. **1**

Heat loss by conduction to the surrounding ground averages only 10%. **2**

Evaporation accounts for 70% of total heat loss, even more in exposed, windy areas. **3**

A Typical Pool Cover

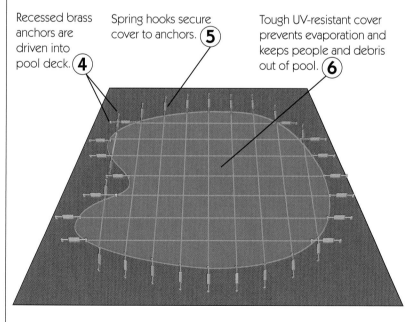

Recessed brass anchors are driven into pool deck. **4**

Spring hooks secure cover to anchors. **5**

Tough UV-resistant cover prevents evaporation and keeps people and debris out of pool. **6**

How It Works

Evaporating water absorbs a lot of energy. Raising the temperature of 1 pound of water 1 F° degree takes just 1 Btu, but evaporating that same pound of water takes 1,048 Btu!

Let's apply those numbers to the average home in-the-ground pool. If the pool is 20′ x 40′ by an average of 5′ deep, its volume is 4,000 cubic feet. Since water weighs 62.4 pounds per cubic foot, the pool contains approximately 250,000 pounds of water. Raising its temperature by 20 F° would require 5,000,000 Btu.

Now let's evaporate just 1 inch of water from the pool. The volume of evaporated water would be 20′ x 40′ x 1/12′ = 66.7 cubic feet. Multiplying by 62.4 pounds per cubic foot, the weight of evaporated water is 4,160 pounds. Multiplying the weight by 1,084 Btu/pound gives us 4,509,440 Btu. Thus the heat loss from 1 inch of evaporation roughly equals the heat required to raise the pool temperature 20 F°! If that doesn't get your attention, how about this? If you are heating the pool with natural gas, those 5,000,000 Btu cost about $100.

So far we have looked only at heat loss. A commercial pool cover of the type shown at left will also prevent dogs, children, and debris from falling in. The savings on your homeowner's insurance and pool maintenance costs alone will pay for the cover.

How It Works

The obvious difference between top-loading and front-loading clothes washers is the way the baskets containing the water and clothes spin. By spinning on a horizontal axis the front loader eliminates the need for a complex transmission. The clothes are agitated simply by tumbling through the force of gravity.

In addition the front-loader consumes less water and spins MUCH faster, removing nearly all the water from the clothes.

These energy saving features require a heavier and more expensive balance mechanism, however.

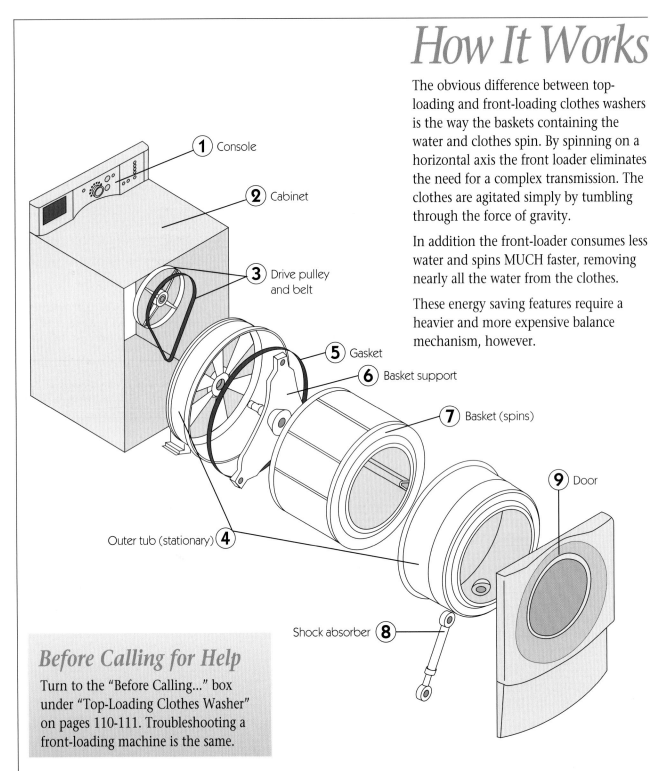

1. Console
2. Cabinet
3. Drive pulley and belt
4. Outer tub (stationary)
5. Gasket
6. Basket support
7. Basket (spins)
8. Shock absorber
9. Door

Before Calling for Help

Turn to the "Before Calling..." box under "Top-Loading Clothes Washer" on pages 110-111. Troubleshooting a front-loading machine is the same.

INDEX